A PARIAH PEOPLE

By the same author

The Day God Laughed

Revolution in Judea

Judaisim on Trial: Jewish-Christian
Disputations in the Middle Ages

The Sacred Executioner

The Mythmaker: Paul and the Invention
of Christianity

Early Rabinic Writings

Judaism in the First Century

Paul and Hellenism

Judas Iscariot and the Myth of
Jewish Evil

A PARIAH PEOPLE

The Anthropology of Antisemitism

HYAM MACCOBY

CONSTABLE · LONDON

First published in Great Britain 1996
by Constable and Company Limited
3 The Lanchesters, 162 Fulham Palace Road
London W6 9ER
Copyright © Hyam Maccoby
The right of Hyam Maccoby to be identified as author of this work
has been asserted by him in accordance with
the Copyright, Designs and Patents Act 1988
ISBN 0 09 475450 0

0094 754 500   *1921*

Set in Linotron Sabon 10½pt by
Rowland Phototypesetting Limited
Bury St Edmunds, Suffolk
Printed in Great Britain by
St Edmundbury Press Limited
Bury St Edmunds, Suffolk

A CIP catalogue record of this book
is available from the British Library

CONTENTS

Preface   7
1 The Pariah Status of the Jews in Christendom   11
2 Max Weber's Theory of the Jews as a Pariah People   20
3 Antisemitism Outside Christendom   38
4 The Jews in Medieval England   51
5 Usurpation and Pariahship   63
6 Caste in Judaism   74
7 Paul and the Formation of the Usurpation Myth   82
8 The Development of the Christian Usurpation Myth   93
9 The Pharisees in the Usurpation Myth   106
10 Sacrifice in the New Testament   116
11 The Stigma of Deicide   129
12 The Meaning of Sacrifice   142
13 The Anthropology of the New Testament   155
14 Did Antisemitism Begin in the Middle Ages?   166
15 Were the Jews a Caste?   176
16 Sin-eaters and Others   189
17 Conclusion: the Holocaust was no Mystery   198
   Endnotes   208
   Bibliography   222
   Index   229

PREFACE

There have been many theories purporting to explain the phenomenon of antisemitism. Often it is suggested that Jew-hatred is somehow the fault of the Jews: they are too clannish, they have a religion different from the norm, they are engaged in a conspiracy to take over the world, they are the founders of capitalism, they are the founders of communism, they have something wrong with their blood, they have long noses, or bad breath, or pale faces, they dress differently, or (even more cunningly) dress the same as others. They are cowardly pacifists (as shown by the meek way they marched into the gas-chambers, naked under the machine-guns), and also militaristic bullies (as they showed when they finally managed to obtain weapons to use against their enemies).

What is it that makes people blame the Jews for everything that is wrong in their lives, as well as for antisemitism itself? Is this tendency world-wide, or confined to certain areas of the world? What is there about the relation between Judaism and its offshoots that has set up this syndrome of hate?

The massive slaughter of Jews in the Holocaust has prompted a sense of guilt among Christians about antisemitism. Unthinking antisemitism, endemic in Western literature up to the Second World War, has now been halted. Even though critical attitudes to Christian tradition have become widespread in post-war Europe and America, medieval religious antisemitism has reappeared in Eastern Europe where, paradoxically, official atheism prevented the development of

7

critical modern reading of religious texts. In South America, antisemitism of the medieval kind is rife.

Even better than to examine antisemites is to examine the society in which antisemitism occurs. Is antisemitism somehow a necessary element in a certain kind of society? Does antisemitism have a function to perform that helps to knit society together, release its members from dysfunctional guilt, and enables them to achieve hope for the future? To turn the spotlight away from the Jews themselves and from individual antisemites, and turn it instead on the society itself is in principle an anthropological enquiry – not merely sociological – because it brings into play factors that operate in all societies, Western or Eastern, modern or ancient. In this enquiry, the comparison between the role played by the Jews in Western society and that played by the Untouchables in Hindu society is important, because the Untouchables represent a paradigm of a disadvantaged group that is essential to the whole religious fabric and ethos of the society concerned. What is fundamental to the notion of a pariah class is that its role is built into a religious scheme of hierarchy; this distinguishes it from a mere oppressed class, such as Afro-Americans in the American South, whose role actually went counter to the prevailing democratic ethos of American society.

The present study thus regards antisemitism as a phenomenon that is not mysterious. It can be explained by comparative study of various forms of society in ancient, medieval and modern history. In other interpretations, the proximate causes often adduced, such as economic friction or xenophobia, are shown to be too weak to be adequate to this extraordinary and persistent phenomenon. Though composed of elements that can be found elsewhere, the particular combination that forms antisemitism, originating from a particular historical concatenation of events, is unique.

In previous books I have explored aspects that are essential to the present study: the Jewish-Christian conflict, the development of the New Testament, the Judas Iscariot myth, the mythology of sacrifice, the plight of the Jews in medieval Christendom. In this book, I develop my findings into a comprehensive theory of antisemitism.

I wish to acknowledge the warm and inspiring support of my colleagues and students at the Leo Baeck College. I should like to thank my friend Daniel Brin, editor of *Heritage*, Los Angeles, for his unstinting support for my work, and for the inspiration of his example. My special thanks go to Mary Douglas for her generous help and stimulating criticism in our continuing exchange of ideas. The debt I owe to my wife, Cynthia, for her constant help, creative comments and loving support is beyond expression.

Hyam Maccoby, Kew, 11 March 1996

CHAPTER 1

THE PARIAH STATUS OF THE JEWS
IN CHRISTENDOM

Let us suppose that an anthropologist from some civilisation in outer space were to land on earth, and were to adopt as his scientific task the investigation of antisemitism. His report might run, in part, as follows:

'There is a group of people, called Jews, who have a peculiar status in many countries of Earth. They form a distinct community by virtue of a shared religion and history and attachment to a land in the Middle East where at one time they were a sovereign people. But like many other peoples, they lost their land and settled in other countries, retaining their identity through their religion, but in all other ways acting, as far as they were permitted, as citizens of their country of residence. During the backward period known as the Middle Ages, they were denied both citizenship and admittance to the honourable professions, and subjected to sporadic and sometimes bitter persecution. Yet even during this period, their talents and usefulness were acknowledged at times of greatest need, and many of the cultural achievements of the Middle Ages can be attributed to them. Short periods when Jews were allowed to flourish alternated with longer periods when they were harassed, massacred or brutally expelled from their homes. But when more enlightened attitudes prevailed, they were given full citizenship and allowed to partake in the culture of their countries of residence. They responded to this liberty with enthusiasm, and many of them made distinguished contributions to the culture into which they had been admitted. They demonstrated their loyalty with eager gratitude, and laid down their lives in disproportionate numbers in defence of the state in wartime.

They were disappointed and amazed, however, to find that the more they were officially accorded public acceptance, the more they became the targets of paranoid fantasies in which they were accused of plotting against their host societies and aiming to achieve power over the whole of Earth. These paranoid fantasies, all of which were characterised by the ascription of awesome power to the Jews, were quiescent during periods of prosperity, when more rational attitudes, on the whole, prevailed. But when any country was afflicted by political or economic crisis, the movements, previously weak, which were based on anti-Jewish paranoia, became strong, and at times even took over the administration of the state. At such times, there was no limit to the rage and cruelty with which the Jews were treated. Moreover, even in prosperous times, there were many indications that, despite their emancipation in the legal sense, the Jews were regarded with contempt and suspicion. The result of this has been that some Jews, despairing of genuine acceptance, conceived the notion of abandoning the host societies and returning to their place of origin in the Middle East. This resulted, however, in further paranoia. The Jewish attempt to return home was interpreted as one more move towards Jewish world domination, and the word "Zionism", coined by the Jews to designate their attempt, became an additional term of opprobrium in the vocabulary of their enemies.

Any rational assessment would see the Jews as inoffensive people, many of them gifted and hard-working, who are eager to be allowed to lead useful lives. The belief in large-scale Jewish power is pure illusion. The Jews are one of the least powerful communities on Earth. Yet like every other weak community, they have some prominent individuals who have gained wealth or position in society. In Israel, Jews have gained sovereign political power for the first time in 2000 years, but in a precarious and embattled fashion. In America, Jews have lobbying powers like other minorities. Yet every minor acquisition of power by Jews is experienced by anti-Jewish elements as confirmation of a Jewish

THE PARIAH STATUS OF THE JEWS IN CHRISTENDOM

conspiracy to dominate Earth. This form of paranoia is different from that associated with other xenophobic manifestations. Colour-prejudice, for example, is characterised by contempt rather than fear, and is never associated with fantasies of cunningly organised plans for world domination.

My task as an anthropologist is to enquire into the role of the Jews in the wider society of which they form a part. It is a role that is not consciously formulated by the host society, and certainly not by the Jews, whose attitude towards the hostility which they encounter is one of incomprehension. Nevertheless, it appears that to the host society, the Jews are not just outsiders who are difficult to assimilate, but an integral element in the society itself, which would not be able to function fully without the Jews as perennial scapegoats, and as the focus of power-fantasies. The Jews, as an essential ingredient in their "host" society, are in fact its oldest element. It has been pointed out that the Jews have a longer record of residence in the city of Cologne than any other group; yet in all the ethnic changes that have taken place there, the Jews have been regarded as the perennial outsiders. The conclusion is that it is the Jewish time-honoured fate to contribute to the peace of Cologne by enacting a special and necessary role as outsiders.

The anthropologist's task then is to ask, "Why are the Jews so necessary to their 'host' society?" The word "host" can go into inverted commas, because in fact the Jews are an integral and ancient part of the society, though their traditional role is to act the part of the perpetual alien. Why does a society need to contain within itself a group that is refused official integration? Why, in particular, is such a group credited with almost supernatural powers for evil?

We may expect to find enlightenment on this question in two ways. One is to examine the history of the Jews in the broader society. How did the Jews come to occupy a niche in the non-Jewish community? It is only to be expected that the present anomalous situation in which Jews are officially equal citizens, yet in fact are the target of resentment when they exercise equality, derives from an earlier situation in which Jews were officially perennial (yet necessary) aliens.

The second approach is synchronic rather than diachronic. What parallels can we find to the Jews in other communities on Earth? In what other societies can we discern a class of people who are hated, feared and despised, yet who may perform an essential function in the society? Can we find a parallel to the resentment felt against the Jews when attitudes of enlightenment and enfranchisement conflict with atavistic hatred?

I intend to pursue these two lines of enquiry, confident that my detachment from the issues will enable me to arrive at the truth. I note indeed that Earthlings who have attempted the task have shown amazing inability even to see the dimensions of the problem, but have always attempted to explain away the special hatred felt for the Jews as caused by trivial circumstances and easily-overcome irrationalities, rather than as endemic in the structure of the host society.'

The detachment claimed by the extra-terrestrial anthropologist is certainly very hard to attain by any earthling, much less by someone deeply and personally involved in the complex situation known as 'antisemitism'. In the eighteenth century, when Enlightenment thinkers sought a detached view of European civilisation, it was a frequent device to compose a series of letters purportedly written by a Chinese tourist, describing for his family and friends in China the strange vagaries of Western life. None of these compositions, however, show any realisation of the sheer strangeness of the role of the Jews in this culture.

As a Jew, I am heir to a long tradition of incomprehension of antisemitism. The Jews, in a history of about 4500 years, have undergone so many episodes of hostility that they have ceased to analyse any particular episode, and have put them all down to a generalised and inexplicable hatred. When Christians persecuted Jews in the Middle Ages, this, in Jewish eyes, was just another tribulation like earlier persecutions by Egyptians, Philistines, Assyrians, Babylonians, Greeks and Romans. Indeed, the Christian Church and its secular arm were regarded by Jews as the continuation of the Roman Empire, and were therefore given the name of 'Edom'. This name is equivalent to Esau, who was the twin brother of Jacob, with whom he struggled in his mother's womb. It was a Jewish belief that the progenitor of Rome was none other than Esau, and that therefore the rivalry of Jacob and Esau had assumed the dimensions of a national conflict bestraddling history, in which the Jews were doomed to suffer under Esau's wrath until the millennium, when Jacob would be liberated. There was a theory of 'the Four Kingdoms' (based on the apocalyptic scheme of Daniel) in which the last of the persecuting kingdoms was Rome.

Thus it is true but not entirely adequate to say that Jews regarded Christian persecution as merely the renewal of old enmities of the ancient world. Jews did recognise that there was something special about Christian hatred. There was a mythical, cosmic tinge to this hatred, something intimate and archetypal, which could be symbolised only by the image of a conflict of twin brothers, locked in combat from the womb to the end of time. Egyptians, Assyrians, Babylonians and even Greeks could come and go, but Esau-Rome had been there from the beginning and would be there to the end.

Yet it is also true to say that Jews entirely failed to comprehend what made Christian hatred unique. Jews thought of it as some kind of national rivalry. Jewish endurance of Christian persecution could be seen as resistance to the claim of yet another military power to dominate the earth. They failed to understand that Christianity was primarily a religion, not a political power. It was a variety of Judaism, and this made the contest far more bitter than if it had been a matter of mere political oppression. The contest was about who could truly claim the name of 'Israel'. It was a struggle not for domination, but for the birthright. And in particular, it was a struggle in which the Christian claim to the birthright included a scenario of dispossession in which the Jews were cast for a role of degradation and necessary evil. Jews, absorbed in the contemplation of their own religion, did not understand Christianity, and above all did not understand the role that they, the Jews, had come to occupy in the Christian imagination and theology.

So, if the Jews were pariahs in medieval Europe it was in a way that must be differentiated from the basic meaning of pariahship as found in Hinduism, from which the word 'pariah' derives. For in the classical period of the caste system (before the modern movement against Untouchability) the pariahs of India accepted, generally speaking, their pariah-status as their earthly ordained lot. They believed that if they performed their lowly duties with a willing heart, they would be reborn in their next life in a higher caste. The Jews in medieval Europe were not pariahs in this sense, for they never accepted the lowly status imposed upon them, regarding their sufferings as due to oppression, not to the 'nature of things'.

Yet from the standpoint of Christian theory, the Jews were indeed pariahs, and since Christian theory was what counted in practice, not the Jews' own self-estimation, the plain fact was that in Christian medieval society the Jews were a pariah class. Moreover, Christians even fantasised in various bizarre ways that Jews did accept their pariah status – a fantasy that implanted the de facto societal role of the Jews even more firmly.

The basis of Jewish pariah status was the pronouncement of St Augustine on the Jews. This consists of a rationale for the continued existence of Jews within Christendom. According to Augustine, the Jews had some important services to offer to Christians. One of these services is to prove by their sufferings the truth of Christianity. Once a sovereign people, the Jews had sunk to the status of wanderers and slaves. This showed that they were being punished for their rejection of Jesus and the crime of deicide, and this was a highly useful proof that Jesus was indeed what he claimed to be, God incarnate. Thus the Jews were living proof of the truth of Christianity, and as such had to be preserved from extinction. So far, this was a humanitarian message, for if the Jews had been declared to be merely heretics, that would have been their death warrant. Heretics such as the Albigenses were exterminated to the last man, woman and child. The Jews were spared this fate because they were considered to have an important contribution to make to Christian society.

There was also another way, according to Augustine, in which the Jews were 'witnesses' to the truth of Christianity. The Jews were the transmitters of the Old Testament, which they had preserved for centuries before the birth of Christianity. The Old Testament was the authentication and legal confirmation of Christianity before the nations of the world: in these oracles, the advent of Jesus was prophesied together with the triumph of the Church and the downfall of its enemies. Without the authentication given by the Old Testament, the Church might be denounced as a charlatan sect which had manufactured its own credentials. The Jews, by their survival, testified to the historical pedigree of the Old Testament and thus unwittingly and unwillingly proved the age-old inevitability of the coming of what might otherwise have been thought an upstart religion. The Jews, in Augustine's phrase, were the 'slave-librarians' of the Church. 'By the evidence of their own Scriptures, they bear witness for us that we have not fabricated the prophecies about Christ.' (*City of God*, 18:46).

The Jews, Augustine believes, must survive for another very important reason – that history cannot be consummated without them. Paul, in his Epistle to the Romans, had prophesied that the Jews would be converted to Christ at the end of days. Thus the much hoped for 'conversion of the Jews', to which Christian thinkers and reformers refer during the course of many centuries, became identified with the hoped for Second Coming of Christ, the two events being indissolubly connected. At the time of the Second Crusade (1145–48), when it seemed that massacres of Jews would occur as in the First Crusade, St Bernard of Clairvaux intervened to save the Jews, citing this belief, and arguing that the Jews must be preserved to play their role in final salvation. Here we have an important phenomenon: a group that is despised and regarded as damned, yet which is regarded as essential for the salvation of Christians. Such paradoxes demand a search for parallels in other cultures in order to arrive at a satisfactory explanation.

The Jews, then, again in Augustine's words, continue to exist 'for the salvation of the nation [i.e. Christendom] but not for their own'. While their survival was thus ensured, their misery was no less a requirement for their 'witness' to Christianity's truth. They helped to bring salvation to Christians, but they themselves were beyond salvation, whether in this world or the next (for only their millennial descendants would be saved; they themselves were condemned to eternal hellfire). If, by chance, Jews should manage to raise themselves above a condition of misery in some Christian country, this was an unnatural situation that had to be remedied. It became a Christian duty to oppress the Jews.

According to St Thomas Aquinas, the greatest expounder of

Christian doctrine, the Jews 'in consequence of their sin, are or were destined to perpetual slavery; so that sovereigns of states may treat their goods as their own property; with the sole proviso that they do not deprive them of all that is necessary to preserve life'. He counselled, however, that robbing the Jews of everything except the bare necessities of life might 'cause the name of Christ to be blasphemed' and that therefore 'it would seem more correct to forgo what is permitted by the law'. The Jews, therefore, were permitted to live and enjoy (to a limited degree) the use of their possessions, but not because they were considered to have human rights, but out of a special saintly morality going beyond the letter of the law. The killing of any particular Jew was not a sin; only massacres or wholesale starvations that might lead to the annihilation of the Jews were deprecated, as endangering the Second Coming, or the Jews' role as 'witnesses'. It is hardly surprising that this very limited scheme of protection for the Jews proved frequently inadequate. To kill or rob a Jew was wrong in the 'law of the saints' but not in ordinary morality.

Ironically, however, Aquinas's definition of the Jews as slaves worked to some extent in their favour. For this meant that the most powerful Christian figures, the Kings and aristocrats, saw the Jews as property, of which their power gave them the right of annexation. Thus the Jews frequently became the personal slaves of powerful people, who then had an interest in preserving their property. Jews, like deer, were regarded as appurtenances of the rich; unlike deer, they could be manipulated as valuable sources of revenue. Anyone who arbitrarily killed or robbed a Jew, then, was liable to incur the wrath of some potentate who had reserved the right to kill or rob his Jews for himself, but often limited his extortions on the principle of not killing the goose that laid the golden eggs. King John, in his periodic bouts of insolvency, might extract a Jew's teeth or his eye in order to extort the last penny of his wealth (from which practice the phrase 'as valuable as a Jew's eye' is derived), but woe betide any lesser person who had recourse to this source of income. Meanwhile the Jews would have only one oppressor instead of many.

While the law of supererogatory virtue (i.e. virtue that goes beyond normal obligation), or at times the greed of potentates, did protect the Jews from annihilation, and even in settled times from undue oppression (though in times of general distress they were the primary scapegoats), it also prevented the Jews from making any secure progress culturally or economically. For any appearance of Jewish success or prosperity aroused anger and fear among Christians, since this was a blasphemous denial of the Jewish role of subjection and suffering. The history of the Jews in the Middle Ages is thus one of ups and downs. For brief periods, Jews might prosper, as in the Golden Age of Spain (12th century). As a hard-working, talented people, whose religious philosophy encouraged earthly endeavour, the Jews blossomed both culturally and economically whenever they were permitted to do so. This was noted by Christians, who in time of need were not reluctant to use Jewish talents for their own purposes. The Golden Age of Spain happened because both Christians and Muslims needed the Jews at this time. When the time of need passed, the Jews were brutally oppressed by the Christians and finally expelled. This story was repeated again and again in Jewish-Christian relations; another prominent example is the history of the Jews in Poland. But it also happened countless times on the minor level of individual towns, which would cordially invite the Jews to settle when prosperity was low, and expel them when, by Jewish effort, the economy improved.

An excellent example of the way in which the Jews were treated as a milch cow, to be discarded when the milk ran dry, is the history of the Jews in medieval England. There could hardly be a better illustration of the function and status of the Jews in medieval Christendom, and in Chapter 3, this episode in the sad history of the Jews under Christian rule will be more closely examined.

However, it is necessary first to examine in some detail the theory of Max Weber which first attempted to explain the history of the Jews in terms of pariah status.

CHAPTER 2

MAX WEBER'S THEORY OF THE JEWS
AS A PARIAH PEOPLE

Max Weber never put forward an explicit theory of antisemitism, but his concept of the Jews as a pariah people has obvious implications for the study of antisemitism and has been influential in that field. Since in this book, which is chiefly about antisemitism, I also put forward a theory of the Jews as a pariah people, it is important to state at once how my theory differs from that of Weber.

The basic difference is that Weber argues that the Jews made themselves into a pariah people, by their adoption of a separatist religion; while I argue that there is nothing in Jewish religion that makes for pariahship, that the Jews became pariahs only because they were cast in that role by Christians, out of a mythic compulsion arising from Christianity itself.

Weber argues that the Jews were traumatised by the disaster of the Babylonian conquest and destruction of the First Temple. Up to that point, they had felt secure in their covenant with God. But the Babylonian defeat was made bearable and intelligible by the new concept that it was caused by their own sins – defined as failure to observe ritual and ethical commands contained in holy writings. The holy writings first appeared in canonical form during this period of defeat, and the priestly writers shaped them into a code of conduct that marked out the Jews as a law-based religious community, rather than as a nation. It was the strict observance of this law that enabled the Jewish community to survive defeat, instead of becoming assimilated into the surrounding nations. But it also meant that the Jews were no longer a nation in the normal sense, but a guest-community living parasitically within a wider society, marked off from their host-nation by their own distinctive code, but fostering hopes of final revenge for their defeat, the recovery of their power in a much enhanced form.

Weber reinforces this picture by a comparison between the position of the Jews in Gentile society and the position of the pariahs[1] in Hinduism. He remarks that the pariahs in India follow a strict code of conduct, by which they hope for eventual salvation from their role of subservience and humiliation. This salvation, however, is purely individual, and takes the form of rebirth into a higher caste; whereas the Jewish hope of salvation is on a communal level, and is to be experienced by the descendants of the defeated people, not by themselves individually. Nevertheless, Weber sees significant similarities. Both Jews and Indian pariahs live as a despised minority in a dominant society, both groups adhere strongly to their present status which they reinforce by separatist practices, and both groups nurture hopes of salvation, as a result of this faithful observance.[2]

While I reject emphatically Weber's concept of the Jews as a pariah people, I do not reject the term 'pariah people' itself, since, properly understood, it gives a strong clue to the meaning and purpose of antisemitism. To explore the function of the Jews as a 'pariah people' in Christendom is to adopt an anthropological method, for the first time, in the explication of the phenomenon of antisemitism. Weber's attempt, in spite of its apparent aim, cannot be regarded as anthropological, because he regarded the Jews as creating their own pariah status. It did not occur to him to ask the question, 'What function was performed in Christian society by the pariah status of the Jews?' This is as if he were to discuss the position of the pariah class in Hindu India without considering the way in which their status is dictated by Hinduism, or the function which they perform in the general social scheme of Hindu society. Indeed one cannot help marvelling at European anthropologists who traversed the earth to analyse societal phenomena in so-called primitive communities, yet failed to recognise in their own society a phenomenon that was crying out for an anthropological approach.

A by-product of Weber's picture of Judaism is that he sees the Jews as chiefly motivated by 'resentment'. Their religion is powered by a deep consciousness of defeat, but instead of accepting defeat both for themselves and for their god, as in the case of other defeated communities, the Jews procure their own continuance by a dream of eventual victory when their enemies will be humiliated and the Jews will attain world dominance. Thus all the moral and ritual prescriptions of the Torah are grounded in this 'resentment', for they are the means by which the Jews propitiate Yahweh and ensure that his favour will eventually return. Weber claims to find this yearning for revenge particularly in the Psalms.

Weber's doctrine of 'resentment' is his legacy from Nietzsche, who coined this term to express his distaste for both Judaism and Christianity, as religions of the disadvantaged and weak, projecting their dreams of overthrowing the strong and noble, the true lords of humanity.[3] Nietzsche has been defended from the charge of antisemitism because he occasionally expresses admiration for the Jews. This admiration, however, seems to be based on his theory that the Jews do not really believe their own doctrine of humility, but only use it for the purpose of gaining the ultimate victory; Christianity, on the other hand, really believes in humility, and is thus truly contemptible. Christianity takes seriously what Jews regard only as an instrument employed by their indomitable will to power. The idea that Christianity was set in motion by the Jews as a means of sapping the strength of their adversaries is distinguishable from the antisemitic fantasies of Hitler only by Nietzsche's inclination to applaud such sinuous cunning. Somewhat similar to the Nietzschean brand of antisemitism is modern Japanese antisemitism, which developed for the first time as a result of the Nazi-Japanese alliance. Japanese antisemitic literature shows a curious half-admiration for the Jews' alleged success in dominating the world – a nuance that probably derives from Japan's own dreams of world-domination.

Weber's theory of Judaism ignores a great deal of Jewish history. He traces the 'pariah' status of the Jews to the destruction of the Jewish state by the Babylonians in 586 BCE, when for the first time, the Jews became a religious community instead of a nation, turning in on themselves in quietistic style. Weber, however, ignores the fact that the Babylonian disaster was by no means the end of the Jews as an independent national and political entity. Under the Hasmonean kings, the Jews threw off the yoke of a foreign empire. If observance of the Torah was a means of coping with subservience and loss of power, it is hard to see how the Torah became the inspiration of Judas Maccabaeus in his heroic military victories against the Seleucid Greeks (161 BCE). The Hasmonean John Hyrcanus (135–104 BCE) was a conqueror who ruled over a kingdom larger than that of King David, at a time over four hundred years later than the Babylonian defeat. Similarly, the three great wars of independence fought by the Jews against Rome cannot be explained if Judaism was essentially an expression of defeat.[4]

One must conclude that Weber was reading back into the ancient world a picture of the Jews derived from his own time, when the Jews had been beaten into submission by centuries of Christian persecution, including exclusion from all honourable professions, and had only recently begun to acquire a more respectable image through long-delayed and much-grudged laws of emancipation. It was easy to see downtrodden Jewish pedlars or pawnbrokers who salvaged their self-respect through study of the Torah and Talmud as using this literature as a quietist haven and oasis of revenge; it was much harder for Weber to see the Torah and Talmud as the instruments of realistic and activist political and moral theory, preserving in the Jews a national and ethical consciousness, grounded in principles far deeper than revenge. Indeed, Nietzsche's and Weber's theory of Jewish revengefulness is itself easy to understand as a continuation of the medieval concept of the vengeful Jew (Shylock, for example) – an image projected by the guilt-feelings of a persecuting society.

But what are we to make of Weber's picture of Judaism, beginning with Ezra, as a separatist religion, in which a multitude of laws built a hedge against the outside world? This picture is, in fact, familiar in another context, namely that of the Christian polemic against Judaism. It was always the contention of Christian theologians, beginning with Paul, that the legal orientation of Judaism was a sign of its degeneracy. The figure of Ezra (5th century BCE), as the father of legalism, and the pivotal figure marking the end of prophetic inspiration, is important in the religio-historical schema of Wellhausen, whose scientific work on the documentary theory in his *Prolegomena to the History of Ancient Israel*, 1885, and *Die Composition des*

Hexateuchs, 1889, was enlisted in the cause of an ancient Christian periodisation. Weber actually did not swallow Wellhausen whole. He was aware of the fact that Wellhausen's dating of the documents was much influenced by Christian prejudices. Weber's own dating allows much advanced and positive religious thought to have taken place before the Exile, especially in relation to the concept of covenant.[5] But he concurs with Wellhausen in his view of the role of Ezra, as ushering in a new narrow age which was to result in the alleged particularism, separatism, pariahhood and 'resentment' of Pharisaic and rabbinic Judaism, in contrast with the universalism of Christianity.

The chief feature of Ezra's career leading to this conclusion is his campaign against intermarriage. According to Weber, Ezra, by banning intermarriage with non-Jews, created the pariah status of the Jews, which he reinforced by separatist dietary laws directed against commensality with non-Jews. Weber has to admit that certain books admitted into the Hebrew canon cannot be fitted into such an outlook. The book of Jonah, for example, depicts a Jewish prophet who is sent on a mission to Gentiles. The book of Ruth traces the descent of King David to an ancestress, Ruth, who was a Moabite convert. The book of Job, pondering the problem of theodicy, makes its protagonist a non-Jew and makes no mention of any specifically Jewish concerns. The inclusion of these books in the canon is explained by Weber, as by other proponents of the theory of Jewish degeneracy and separatism, on the lines that there was a faction of Jews who opposed Ezra, and who managed somehow to squeeze their universalistic writings into the canon, though the later evolution of Judaism ignored them; their true line of succession being found in the intertestamental Pseudepigrapha and the New Testament.

Weber avoids the mistake, made by many other authors following a similar line, that Ezra's Judaism banned the entry of converts into the Jewish community. He is aware of too much evidence, both before and after Ezra, of a continual stream of converts into Judaism, and of a continual activity of proselytising, or at the very least of the welcoming of proselytes, by the allegedly separatist community. But Weber considers that proselytisation is compatible with separatism, because once converted, the proselytes are cut off from their former communities and are bound tightly into the Jewish community by strict laws of marriage and commensality. Thus proselytisation, in Weber's view, does not argue any universalism of outlook, but only serves to increase the numbers of the pariah community.

Weber must be applauded for not joining the large band of scholars who have argued that Ezra was opposed altogether to admitting converts into Judaism. This view is based on Ezra's (and Nehemiah's) action in compelling those Jews who had married 'foreign wives' to send them away. If Ezra accepted the idea of conversion to Judaism (as advocated in the book of Ruth), why should such an action have been felt necessary? Why did Ezra not instead urge the Jews to convert their foreign wives to Jewish practice and belief? The answer given is that Ezra was a racialist, who regarded proselytism as a contamination of the purity of the Jewish race. This picture of Ezra as a racialist has been reinforced by highlighting the expression 'the holy seed', used in Ezra 9:2[6], which has been taken to be equivalent to Nazi expressions about the purity of the Aryan race. In fact, this importation of modern racialist theory into the ancient world is an anachronism. The biblical historical records show that the Israelites were of mixed racial origins, containing a large admixture of Egyptian, Canaanite, Kenite and other elements. The very lists given by Ezra himself of the returnees from Babylon show that many of them were of Canaanite origin. Yet all these returnees were regarded as part of 'the holy seed'. This expression does not refer to racial purity, which has never been a value in any kind of Judaism. It refers to those persons who have the right to contribute to the genetic stock of the Jewish community. Converts, by the fact of their conversion, become 'holy seed', being permitted to marry other Jews, and therefore to contribute to the Jewish genetic future. The expression 'holy seed' is thus compatible with any degree of racial adulteration of the Jewish community – even with the near-total loss of Semitic genes.

Why, then, did Ezra and Nehemiah, so peremptorily demand that the 'foreign wives' should be sent away, without offering as an alternative that they, or at least some of them, could be converted? The answer lies in the religio-politics of the time. As can be seen from a close reading of Ezra, taken together with the religious polemic of II Kings 17, the point at issue was whether Judaism could be combined with polytheism. The 'people of the land' of the time were descended from the non-Jews transported to Palestine by the Assyrian policy of exchange of populations two centuries before. These people had developed a syncretistic form of religion, in which Yahweh was worshipped together with the gods brought from their previous homes in North Babylonia. What Ezra and Nehemiah were trying to stamp out was not so much polytheism as heresy. The 'foreign wives' could not be converted to Judaism because they and their families already claimed to be Jews. This is why, indeed, so many alliances had been made, even by the Temple priests: it was not so clear, before the arrival of Ezra and Nehemiah, that the syncretistic form of Judaism was unacceptable. Ezra's and Nehemiah's campaign should be thought of not as racialism, but as the assertion of uncompromising monotheism. The expulsion of the 'foreign wives' meant the expulsion of their parents and relatives too from the Israelite faith, as idolaters posing as Jews. This was the first great religious schism in history, involving considerations of theology, not race.

The correct analogy, therefore, is not between Ezra and Hitler, but between Ezra and Pope Innocent III, who outlawed the Albigenses, though Ezra's action was far less violent, consisting of a refusal of admittance to Jewish status, not a call for extermination.

The comparison with the history of Christianity is also enlightening with regard to Weber's thesis, according to which the policy of Ezra, while not racialist, was the foundation of the 'pariah' status of the Jews.

It is hard to see how Ezra's policy differs from that later adopted by the Christian Church to safeguard the continuance of the Christian faith. If Ezra turned the Jews into a pariah community, then the same appellation must be given to the Christian Church. There was a Jewish law against Jews marrying non-Jews (a law long pre-dating Ezra, being found in Deuteronomy), and the Church too enacted a law forbidding Christians to marry non-Christians.[7] There were Jewish dietary laws that had the effect of restricting social contacts between Jews and non-Jews, though, as Weber, with characteristic punctiliousness, admits, there was never any law forbidding commensality between Jews and non-Jews if the meal consisted of permitted foods. In the case of Christianity, however, many laws were passed by councils explicitly forbidding commensality with non-Christians, even though there were no Christian dietary laws.[8]

A monotheistic religion is bound to have laws forbidding intermarriage with unconverted polytheists. Polytheistic religion does not need such laws, since it is hospitable to all gods. Two spouses from different polytheistic backgrounds can worship different gods, or switch without much difficulty to the other spouse's god, or amalgamate their god-worship. A monotheist regards polytheistic worship as wrong, and cannot accept the possibility that his children will not be monotheists. On the other hand, two rival monotheistic religions are likely to forbid intermarriage with each other because it is the nature of such rival religious communities to be locked in conflict about which of them has the true succession or apostolic chain. Even two rival branches of the same monotheistic religion are likely to forbid, or at least restrict, intermarriage; an example is that of Roman Catholicism and Protestantism.

These bans on intermarriage, so characteristic of monotheism, have nothing to do with racialism or with pariahship. They arise from the claim to unique truth, which demands the preservation of the community dedicated to its transmission. The presence of persons within the community, contributing to its future by the procreation and education of the young, who do not subscribe to the community's truth-claim, would be fatal to the continued existence of the community.

Judaism, as it happens, is *less* separatist in this respect than Christianity, for Judaism does not include the belief, characteristic of classical Christianity, that all persons outside the religious communion are damned. Thus the early Christian community separated itself from the surrounding pagan world in a far more radical way than Judaism, which always acknowledged that salvation could be obtained outside the Jewish communion by God-fearing Gentiles such as Naaman, Job, Cyrus, and the repentant citizens of Nineveh in the book of Jonah. Moreover, the Christian community dreamed of a more radical victory over non-Christians, for it envisaged the eventual domination of the entire world by Christianity, while Jewish eschatology looked forward only to world-wide conversion to monotheism, not to Judaism. Such considerations do not seem to have occurred to Weber, who never realised that his criteria for a 'pariah' community applied even more strongly to Christianity.

Indeed, it seems that the very pluralism of Judaism is what stamps it, for Weber, as separatist and non-universalist. Since Christianity wished to convert the whole world, and to a large extent succeeded in doing so, this absolves it, for Weber, from the charge of pariahdom and characterises it as a universalist religion. The early history of Christianity as a radically separatist community is forgotten in consideration of its later conquest of Europe, where the Jews remained as a small and distinct minority.[9] But pariahdom is not a matter of minority status or failure to convert others on a large scale. Such failure may indeed be the index of a lack of fanaticism in the mode of self-separation from the world at large. The Jewish mode of self-separation is that of a dedicated group, like the orders of monks and friars within Christianity, which do not condemn non-members to damnation. The Jewish holiness code is intended for Jews only (including, of course, those Gentiles who opt to become Jews), and non-Jews are not regarded as sinful because they do not observe it. This kind of self-separation is by no means incompatible with universalism. On the contrary, Judaism's eschatology concerns all the nations of the world, but without seeking to destroy their independent status or dictate their modes of worship, as long as they become monotheistic and observe the minimum code of ethics, or *lex gentium*, known as the Seven Laws of the Children of Noah.[10]

The concept of pariahdom, as defined by Weber, is thus inappropriate to the Jewish mode of self-separation, though it does have some validity when applied to early Christianity, before its radical self-separation and refusal to recognise any validity outside itself resulted in a successful process of destruction and incorporation of most of the religious communities within its orbit.

The above discussion enables us to enter more deeply into the question of whether Judaism, as Weber argues, is chiefly characterised by 'resentment' and feelings of revenge. This view is really quite a traditional one, since Christian writers have always contrasted Judaism's alleged morality of revenge ('an eye for an eye') with Christianity's alleged morality of forgiveness and love. This contention (though it still plays a large role in Christian textbooks) can be seen without great difficulty for what it is: a polemical weapon in Christianity's perennial campaign to supplant Judaism. But when the same contention is put in the language of objective sociology, it becomes far more dangerous, since it easily enters the pseudo-scientific formulations of antisemitism. We are often told that it is naive of Jews to take offence when told by Weber that their religion is fundamentally an expression of pariah resentment and desire for revenge. The terms 'pariah' and 'resentment', we are told, are in Weber's hands merely sociological terms with restricted definitions and without any derogatory intention. This, however, would be to underestimate the extent to which religious animosities can survive unconsciously in post-Enlightenment would-be scientific transformations, and become even more virulent because released from theological restraints. In Weber's case, the legacy of the Christian polemic against Judaism is especially noticeable, since he departs from his Nietzschean source by applying the concept of 'resentment' only to Judaism, and not to Christianity, which he explicitly absolves from 'resentment'.

Weber did a great deal of reading of Jewish literary sources; but, characteristically for his day, he made no effort to undertake field work in contemporary Jewish communities, or even to study the history of the Jews as living communities in Europe and the Orient in post-Talmudic times. Less forgivably, he did not consult Jewish scholars about the meaning of the Jewish texts over which he pored. The result is a judgement of the Jews and Judaism that is quite false to the tone of Jewish community life. Jews have never isolated themselves from non-Jewish society in order to harbour brooding dreams of revenge. The history of the Jews throughout the Middle Ages and modern times shows that whenever relentless outside oppression relaxed, they blossomed into full and enthusiastic participation in the cultural achievements of their host society. The tone of Jewish society is not consciousness of defeat, but on the contrary, expectation of success, so that setbacks and societal demotions are always regarded as temporary nuisances. No Jewish family ever reconciles itself to a lowly position in society, and even if the parents are resigned to being, say, pawnbrokers or petty shopkeepers, their children are expected (given that the wider society allows Jews to have career opportunities) to acquire high educational qualifications and enter respected professions. Even before the emancipation brought long-delayed rights to the Jews, they occupied high positions in host societies whenever allowed the opportunity to exercise their talents; for example, in medieval Spain, medieval England, and late-medieval Poland, Jews occupied a high proportion of managerial positions. Periods of Gentile toleration were invariably followed by explosions of violent intolerance, when the growth of a Gentile managerial class rendered the services of the Jews no longer essential, and underlying feelings of hostility to Jews as an accursed community no longer needed to be suppressed.

This history is not that of a pariah class, nursing hopes of revenge. On the contrary, it is the history of a community of very high morale, forward-looking and optimistic, and little concerned about brooding about the past. The lowest point of Jewish morale was in the 18th century, when emancipation came to everyone except the Jews, who – from the aspect of status and secular education – remained in the Middle Ages, though individuals such as Moses Mendelssohn and Salomon Maimon managed to acquire literary and scientific knowledge and even came to the forefront of culture. Not long before Weber's time the Jews had begun to enter an era of emancipation. Even their Gentile wellwishers expected them to take centuries to catch up to the standard of European culture. In the event, it took only one generation of emancipation for the Jews to reach such a high participation in the professions as to excite antisemitic envy. The complaints then made were not that the Jews were an indrawn, backward, revenge-brooding community, but that they were dominating Gentile society by their excessive participation in it. Weber did not offer any explanation of this rapid integration of the Jews into Western emancipated culture. His analysis, despite its purportedly broad historical sweep, is very much tied to a perception of the Jews that was rooted in the recent pre-emancipation past.

Weber's much-praised researches into Jewish literature, on which he based his claim that Judaism is a religion of 'resentment', were largely confined to the Hebrew Bible and the intertestamental literature; he knew little about the rabbinic literature, despite his sporadic attempts to study it (though indeed what he found there led him to modify previously-held views). He found his chief evidence in the Psalms, of which he declared, 'The religion of the Psalms is full of the need for vengeance ... The majority for the Psalms are quite obviously replete with the moralistic legitimation and satisfaction of an open and hardly concealed need for vengeance on the part of a pariah people.' It is interesting to enquire how this result is arrived at. About a third of the Psalms are individual petitions for help, expressions of gratitude or joy; these poems do not refer at all to the position of the Jewish people as a whole, and through the centuries, Jews and Christians alike have used them as moving expressions of individual devotion. It was a nineteenth-century theory that all the Psalms should be regarded as written for cultic worship, and that none of them should be regarded as expressions of personal, individual feelings. This view is still held by some present-day scholars, as part of the theory of form criticism[12]; but many scholars now recognise that many of the Psalms expressing individual anguish or devotion are just what they appear to be, and that their cultic use in public worship in the Second Temple period was a later development.[13] Weber's adoption of a questionable current theory enables him to enlist these psalms as calls for national revenge. He also used a now-obsolete dating of the Psalms[14], by which they are largely the product of the post-Exilic situation of the Jews.

Again, many of the Psalms are concerned with the question of theodicy. Why do the righteous suffer, and the wicked flourish? The answer given is that in the long run the wicked get their deserts and the righteous are rewarded. Weber interprets this solution as an expression of revenge in every case, an interpretation that seems, at the least, eccentric. The concern of the psalmist can be much more plausibly interpreted as a genuine perplexity about how the evils of life can be reconciled with the goodness of God. Weber notes that the book of Job, unlike Psalms, regards the problem of evil as insoluble; he concludes, therefore, that the author of Job was produced by 'the upper classes', and does not share 'the theodicy of disprivilege'. Yet Weber attributes the doctrine of 'resentment' to Ezra and Nehemiah, who both belonged to the upper classes, and, in general, does not distinguish elsewhere between various classes among the Jews, apparently considering the whole community as united in consciousness of national calamity. Nor does Weber address the question of how Job was included in the canon if it presents a theodicy diametrically opposed to that which allegedly shaped Judaism so decisively.

The Psalms undoubtedly do contain some cries for revenge, as does every body of literature, ancient or modern, that attempts to cover the gamut of human emotion. But we do not regard Milton as a poet of revenge just because he began a poem with the line 'Avenge O Lord Thy slaughtered saints', or because he devoted a long poem to the task of 'justifying the ways of God to man' with the conclusion that everything would come right in the end. More characteristic of the Jewish ethos is the Midrashic story that, when the Israelites were singing their exultant song of triumph over the Egyptians at the Exodus, God refused the angels permission to join in, saying, 'My children, the Egyptians, are drowning in the Red Sea.' This story is indulgent to the human passions of revenge and triumph experienced by an oppressed people experiencing longed-for liberation, but puts these passions firmly into perspective from a universal standpoint.

All in all, it appears that Weber's portrayal of the Jews is merely the age-old Christian anti-Jewish polemic disguised as sociology. In particular, there is the common feature of a drastic and exaggerated periodisation of Jewish history, by which the Jews, at a certain dramatic point, plunge into a disaster which leaves them marked by defeat and subjection. In the Christian schema, this point is the destruction of the Second Temple by the Romans in 70 CE, which Christian literature, from the Gospels onwards, interpreted as a punishment for the Jewish crime of deicide. There is a widespread myth that the entire Jewish population of Palestine was deported into exile at this point, and that the Jews then ceased to be a normal nation. Such a depth of disaster and disinheritance fits the Christian conception of the Jews as undergoing a curse because of their rejection of the divinity of Christ. The historical truth is very different. The Jews continued to form the majority of the population of Palestine right up to the Muslim conquest of the 7th century CE. There were thus over five centuries of Jewish history in Palestine that have disappeared from the Christian myth. These include the Bar Kokhba Revolt, when the Jews defeated the power of Rome and achieved independence for a period of two years (135–7). They also include the golden age of the Patriarchate of Rabbi Judah the Prince, the compiler of the Mishnah, when the Jews, reconciled to Roman power, achieved peaceful and prosperous status as a Roman province (200–230). The Patriarchate continued until 425 CE, and came to an end only because the Roman Empire had become Christian and intolerant. During the short reign of the Emperor Julian the Apostate, the Jews even began the rebuilding of the Temple, which was halted by the death of the Emperor and the resumption of Christian oppression. The period of the exile and subjection of the Jews of Palestine began not in the 1st century, but in the 7th, through a combination of Muslim internecine war, which made Palestine uninhabitable for non-Muslims, and Christian theological intolerance, which allowed Jews to live in Christendom only as a disprivileged class. Meanwhile, the Jews of Babylonia, where a settled and tolerant Muslim regime allowed the large Jewish population a considerable measure of self-rule under their Exilarch, enjoyed a long period of peaceful development and cultural achievement (the Talmudic and Geonic eras) until the 11th century.

Weber, however, not only adopts the Christian myth, but greatly exaggerates it by dating the degradation and depoliticisation of the Jews not from the destruction of the Second Temple, but from that of the First Temple, more than six hundred years earlier.

Another feature of Weber's theory of the Jews must be mentioned, for though ostensibly a matter of economics, it too contains theological overtones and a strong dash of anti-Judaism. This is Weber's contribution to the question of how far the Jews were responsible for the growth of capitalism. Werner Sombart, in his book *The Jews and Modern Capitalism*, argued that the Jews were mainly responsible, because of their development of a rational, value-free approach to economic affairs. Weber, however, in his celebrated *The Protestant Ethic and the Spirit of Capitalism*, had put forward a different view, which he defended against Sombart in subsequent years.

Weber's view was that, though the Jews had indeed made an important contribution to the development of capitalism by the introduction of rational methods of financing, they had failed to discover the main requirement for capitalism proper, namely the organisation of mass production. This discovery was reserved for the Protestant entrepreneurs who set up the first factories. Weber thus set himself the very

33

interesting task of explaining why the theology of Protestantism was conducive to this all-important economic development, while that of Judaism was not. Here again Weber made use of his theory of the Jews as a pariah people actuated by a religion of pariahdom.

Weber gives two main reasons why the Jews failed to arrive at the ideas necessary for capitalism. The first is that Judaism did not contain the theological idea of predestination; the second is that Judaism, because of its pariah structure, has a two-tier system of morality in business matters, by which non-Jews were not treated with the same moral scrupulousness that was applied in dealing with fellow-Jews.

The way in which the doctrine of predestination is held by Weber to have conduced to the growth of capitalism need not detain us long here. Suffice to say that Weber thought that this doctrine contributed significantly to the Protestant merchant's feeling that his business activities had religious sanction and holiness. It is true that predestination plays no part in Judaism, but it may be thought that such a doctrine could just as easily lead to lassitude as to purposeful activity. The Jewish doctrine of free will certainly does not give anyone assurances of success, but it does prevent people from excusing failure as preordained, and may thus act as a spur to effort.

More important in our present context is Weber's emphasis on an alleged double standard in Jewish business practice. This again, he argued, prevented the Jews from feeling any sense of vocation in their business activities, which they regarded as outside the scope of their religious life. Thus, while the Jews did apply rationalism to economic activity, they did so in a piecemeal way, and never fused their economic rationalism with their religious fervour as Protestants did. The conviction that successful entrepreneurship was an expression of central religious feeling and consciousness of salvation was the mainspring of the growth of capitalism, and this feeling, according to Weber, existed only in Protestantism.

If some Jews were less scrupulous in their business dealings with non-Jews than with their fellow-Jews, this is much more easily explained as an instance of the universal trend to favour one's own in-group. On the other hand, one could easily multiply instances of Jewish religious exhortation to be *more* scrupulous in dealing with non-Jews than with Jews.[15] One could also give many instances of non-Jews expressing a preference for doing business with Jews because they experienced Jewish businessmen as honest and reliable. Jewish rationalism, on the whole, has expressed itself in business by the realisation that cheating does not pay in the long run because it loses customers. The success of Marks & Spencer's, for example, by innovations of customer-trust, willingness to replace unsatisfactory goods etc., can be paralleled throughout the history of Jewish commerce. Of course, there have been many hostile expressions about Jews as dishonest and grasping, but these have come most often from rival businessmen who resented Jewish competition, and disliked what they regarded as brash Jewish methods of cutting prices, providing cheaper substitutes, and advertising goods. Customers, on the contrary, have not disliked the Jewish practice of reducing prices by innovative methods of production, and have in fact shown their appreciation of these methods by flocking to buy Jewish wares.

The idea that Jewish religion itself sanctions the cheating of non-Jews has arisen largely from misrepresenting certain religious texts in the Bible and Talmud. It is certainly true that there is a certain discrimination in these texts between Jews and non-Jews, in that a Jew is commanded to treat his fellow-Jew more like a member of his own family than as a business rival or even just a fellow-citizen. But a high standard of intra-familial love does not necessarily imply an attitude of hostility or exploitation towards those who are not members of the family.

An example is the Jewish attitude towards the taking of interest on loans. The Bible says plainly that interest may be charged on loans to non-Jews, but not on loans to fellow-Jews. This has very often been interpreted to mean that Jews are permitted to exploit and cheat non-Jews. But this interpretation depends on the very foolish idea that to charge interest on a loan is inherently immoral. It is obvious, as the whole modern world has accepted despite centuries of Christian self-torture on the subject, that a businessman is quite entitled to charge interest on a loan in consideration of both the loss he suffers by depriving himself of the use of the loaned amount, and the service he supplies to the borrower whom he enables to engage in a profitable enterprise. Yet there still remains a category of loans in which it would be boorish and insensitive to charge interest: namely, loans to

close friends and relations who need the money not to fund an enterprise, but to extricate themselves from financial difficulty. The Bible
exhorts Jews to regard all loans to fellow-Jews as coming into the
latter category. But the Bible does not regard interest on loans as
wicked in itself, and therefore permits it in an extra-familial business
context. The Christian Church, however, partly basing itself on some
superficial remarks by Aristotle and partly on misinterpretations of
both the Jewish Bible and the New Testament, outlawed interest
altogether, thus making any large-scale business enterprise impossible. The solution that was found was to hand over banking activities
to the Jews, who, in Christian theory, were damned anyway (see
pages 53 to 57).

To Weber, the fact that Judaism enjoins a special standard of loving, caring behaviour to fellow-Jews is proof positive that Jews have
made themselves into a pariah people. The alleged double standard
is, in Weber's view, what prevented the Jews from being the founders
of capitalism, which demanded the more universalistic approach
found in Protestantism. On the other hand, Sombart, agreeing that
the Jews have a double standard, saw this as the very thing that
enabled the Jews to be the founders of capitalism, since it released
them from medieval moralistic market restriction, and rendered possible the coldly rationalistic, exploitative approach to business that
was characteristic of capitalism.

Whether it was Judaism or Protestantism or neither that produced
capitalism is a question that we may thankfully shelve in our present
enquiry. We do need to ask the question, however, 'What is a double
standard?' Every dedicated group has sought to intensify the bond
between members of the group by adopting a special standard of
loving behaviour towards each other. It is only when people outside
the group are regarded as legitimate targets of selfish, exploitative or
dishonest behaviour that we can talk of a 'double standard', with the
implication that people outside the group are not regarded as fully
human and are not included within the scope of ordinary human
ethics. When those outside the group are regarded as fully ethical
subjects, while those inside have undertaken to observe a supererogatory code, what we have is not a 'double standard', but a band of
brothers and sisters dedicated to a common cause. Such groups would

include, for example, the Catholic orders of monks and friars, the utopian groups formed by Robert Owen and Coleridge, and the community depicted in Plato's *Republic*.

The Jewish doctrine of the *lex gentium*, or the Seven Laws of the Children of Noah, ensures that the special provisions of the Holiness Code and the utopian provisions of the Holy Land (such as the cancellation of debts every seventh year) do not give rise to a 'double standard'. Instead, these special provisions are part of the Jewish self-image as a dedicated people, or 'kingdom of priests', whose special obligations towards each other would be meaningless if unaccompanied by an ethical attitude towards the whole of mankind.

To speak of such a group as forming itself into a 'pariah' community by the exercise of its special code is thus a reversal of its intention. The pariah caste of Hinduism accepts its lowly status, reconciles itself to the performance of humiliating tasks which deprive it of purity, and hopes that by obedience to the rules imposed upon it, the individuals who compose it will be reborn into a higher caste. The Jews, on the other hand, think of themselves as Brahmins, not as pariahs. Their purity code is one appropriate to the highest, not the lowest, caste. When they suffer oppression and humiliation, they regard these as inappropriate to their status. However patiently they bear these tribulations, they regard them as mere temporary setbacks, and whenever oppression is temporarily lifted, they gravitate immediately and naturally to high cultural positions. Above all, they do not regard their eventual salvation as an escape of individuals from their caste, but rather as the vindication and restoration of the caste as a whole to its true position in society. On Weber's definition of 'pariah' it is impossible to differentiate between a pariah caste and a Brahmin caste that happens to fall on hard times.

Yet it is undoubtedly the case that the Jews have functioned as a pariah caste in Christian society. To this extent, we can accept Weber's terminology. But this pariah status has been imposed upon the Jews, not accepted by them as forming any part of their self-image. The cause lies not in Judaism, but in Christianity.

CHAPTER 3

ANTISEMITISM OUTSIDE CHRISTENDOM

Weber's theory of the Jews as a pariah community, though expressed in sophisticated sociological terms, is simply an example of the well-worn popular theory that antisemitism is the fault of the Jews. Though Weber himself did not draw this conclusion explicitly, his terminology recalls familiar charges against the Jews as provoking hostility by their separatism, stubborn insistence on retaining their distinctive observances, and refusal to enter into relations of easy friendliness with their neighbours.

There is an obvious test of this theory, and that is to ask whether in fact the Jews have met with hostility everywhere, or only in certain well-defined areas. If we turn to the area from which Weber took his 'pariah' terminology, namely India, we encounter the surprising fact that in this very area, the home of pariahdom, the Jews have never been treated as pariahs.

The Jews of Cochin, on the Malabar Coast of South Western India, formed a large, pious community, showing all the features that, according to Weber, should have made it into a pariah group. Yet this community lived for centuries in the midst of Indian society without ever encountering antisemitism. On the contrary, ·it was a highly-respected community, living on terms of great friendship with its Hindu neighbours, and enjoying the favour of the Rajah and other high Hindu officials. On all important public occasions, Jewish representatives were invited, as a matter of course, to attend, and given positions of honour, with due consideration for their religious dietary requirements. The Jews responded by their loyalty, and gave valued military service to the Rajah against his enemies, though it was accepted that the Jews would not fight on the Sabbath.

The first time that the Jewish community of Cochin experienced antisemitism was when the Portuguese arrived in the 16th century. The insults and violence directed to the Jews by these Christian colonists from the moment they arrived, including the burning of Jewish synagogues and sacred books, were found astonishing and distressing by the Hindu community, and were the subject of protests by the Hindu authorities. Throughout the period of Portuguese rule (1502–1663), the Jews were subject to Christian oppression, but were saved from total disaster by the repeated intervention and protection of the Rajah. The sufferings of the Jews ceased when Portuguese rule gave way to that of the Dutch (1663–1795). Holland, a leader of the Enlightenment in Europe, had given safe haven to Jewish refugees from the Spanish Inquisition and fostered a flourishing Dutch Jewish community; and the same spirit of enlightenment was extended to the Jews of Holland's overseas empire.[1] The better treatment accorded to the Jews of Cochin under the Dutch can largely be attributed to the secular movement of toleration which was working towards the emancipation of the Jews in Europe.[2]

A similar story could be told about the Jews of China. The popular adage, beloved of pub orators and even of respected authors such as H. G. Wells, that Jews have suffered antisemitism wherever they have gone, and that therefore they must be somehow responsible for it themselves, is not borne out by the historical facts, and is the fruit of an ethnocentrism that regards the world outside Christendom as nonexistent. It is true indeed that wherever the Jews have gone in Christendom they have encountered antisemitism. It is also true that even areas in Christendom which Jews have never entered and in which the Christian inhabitants have never seen a Jew, are permeated with antisemitism. The obvious corollary is that Christendom itself is the locus of antisemitism, the origin of which should be sought in Christian belief and mythology.

Against this, it may be urged that antisemitism, though not worldwide, is nevertheless found outside the area, and era, in which Christian beliefs have predominated.

The earliest example of non-Christian antisemitism may be thought to be the genocidal scheme of Haman, as depicted in the biblical Book of Esther. This purports to be an incident in the history of the Persian Empire where the adversary of the Jews, Haman, describes the Jews in typically antisemitic terms: 'There is a certain people scattered abroad and dispersed among the people in all the provinces of thy kingdom; and their laws are diverse from all people; neither keep they the king's laws: therefore it is not for the king's profit to suffer them. If it please the king, let it be written that they may be destroyed.' (Esther 3:8). This episode is vaguely dated, but may be intended to refer to the 6th century BCE, i.e. about six centuries before the birth of Christian antisemitism. Yet the grounds offered for the proposed annihilation of the Jews are uncannily similar to Weber's characterisation of the Jews as a pariah people even at this date, and may have contributed to Weber's ascription of the origin of Jewish pariah status to as early as the Babylonian Exile.

However, we may discount the alleged antisemitism portrayed in the Book of Esther, for this book was actually written in the Hellenistic period, and the author retrojects the antisemitism of his own period into the earlier Persian Empire, which, as we know from authentic historical sources was actually very tolerant and friendly to the Jews. Indeed, the mythical Haman, advising his Emperor to annihilate the Jews, is most probably a disguised version of a Hellenistic antisemite of the 2nd century BCE.

The real beginning of antisemitism is indeed to be found in the Hellenistic culture of Alexandria, Antioch, Rome and other centres in the Greek and Greco-Roman Empires from the 3rd century before the birth of Christianity. The genocidal advice attributed to Haman was actually given to the Seleucid emperor Antiochus Sidetes in 133 BCE, while besieging Jerusalem in the time of the Jewish king John Hyrcanus. Some officers urged the emperor to destroy not only Jerusalem but the whole Jewish people, since the Jews were the only people in the world that refused to associate with other peoples; they reminded him also of the previous attempt by Antiochus Epiphanes (175–164 BCE) to stamp out Judaism as inimical to humanity (Diodorus, *Bibliotheca*, 34:1, 1ff.) Here again the same note is sounded: it is Jewish separatism that arouses the hostility of Gentiles. Hellenistic antisemitism led to periodic massacres of Jews in the great Hellenistic cities. Antisemitic writings were produced in Alexandria by writers including Manetho, Apion and Chaeremon.

The most dangerous and far-reaching Hellenistic expression of anti-semitism is that found in certain writings of the Gnostics, whose movement stems from the pre-Christian period. In these writings, the Jews are not merely attacked as antisocial and misanthropic, but are given a cosmic role as the acolytes and devotees of an evil deity. The general theory of Gnosticism is that this evil world of ours was created by an evil, or at least limited and self-deluded, god known as the Demiurge (or Creator). The special antisemitic theory held by some Gnostics was that this evil god is no other than the God of the Jews, and that it was he who gave the Jews the Torah, in the name of which they impede knowledge (*gnosis*) of the true High God. This is the first appearance in history of the antisemitic image of the Jews as the people of the Devil. It is also the first appearance of the antisem-itic image of the Jews as unspiritual, materialistic and bound to the limited values of life on this earth.

Hellenistic pre-Christian antisemitism was indeed very important in the history of antisemitism. It was based on the cultural rivalry between Hellenism and Judaism. Hellenists, in their way, were often just as enthusiastic about spreading the values and practices of Hellen-ism as a universal culture as Christians, later on, were about spreading the Gospel. For example, Antiochus Epiphanes, who sparked off the Hasmonean revolt by desecrating the Jewish Temple, was a genuine devotee of Hellenistic culture, and was outraged at the Jewish refusal to adopt it wholeheartedly. A later persecutor of Judaism was the Roman Emperor Hadrian, who again regarded Jewish practices such as circumcision, the Sabbath and dietary observances as an affront to the Hellenistic ideal of cultural uniformity. Not that Hadrian opposed the concept of toleration: on the contrary, he prided himself on his receptiveness to all faiths, and set up a Pantheon to which all nations under Roman rule were invited to contribute statues of their gods. The Jews too were invited to send a statue of their god, Abraham; and when they refused to do so on the grounds that Abraham was not a god, and that the God the Jews worshipped could not be portrayed in a statue, Hadrian felt this to be an insult to his great ecumenical project. Hadrian, as the leader of a nation that despite its imperial conquests (including that of Greece) had surrendered totally to Greek culture, resented the intransigence of a nation that insisted on not only retaining its own culture but on asserting its superiority. Though ostensibly tolerant, Hellenism was actually intolerant of any real divergence from its norm, or challenge to its supremacy. Here the Hellenists, with their ideology of imperialist mission, differed from the authentic Greek intellectuals of earlier days, who, in so far as they were aware of Jewish culture, regarded it with admiration.

Thus there was a deep and bitter conflict between Hellenism and Judaism, arising from the Jewish claim to be the chosen people of God and consequent denial of Hellenistic cultural pre-eminence. Hellenistic resentment at the Jewish claim could take two forms. One was simple rejection, as in the scornful diatribes against the Jews as mere barbarians who were incapable of benefiting from the light of Hellenism. Another, however, more significant for the theme of this book, was the method of usurpation. This reaction to Judaism consisted of asserting a rival claim to that of the Jews, but in a style clearly derived from the discourse of Judaism itself. The Gnostics were the inventors of this kind of supplanting reaction. They set up a rival chosen race, 'the seed of Seth', and thereby relegated the Jews to the position of false claimants. Using the Jewish Scriptures, especially Genesis, as their text, they developed a doctrine of election that bypassed the Jewish succession from Abraham onwards. Non-Jewish biblical characters such as Seth, Melchizedek or even Cain became the heroes of the story, members of a line of enlightened ones, possessors of *gnosis* derived from the High God, who opposed the unspiritual teachings of the flawed Creator-God of the Jews.

The latter reaction shows that many Hellenists were unable to adopt an attitude of simple scorn towards the Jews. They were impressed, in spite of themselves, by the confidence of the Jewish stance, and their response was to take it over, ejecting the Jews in the process.

This response was the precursor of the Christian supplanting of the Jews, in which the Jewish Bible was adapted to the purposes of the Christian Church, though in a much more thoroughgoing fashion than that achieved by the Gnostics. The Jews were thereby ejected from the position of being God's people, and their place was taken by the new Israel, Christendom. Instead of selecting certain aspects of the Jewish Bible, as the Gnostics did, Christians took over the whole of it, and reinterpreted it so drastically that it became a Christian Bible. The Jews themselves were vilified for not acquiescing in this reinterpretation, and relegated to a lowly position in the cosmic scheme.

Thus Christianity should not be thought of as introducing a new form of antisemitism unconnected with that of Hellenism. On the contrary, Christian antisemitism shows strong links with Hellenism. It should be thought of as the variety of Hellenistic antisemitism that survived into the medieval and modern world. The previous existence of Hellenistic antisemitism is no disproof of the centrality of Christian antisemitism in any study of the subject, since they are related to each other as precursor and successor. We shall see, however, that Christianity, much though it owes to Gnosticism, added certain features to what it found there, and thus produced a unique brand of antisemitism.

There is, however, one form of antisemitism that has little to do with either Hellenism or Christianity, and must be reckoned an independent variety. This is the antisemitism found in the religion of Islam, which began in the 7th century CE with the appearance of the prophet Muhammad in Arabia. In the Quran, the Jews are stigmatised as the enemies of Muhammad, who defeated them militarily in Arabia. Judaism, in Islam, became a permitted religion, but Jews were subject to special taxes and disprivileged in many ways. Sporadic persecution of Jews has taken place throughout Muslim history, though at a much less severe level than in Christendom. In recent years, however, political conflict between Jews and Muslims over the establishment of the state of Israel has led to the proliferation of antisemitic literature in the Near East, and the adoption by Muslims of antisemitic attitudes and materials previously associated with the Christian tradition (e.g. *The Protocols of the Elders of Zion*).

The common characteristic of Muslim and Christian antisemitism is that both derive from a theology of displacement. Islam, like Christianity, makes a counter-claim to that of Judaism, and seeks to

43

supplant the Jews from the position of the chosen people of God. Here again, Islam adopts a Jewish discourse, but seeks to occupy the position of the Jews in that discourse. The Jews become the object of hostility, because they do not acquiesce in their own displacement, and do not adopt the new religion which is claimed to be the 'fulfilment' of their own. Just as Christianity took over the Jewish Scriptures, interpreting them as prophecies of the coming of Christ, and supplementing them by new Christian Scriptures, so Islam assigns a prophetic value to the Jewish Scriptures, incorporating their material in an interpreted form in its own Quran, though with the proviso that the Jewish Scriptures have been corrupted by the Jews, and therefore cannot be fully accepted. (Here the Islamic strategy comes halfway between that of Gnosticism and that of Christianity: Gnostics, while using Jewish Scripture for their own purposes, regarded it as flawed from the beginning; Christianity regards Jewish Scripture as totally inspired, but as falsified by Jewish interpretation; Islam regards Jewish Scripture as totally inspired in its earliest form, but as having become flawed through the editing of Jewish scribes, who inserted inauthentic material and omitted material prophetic of Muhammad.)

We may freely accept, then, that antisemitism is not confined to Christendom, but also exists, in a different form, in Islam. But this leads us to frame a first formulation of the origin and scope of antisemitism, one which will require further refinement and nuancing, but which is nevertheless an important guiding principle: *antisemitism arises in areas dominated by a religion derived from Judaism.* This principle leaves room for much elaboration, for the type of antisemitism that arises depends on the character of the relationship between the supplanting religion and the religion of origin. It also depends, as will be explained, on the type of *usurpation myth* that arises in the supplanting religion to explain the need for a new form of the religion, for a new personnel for the chosen people of God, and for the reprobation and expulsion of the previous personnel.

One objection, however, that may be made against the principle enunciated above is that it takes no account of the earliest form of antisemitism, namely Hellenistic antisemitism, which arose from cultural rivalry and simple dismissal of Jewish religious claims, not

44

from the attempt to supplant the Jews from within their own frame of discourse.

Here it is necessary to enter more deeply into the definition of antisemitism, in order to distinguish various levels.

In general, antisemitism means simply hatred of Jews. It is hardly necessary, at this date, to point out that it does *not* mean 'hatred of Semites'. Hitler's close friendship and alliance with the Mufti of Jerusalem proves that he was no enemy to Semites, but only to Jews, and this is true of all antisemites. The name 'anti-Semite' was coined by Wilhelm Marr[3] to give a pseudo-scientific genetic or racialist veneer to Jew-hatred. Some well-meaning but fatuous writers (e.g. Arthur Koestler and Hugh Montefiore) have taken the racialist theory so seriously that they have proposed an easy solution to antisemitism: prove that the Jews are not really Semites (being of Khazar or mixed descent) and antisemitism will disappear. Unfortunately, since the equation between Jews and Semites was never more than a ploy, this solution has no chance of working. James Parkes proposed that the word should always be written 'antisemite' rather than 'anti-Semite' in order to mark the hollowness of the idea that there are any people who are genuinely opposed to Semites as such (i.e. not only Jews, but also Arabs, Phoenicians, Akkadians, Babylonians, etc.). It is unfortunate that the word has become so well-established that it is now impossible to exchange it for a more appropriate expression such as 'Jew-haters'. Given that the word has come to stay, we must reconcile ourselves to such apparent absurdities as 'Arab antisemitism', or the apparent anachronism of 'Hellenistic antisemitism' at a time when racialist theory did not exist. The most we can do to obviate absurdity or anachronism is to use the spelling 'antisemitism', as Parkes suggested, to indicate that the word is not to be taken literally as meaning 'hatred of Semites', but as a code expression for Jew-hatred. Meanwhile, it is to be hoped that the expression will cease to be used as an excuse for opportunistic semantic legerdemain: e.g. 'How can Arabs be antisemites? They are Semites themselves.'

If antisemitism means hatred of Jews, how does it differ from mere xenophobia? The answer is that at the lowest level, antisemitism is indeed merely a form of xenophobia, and is parallel to such expressions as Anglophobia. At this level, Jews are merely disliked because they are different, just as Englishmen may dislike Frenchmen, or even Welshmen. Much of Hellenistic antisemitism was at this level. But much of it also rose above this level, becoming instead an antagonism of an ideological kind, Hellenists believing that the Jews represented a threat to the Hellenistic cultural claim to be the highest form of civilisation. This ideological antisemitism rose to yet another level in Gnosticism, where the Jews were regarded as the earthly representatives of an evil cosmic power; and to yet another level in Christianity, where the Jews were believed to have performed a deed of preternatural wickedness, the murder of the Incarnate God. Gavin Langmuir has argued that it is only at this irrational and paranoid level that antisemitism deserves its special and unique place, demanding a special term, among the various kinds of xenophobia. I would agree that this ultimate form of antisemitism is the most interesting and important to the historian, sociologist and anthropologist. A special paranoid loathing attaches to the Jews on this final level that cannot be paralleled in any other xenophobic hatred, and it was this that brought about the Holocaust, after many centuries of indoctrination. Yet there are terminological difficulties in confining the term antisemitism to this level only, and I would suggest that the term should be applied at every level, but with the reservation that only at the *demonising ideological level* does antisemitism present a unique problem.

Before modern times, there were only three forms of demonising ideological antisemitism, Gnostic, Christian and Islamic, of which the Christian form was by far the most virulent, being fortified by a uniquely horrifying usurpation myth. A detailed comparison of these three pre-modern forms is beyond the scope of this book. Here it is sufficient to note that all three are Judaism-dependent forms of religion, and we may amend our formula as follows. *Demonising ideological antisemitism is confined to populations adhering to religions derived from Judaism.*

The existence of virulent forms of modern antisemitism, apparently not associated with Christianity, is often cited to prove that demonising antisemitism is not necessarily religious in origin. Nazism displays itself as a non-Christian, pagan, or even anti-Christian doctrine in the spirit of Nietzsche. Similarly, the other manifestation of modern ideological antisemitism, that of Marxism, with its more recent off-spring, New Left antisemitism, is clearly in aim and self-definition non-Christian. However, any historical examination of the origins and thought patterns of Nazi and New Left antisemitism shows how indissolubly continuous these manifestations are with Christian anti-semitism. The Nazi antisemitic propaganda consisted of the repetition of antisemitic slanders concocted against the Jews in the Middle Ages and even earlier: e.g., the blood libel alleging that Jews used Christian blood for ritual purposes. Hitler consciously based his stance on the antisemitic outpourings of Luther. While Nazism was not a Christian movement, its antisemitism was the fruit of centuries of Christian antisemitic propaganda, which was especially virulent in Germany, the main home of the Passion Plays. The Nazis knew that to play the antisemitic card was a political ploy that would rouse a ready response in the Christian population not only of Germany, but of Europe generally. Without the tacit and often open support of this popu-lation, the Holocaust could never have been implemented.

Marxist antisemitism was not so consciously designed to appeal to ingrained Christian prejudices, yet its origins may be easily traced. Marx himself was a Jew, but was baptised and brought up as a Christian. His whole education was Christian, and his knowledge of Judaism was only that contained in Christian sources. Though as an adult he shed his Christian belief, he retained a negative Christian image of the Jews as essentially 'hucksters' whose whole religion centred on money. It was therefore easy for him to identify Judaism as the heart and soul of capitalism, an identification he shared with other socialist antisemites including Proudhon and Charles Fourier. This identification is traceable ultimately to the Christian image of Judas Iscariot, the archetypal Jew, who sold his master for money, juggled with the funds of the twelve apostles, and is always portrayed in Christian art as carrying a money-bag. In New Left antisemitism, the image is carried a stage further: the Jews are not merely the organisers of internationalist capitalist finance, but the spearhead of the capitalist imperialist Zionist conspiracy against the innocent and deprived nations of the third world.

The paranoid nature of these images is illustrated by the fact that right-wing supporters of capitalism have found it just as easy to portray the Jews as the spearhead of the forces of international communism. Some have even portrayed the Jews as combining both operations: furthering both capitalism and communism simultaneously as concerted manoeuvres aimed at the disintegration of the Gentile world. The total picture of modern antisemitism shows a strong tendency to identify the Jews with whatever diabolic force is required by a dualistic ideology: where theory demands a wicked political group working against justice and progress, that group is discovered to be the Jews. It cannot be a coincidence that this dualistic schema echoes that of traditional Christianity. This phenomenon arises from the fact that when a belief system collapses, it does not disappear, but persists in the form of unconscious fantasies and prejudices, which may be all the stronger for being inaccessible to rational analysis. The Jewphobia of modern political ideologies should therefore be regarded as *post-Christian antisemitism*. It should not be equated with the pre-Christian antisemitism of the Hellenistic world. For it bears all the special characteristics of Christian antisemitism, of which it is the unacknowledged child. Nazi antisemitism, for example, should not be written off as a reversion to paganism, in virtue of Wagner's and Hitler's expressed admiration for Norse mythology. This is an undeserved slur on Norse pagans, who were never antisemitic until they became Christianised.

A final version of our formula will thus read: *Demonising ideological antisemitism is confined to populations adhering to, or having a historical background of, religions derived from Judaism.*

An added complication is that Western civilisation, through its successful use of technology, has had an important influence on non-Western societies, especially in the 20th century. This influence has also extended to Western ideologies, especially Marxism, which became the ruling creed of China and other Eastern countries. Together with technology and the communist creed, Marxism brought to these countries for the first time the tenets of antisemitism, now masquerading as 'Zionist imperialism'. Since, however, antisemitism has no real roots in Eastern countries, it became an empty formula there and is not likely to survive further political developments.

A somewhat more serious phenomenon was the antisemitic effect of the Nazi alliance with Japan. Antisemitism seemed to strike a chord in the Japanese psyche, even though unknown before the Nazi alliance introduced antisemitic literature into Japan. Even after the Japanese defeat and the establishment of democracy, antisemitism persisted in the form of a best-selling popular literature retailing the machinations of a world-wide Jewish conspiracy. Indeed, the appeal of this literature may be intimately connected with the Japanese defeat and the need to find some diabolic reason for it. In an extraordinary way, too, the fantasy of Jewish world domination acted as a substitute for the previous Japanese dream of accomplishing this very thing, and also as a model for present-day realistic Japanese efforts towards world domination in the economic sphere. This accounts for the tinge of admiration in Japanese antisemitism, despite its ostensible tone of moral outrage.

All in all, then, the occurrence of antisemitism outside the Christendom–Islam bloc is peripheral and unimportant. It is an unnatural growth grafted on to societies with no tradition of antisemitism. This has happened because of Western cultural, technological and political influence, and is unlikely to take permanent root.

Nevertheless, it may still be asked why the Jews of Hindu India did not encounter antisemitism. Why was there no cultural rivalry between Judaism and Hinduism, similar to that between Judaism and Hellenism in the ancient world? Granted that the special edge of religious supersession and usurpation was lacking, because of the lack of relationship between Judaism and Hinduism, yet one might still expect something of the rivalry that did occur between Hinduism and the other Judaism-based religions – Islam and Christianity. The answer appears to be that Judaism did not present itself as a proselytising religion, as did the others. Moreover, Judaism did not present itself in the guise of military conquest, while both Islam and Christianity did. Hinduism, by its nature, is not confrontational with other religions. It tends to give them a place in its own religious scheme, even assigning a caste-status to communities of foreign origin. The sense of superiority is there, as in Hellenistic culture, but the caste-system allows for so many varieties of life-style and philosophy that foreign cultures can be accommodated at some level. The feelings of superiority are largely concentrated in the top caste, the Brahmins, who are accustomed to making allowance for lower levels of society.

Hellenistic culture, on the contrary, had a drive to uniformity and an intolerance of variety, together with an essential democracy that demanded the same cultural and spiritual level for all. It resented the existence of pockets of cultural resistance, while Hinduism actually welcomes them, as expressing the infinite variety of human possibility.

The excellent record of Hinduism in relation to the Jews has been marred a little in recent years by an unfriendly attitude by Indian governments to Israel. This has been caused not by any essential hostility but by the needs of third-world politics, which demanded solidarity from India with Arab countries with whom, in fact, India has little in common culturally, and much, historically, that is opposed. I have been assured by Indian friends that Government policy in this respect is supported by few representatives of Hindu opinion.

In general, the history of Hindu–Jewish relations provides strong proof that antisemitism is not endemic in human nature and does not arise from irritating or exclusivist features of Jews or Judaism.

CHAPTER 4

THE JEWS IN MEDIEVAL ENGLAND

The astonishing story of the Jews in medieval England is not merely a story of cruel and heartless exploitation of a helpless guest community by an avaricious and hypocritical host power. It is an instance of functionalism, in which, by religious sanction, a whole class of people has been reduced to sub-human and infra-moral status, yet the same class is recognised to have valuable talents which can be a source of great profit to the ruler, who is religiously justified in unlimited exploitation followed by final rejection; and the same class is particularly useful in diverting unpopularity from the ruler in the exercise of his less charismatic activities, such as tax-collecting and collecting interest on loans.

The whole topic is somewhat disguised by the fact that the exploitation of the Jews, in the peculiar circumstances of Church regulation of Jewish status, involved the apparent enrichment of the Jews by the secular power, though in fact the 'riches' of the Jews were held by them as proxies for the King, who through the Jews, levied taxes, extorted high interest on loans, and controlled the movement of money. This has misled some observers into thinking that the position of the Jews in England was actually very fortunate, since they accumulated riches. The subsequent fate of the Jews – massacred, stripped of their wealth, and then expelled – is seen as misfortune, not as the inevitable fate laid out for them from the start.

There is no evidence of Jews in England before the Norman Conquest, and even for some time after it the Jews benefited by the imperfect Christianisation of society. The early Norman King, Rufus the Red, was accused by Christian writers of impiety and 'insolence to God'. One example of this is that he once instituted a debate between Christians and Jews, saying (perhaps jestingly) that if the Jews won he would become converted to Judaism. Relations between Christians and Jews continued to be friendly for some time, as is shown by the record of the courteous disputation between Brother Gilbert Crispin and a Jew (Anselm, *Opera*, ed. 1744, ii, p. 255). But in the 12th century, we can observe the crystallisation of the peculiar role of the Jews in a society based on Christian norms.

As it happens, we have better historical records for the early Middle Ages for England than for any other country, because of the early centralisation of the Government and the absence of civil war, once Henry II came to the throne in 1134, founding what is known as the Angevin (from Anjou) dynasty, called the Plantagenets (from Henry II to John). France, Germany, Italy and Spain cannot be said to be fully existent as political entities at this time and have left few records. Consequently, it is the English records that enable us to see clearly the peculiar position of the Jews in medieval Christian society.

The position of the Jews was determined by the attitude towards them of the Church, which dominated all structures in society. The Jews were regarded as outside the community, being heretics and enemies of Christianity, though having a special dispensation to exist rather than be exterminated. This dispensation, however, gave the Jews no officially-endorsed foothold or role in the economy: they were barred from agriculture, trade, or any kind of public service. The Jews were permitted to live, but not to make a living. The organis-ation of business life through the guilds automatically excluded Jews, since guilds were open only to professing Christians. Even to buy a farm involved a declaration of 'homage' that included allegiance to the Christian faith.

Through the 12th and 13th centuries, the position of the Jews deteriorated as society became more and more under the control of the Church. It was the papacy of Innocent III (1198–1216) that introduced new, debasing provisions further reducing the status of the Jews, including the imposition of the yellow badge, while strength-ening the observance of already existing bans against Jewish partici-pation in normal economic activities. In England, the 12th century

saw the first blood-libel accusations; first the accusations of the murder of Christian children at Easter in repetition of the crucifixion of
Jesus, and then the even more terrible and brutal accusation that Jews
used the child-victims' blood for their own Passover rituals. Thus
the exclusion of the Jews from normal or honourable occupations
coincided with the increasing demonisation of them as sub-human
enemies of Christendom.

The only occupation left open to the Jews was that of 'usurers'.
Some Jews had money, which they had accumulated during times
when they were allowed to be merchants, in the less fanatical times
known as 'the Dark Ages'. This was a somewhat ironical designation
from a Jewish standpoint, since this was a period when Jews were
treated, on the whole, with humanity, the Church's intolerant teaching having little influence over a still largely pagan-minded population. With the capital left in their hands by their previous mercantile
activities, Jews managed to survive for a limited period by financing
the Christian world, or rather by running the money economy at a
time when money was not yet fully established as the medium of
exchange, since the lower classes of society still conducted their affairs
by barter.

The system by which the Jews almost monopolised the handling
of money in medieval England precisely because they were regarded
as damned persons, is one of the most curious creations in the history
of pariahship. 'Usury' was forbidden by the Church, and usury was
defined in such a way that any business enterprise beyond the smallest
was impossible. Not only was it forbidden to lend money on interest,
but even the gaining of profit on a sale was regarded as sinful usury,
though this latter prohibition was hardly taken seriously. The ban
on interest on loans was certainly taken seriously, and this prohibition
meant that banking activities were confined to Jews or to sinful Christians (of whom there were not a few). In theory, even Jews were
forbidden to lend money on interest, but there was little active attempt
to stop them from doing so, since it was found so useful to society
to have a class of people who could handle money without religious
inhibitions, and who, in any case, were regarded as damned souls
because of their rejection and alleged execution of Jesus.

But what is particularly interesting to the student of the vagaries of human self-deception is the way in which the prohibition of usury and its delegation to the Jews resulted in a huge Christian practice of usury by proxy, at least by the Christian ruler. For Christian rulers, of whom Henry II of England may be taken as a typical and well-documented example, showed their Christian disapproval of usury by decreeing that the ill-gotten gains of usurers were to be confiscated by the State on the deaths of the usurers, and not allowed to go to their heirs. These ill-gotten gains included the debts still owed to the usurers, at the time of their death, which were now owed to the King. Somehow the collection of usurious debts by the King was not a sin, since the usury was exacted in the first place by Jews and other sinners (the same law applied to Christian usurers, who, however, had to be open flouters of Christian law rather than unenlightened Jews, and were far fewer in number).

Enormous sums were involved, since all great enterprises in the kingdom, including the building of cathedrals and military expeditions, were financed by interest-paying loans from the Jews, who were, in effect, the main holders of money. The accumulating debts of the middle and upper class, therefore, increasingly became owed to the King, who exacted them as his personal exchequer, though he often allowed a discount in payment. The Jews and the King, in this system, formed an alliance, based on the forbidden practice of usury, which functioned in a similar way to that in which a banking and taxation system functions in a modern economy. At the same time, the King regarded all money in Jewish hands as his own to draw on without interest whenever he needed. He would decree special 'tallages' levied on the Jewish community as a whole, and he also had a long list of occasions on which Jews must pay a fee to the King, which included marriages, deaths, business partnerships, or any other event of importance. The whole 'wealth' of the Jews, gained by 'usury', was a pool of money held in reserve for the King, who was thus able to claim that he himself did not indulge in usury, and even virtuously acted to punish it by his confiscations.

To quote from 'The Laws of Edward the Confessor' (about 1180), '. . . the Jews themselves and theirs belong to the king. And if any detain them or their money, let the king, if he will and can, ask it back as if it were his own' (Howden, ed. Stubbs, ii. 237). The status

54

of all Jews, in other words, was that of slaves, owned by the king. This was their protection from arbitrary violence from all and sundry, but it also meant that the appearance of wealth and prosperity that attached to the Jews (and which added to the hatred of the populace, instilled by the continual propaganda of the lower clergy) was a sham. The Jews no more owned their wealth than a bank owns its customers' deposits. They did, however, have a precarious show of wealth, which they tried to enjoy while it lasted. On this basis, they built houses (the first private stone houses in England), brought up families, created a system of justice, welfare and education, and even reached a high cultural level, with a distinguished roll of scholars and authors.

But no Jew had any surety of having any livelihood even the next day. An illustration of this is the 12th-century comment of the Tosafot on the question of the legality of child-marriages. These were forbidden by the Talmud, yet were practised by the Jews in the Middle Ages. 'As to our custom of the present day of betrothing our daughters while still minors, that is because persecutions wax more frequent every day, and if a man can afford today to give his daughter a dowry, he fears that tomorrow he may not be able to do it, and then his daughter would remain for ever unmarried.'[1]

Indeed, the very practice of usury, by which medieval Jews lived, was available to Jews only through the flexibility of Talmudic law, which allowed some things normally forbidden by its own precepts when the alternative was starvation or extreme hardship. By the law of the Torah, indeed, lending money on interest was permitted between Jew and Gentile, though forbidden between Jew and Jew (Deut. 23:19–20). But the Talmud had extended this law, forbidding even lending on interest between Jew and Gentile, but with the proviso that this Talmudic severity could be relaxed in time of hardship: i.e. when there was no other method of obtaining a livelihood. Curiously, the Talmud also relaxed the prohibition in the case of a scholar, who had no other occupation that would give him similar leisure to study.

Yet in reality, Judaism's attitude towards usury was quite different from that of Christianity. Judaism's view is the modern one, that to exact interest on a business loan is entirely just, since the money so lent is otherwise unprofitable to the lender during the period of the loan; interest is merely compensation for the loss otherwise suffered by the lender. The prohibition against exacting interest from a fellow-Jew was not a matter of ordinary morality, but of supererogatory love. Every fellow-Jew was to be regarded like a member of one's own family, to whom one would willingly lend money without interest to tide over some financial difficulty. This charity began and ended at home: between Jews and Gentiles, normal business relations prevailed, as ruled by the laws of fairness and justice rather than of special love.

Even the Talmud's prohibition against lending on interest between Jew and Gentile was not dictated by any theory of the immorality of usury. It was simply motivated by concern lest Jews should enter too deeply into the Gentile business world and thereby be tempted into assimilation and idolatry. This level of concern was easily overborne by more important considerations, such as the need to avoid penury or starvation, or even the need to find leisure for religious study.

The Christian prohibition against usury, on the other hand, was considered a matter of morality. It was mainly based on Luke 6:35, '. . . lend, hoping for nothing again', but was reinforced by Aristotle's condemnation of usury. It was also supported by Leviticus 23:19, but without the mitigation of the following verse. Indeed, Luke's command had nothing to do with charging interest, but rather with something even more idealistic and impractical: it was an injunction not to expect to be paid back any of the money lent. Even this counsel of perfection can be found in some form in the Jewish sources, in the institution of the seventh-year cancellation of debts (*shemittah*) (Deut. 15:1), again a requirement only between Jew and Jew. But the Christian Church, misinterpreting Luke as talking about interest, abolished all commercial lending at a blow, making no distinction between family and public networks, and so landed Christendom into an impossible economic situation that could be redeemed only by the hypocrisy of using the Jews as bankers, while heaping abuse on them for their damnable usury. The abolition of Jewish law advocated by Paul did not result in a spontaneous law of love, since law, being part of the human condition, could not be abolished. Into the legal vacuum created by Paul rushed a great many laws, derived from various sources including Roman and Germanic law, but also sometimes based on ad hoc interpretations of both the Old and the New Testament. Rabbinic law was rarely consulted. Included in the Scripture-based laws was the indiscriminate prohibition of interest on loans. Other Scripture based laws were the Christian laws against intermarriage of relatives, which were far more severe than the corresponding Jewish laws, based on a temperate rabbinic interpretation of Scripture.

It may be asked, however, why the Jews did not attempt to avoid the hateful role imposed on them by Christian society, especially as even a modicum of foresight would have enabled them to predict the eventual outcome of massacre and expulsion. Joseph Jacobs puts the question as follows: 'It may be allowed to one who is both Englishman and Jew to express his regret both that Angevin England saw no other means of giving its Jews employment except as thumb-screws of the Royal Treasury, and that medieval English Jews had not the manhood to refuse to accept a livelihood, however lucrative, which was only possible by the oppression of their fellow-citizens.'[2] Jacobs here seems to overlook the fact that the activity of the Jews as financiers was oppressive and sinful only in Christian eyes. The Jews themselves regarded these activities as highly useful to the society in which they lived, enabling business projects to be undertaken and great buildings to be erected, tasks normally undertaken (in societies unhampered by childish scruples about usury) by legitimate businesses or by Government investment. Jacobs's question might be re-phrased, however: 'Why did the Jews, knowing how usury was regarded by Christians, allow themselves to be manoeuvred into an invidious role?'

The answer is simply that Jews in medieval Christendom led such precarious lives that they were glad to snatch at any opportunity to secure a livelihood for the immediate future. The only real alternative was to emigrate from Christian countries to Islamic lands, where conditions for Jews, though far from ideal, were more relaxed, and theological hatred of Jews was far less intense. Many Jews did indeed choose this course, and the numbers of Jews in Christendom declined throughout the Middle Ages for this and other reasons (including depletion through massacre and direct restriction by law of the Jewish birth rate). The Jews who remained in Christendom did so through their natural inertia, and also their characteristic ability to set up a warm and stable local environment (through communal and charitable organisation and lively cultural activity) that was hard to leave.

They were like people clinging to comfortable homes built on the edge of a volcano.

The precariousness of the Jews' position in England was shown clearly in the tragic events arising from the coronation of Richard I in 1189. When the leading Jews came to pay homage to the new King at Westminster Cathedral, their presumption was resented by the crowd and a riot started in which thirty Jews died. This incident sparked off even worse riots at various centres, including Stamford and Lincoln. The climax came at York in 1190, when the whole Jewish community died. These persecutions were accompanied by wholesale burning of documents relating to debts owed to the Jews, and it became clear, that at York at any rate, the massacre was instigated for this very purpose by a group of minor aristocrats led by Sir Richard Malebisse. King Richard, who at first showed no concern for the fate of the Jews, suddenly realised that he now faced considerable loss, since a large proportion of money owed to the Jews would have eventually come to him through the regular tallages and confiscations of inheritances.

In these two years of constant persecution, deeply indebted gentry incited the mob of lower classes, who were actually not themselves indebted, because they were outside the money economy and practised barter. But they were easily roused, especially in this period of the Crusades, by appeal to the age-old stereotype of the Jews as Christ-murderers. The lower aristocracy, therefore, had found an easy way to avoid payment of their debts, to the detriment of the Royal Exchequer.

The solution found by the King and his advisers was to set up a new state institution called the Exchequer of the Jews, in which a copy of every Jewish transaction was to be deposited. The King now had his own copy of every debt owed to the Jews, so that people like Sir Richard Malebisse (who received minor punishment from the King for his massacre of the York Jews, but later rose to high office in the King's service) could no longer resort to such an ingenious way of escaping from debt. The Jews were now officially an organ of the state, and the Exchequer of the Jews functioned as the main financial instrument of royal power. The exquisite paradox of Jewish existence in medieval Christendom could hardly be better expressed. The Jews, just because they were slaves and pariahs deprived of all human rights and honour, were indispensable to the running of the Christian economy, and to all outward appearances ensconced at its administrative centre. It is no wonder that the situation could be misread as a cunning plot by the Jews to appropriate the whole Christian apparatus of power.

The influence of the Jews in medieval England can be traced even today in English institutions. The famous Star Chamber at Westminster derived its name from the Hebrew word *shtar*, meaning a document. It was in this chamber that the documents showing that a debt owed to a Jew had been repaid, were deposited. These documents are still extant, written in Hebrew and Latin, signed by the Jewish creditor in Hebrew. Certain expressions still used in English legal practice – such as 'from now until the end of the world' – derive from the Talmudic documentary format used by the Jews of England during this period.

The ruler before Richard I was Henry II, a prudent king who knew well not to kill the goose that laid the golden eggs. He allowed the Jews to accumulate wealth, and then took it away from them in large quantities, but not so extortionately as to disable them from producing more wealth for him. Richard I ('the Lionheart') after his first experience of allowing his Jews to be massacred, learnt from the losses so incurred and adopted a more prudent and protective policy. His successor John, however, was too greedy to preserve the delicate equilibrium. He extorted so much money from the Jews that their viability was threatened. During the disorders of the next reign, that of Henry III, the position of the Jews deteriorated steadily, as the bankrupt King made greater and greater exactions. The next King, Edward I, though personally less villainous than his predecessors, was faced with great expenditures which forced him to continue their policy of squeezing the Jews, until at last they lost all ability to function as money-making machines. At this point, Edward expelled them from England (1290), after going through a pointless exercise of directing the penniless Jews to other professions, such as commerce and farming – pointless because the restrictions preventing Jews from operating in such contexts were still in force.

The wholesale expulsion of the Jews that then took place was only a repetition on a communal scale of what had already been taking place on an individual level throughout the sojourn of the Jews in England. Whenever an individual Jew, overborne by the continual taxes and levies, had sunk into penury, he and his family had been immediately expelled from the country as 'no longer of service to the King'. The Jews were permitted to exist in this Christian country only as the King's cattle, permitted to grow fat in order to provide the King with meat, but, having been allowed by mismanagement to dwindle into unprofitable thinness, discarded brutally.

We have to consider, then, how to categorise, from a sociological and anthropological view, the role of the Jews in English medieval society. They were certainly not outside that society in a functional sense, for they performed an integral and even central role. Yet in every cultural and religious sense, they were complete outsiders, being regarded with contempt and loathing, restrained only by fear of the King, who used his power to protect his cattle. At the same time the Jews were developing their own sophisticated culture, fostered by a high regard for education. Christian society was largely illiterate, but there were no illiterates among the Jews; Jewish women too were highly-educated, and many of them became skilled bankers in their own right, among them Belaset of Oxford, Miriam of Norwich, and many others.

Yet the image of the Jew in the eyes of the Christian masses (who did not come into contact with the Jews as usurers) was descending to a demonic level, chiefly under the influence of the preaching of the lower clergy. It was in this period and area that the blood libel developed and proliferated, bringing great profit to religious centres such as Lincoln Cathedral, which drew thousands of paying pilgrims to the graves of alleged child martyrs. The last traces of pagan tolerance of the Jews were being obliterated, as the Christian masses were inducted into fanatical Christian belief. At the same time, blood-soaked pagan fantasies of vampires and werewolves were pressed into service to support Christian diabolisation of the Jews.[3]

The medieval Jewish role, so clearly evidenced in the English data, thus presents many points of comparison with that of the pariah class of Hindu India. Like the pariahs, the Jews exercised a function in the wider society without being allowed to belong to it. For the

Untouchable castes were excluded from the wider society, being forbidden commensality, intermarriage and participation in religious rites of sacrifice. Yet in Hinduism, the higher castes are not forbidden to benefit from the activities of the Untouchables; on the contrary, the services performed by them, such as cleaning lavatories, the slaughter of animals and the tanning of their skins are essential, though taboo to higher castes.

Similarly, the Jews performed taboo activities that were of different grades of taboo, and were of benefit in somewhat equivocal ways. Thus the whole aspect of usury, though of the greatest benefit to Christian society, was never quite acknowledged as such. The King confiscated the products of Jewish usury and used them for his own purposes, but salvaged his conscience by allowing some discount to debtors and by the pretext that he was depriving heirs of the ill-gotten gains of their parents. In certain other contexts, the use of Jews to perform society's dirty work was more open. Thus, Jews were required in many towns to provide from their ranks the public executioner whenever capital punishment had to be administered. Yet the torture regularly carried out in the Christian legal system was never handed over to be performed by Jews. It seems that such torture was regarded as holy work that did not require delegation to an outcaste, while the guilt of homicide never quite abated even in a legal context, and therefore had to be shunted on to a sin-bearing surrogate.[4]

We may conclude, then, that the Jews were indeed pariahs in Christian society, but in such a way that they could never attain the security enjoyed by the pariahs of Hinduism, who had an assured place in society, however lowly. Moreover, the Indian pariahs, though excluded from the higher castes, did belong to the overall community, with whom they shared religious beliefs, including the comforting belief in transmigration which offered them hope of eventual integration into the regular caste system in a future life. The Jews, on the other hand, were excluded from the community for ever (so long as they resisted conversion to Christianity) and were condemned to everlasting punishment in the afterlife. On the other hand, the Jews, unlike the Hindu pariahs, were able, for a time at least, to engage in taboo activities that brought wealth. In Indian society, the taboo

61

activities of the pariahs were financially petty, and the main wealth-making activities were kept firmly in the hands of the upper castes; moneylending, for example, so far from being taboo, was in the hands of the Vaisyas, the third *varna*.[5] In Christian society, indeed, the situation was eventually corrected, and moneylending was permitted to Christians by various legal fictions and accommodations. Big-time moneylending was then taken over from the Jews by the Lombard bankers, who had close ties with the Vatican. After that, the Jews, still excluded from all honourable professions, sank to small-time lending and pawnbroking, from which they were rescued only by the advent of the Enlightenment which, first in France and later in other countries, admitted them to the professions.

As a pariah people, therefore, the Jews suffered from continual insecurity, being forced to discover and supply some societal need that Christian taboos prohibited or deprecated. In such precarious circumstances, it is remarkable that the Jews were able to survive and even to flourish for periods.

This was because of the nature of their culture, which provided them with a high degree of literacy, and also with a self-respect that precluded despair. They never ceased to regard themselves as princes who had to suffer, temporarily, the condition of paupers. As in England, so in other countries, the Jews provided to half-civilised societies a much needed fund of expertise for the administration of the economy. Eventually, their pariah status would always lead to their downfall in any particular country, but then they would migrate to some other Christian country that was in need of their services. For example, the role of the Jews in Poland in the 15th and 16th centuries presents many interesting parallels to their role in medieval England. As pariahs, the Jews faced catastrophes, as the Hindu pariahs did not, but they also had an openness of opportunity and a mobility that enabled them to reach temporary heights of self-development and societal usefulness. And unlike the Indian pariahs, they did not internalise the norms that relegated them to the status of sinners and taboo-breakers. For Christian taboos, which they made their living by flouting, seemed to them irrational, and they had their own system of ethical norms which provided their lives with meaning.

CHAPTER 5

USURPATION AND PARIAHSHIP

A common way for a pariah group to come into existence is by conquest and usurpation. When a nation or culture is overwhelmed by outside invaders, who take over its territory, the conquered inhabitants may sink to a despised class, serving the conquerors and forbidden to share in the conquerors' privileges. When this happens, it is natural that the conquerors should develop some story to explain their own success and the defeated community's failure, at the same time justifying the conquerors' right to reduce the status of the conquered. This story may be called the *usurpation myth*.

An example may be found in the Bible. The Canaanites were conquered by the Israelites, who took over their land. The Canaanites remaining in the land were given subordinate status as 'hewers of wood and drawers of water', or as outright slaves. Justification for this was found in two ways. First, a story developed about the ancestor of the Canaanite nation, Ham, who sinned by disrespect to his father Noah. Ham was then cursed by Noah, who predicted that the descendants of Ham's son, Canaan, would become slaves of the descendants of Shem, another of his sons (ancestor of the Israelites), who had treated him with respect. Secondly, the Canaanites in general were declared to have forfeited their title to their own land because of their moral degeneration, being guilty of sins such as incest and sodomy.

These two justifications are not exactly compatible with each other. A Midrash offers another incompatible justification, based on the verse, 'The Canaanite was then in the land' (Genesis 12:6), which is

63

taken to mean that originally the land was occupied by descendants of Shem, who had been ousted by the Canaanites: this exegesis thus turned the Canaanites into the usurpers! This kind of re-writing of history resembles present-day Palestinian Arabs claiming to be the original prehistoric inhabitants of a land which they in fact acquired in the Arab conquests of the 7th century of the present era. In the tortuous annals of usurpation myths, a prominent role is played by the claim of the usurper to be the usurped.

The Sudras of India are the subjects of a simpler usurpation myth. Like the Red Indians and the Aboriginals of Australia, they are declared to have forfeited their lands to the invaders simply by virtue of their ignoble way of life. They could have no complaint if a more civilised culture annexed their lands and reduced them to servile status, in which they were enabled to perform useful if menial tasks instead of wallowing in primeval backwardness. Moreover, by being annexed, they were even rescued from spiritual non-being, for they were given the opportunity to enter the wheel of transmigration with the hope of ascending the ladder of the caste-system in future incarnations. It was not denied that the land originally belonged to the people now in low castes; but the Aryan invasion was, so to say, a means of purifying and sanctifying the holy land of India.

Mention of the holiness of the land reminds us of the second justification for the Israelite invasion, cited above. Here too, the holiness of the land forms part of the argument. The Canaanites had to be supplanted because they had defiled the holiness of the land. The corollary, explicitly drawn in the Israelite though not in the Indian theology, was that the conquerors too might expect to be supplanted if they in turn defiled the land. Here the usurpation of the Canaanites by the Israelites is justified by the view that the land, being holy, did not belong either to Israelites or to Canaanites, but to God. Any nation inhabiting this land did so only on sufferance, and on condition that a certain standard of moral behaviour was maintained. Consequently, the Canaanites could not complain about being ejected; God had been patient with them and had refrained from ejecting them until their 'iniquity was complete' (Genesis 15:16).

Usurpation, however, is not always a matter of the occupation of a land. As the case of Christianity and Judaism shows, the very self-image of a community can be the target of a take-over bid. The history of Western religion has been one of massive bids to usurp the claim of the Jews to be the people of God, and to annex the position of being the true Israel. This impulse of usurpation brought with it usurpation-myths of various kinds, Christianity being unique in the complexity of its usurpation-myth, which consisted of elements culled from a surprising multiplicity of mythological motifs.

The Israelite culture was formed as a result of the Exodus from Egypt, where the Israelites had functioned for many years as a pariah class of slaves. It is remarkable that while the impetus of liberation gave the Israelites their self-image as a people chosen by God for perpetual freedom, it was this very self-exultation that aroused such envy and enmity in other peoples that, in the event, they were again reduced to a worse-than-Egyptian slavery. The imposition of pariah status was thus a kind of punishment of the Jews for their temerity and delight in escaping from slavery.

For the effect of their escape, which has never left the Jewish consciousness (being reinforced by continual ritual recall), was to turn the Israelites (later the Jews) into a people dedicated to freedom. The result was that attempts to subjugate the Jews by outside empires never succeeded in subduing the Jewish spirit. This was particularly galling to the intellectual leaders of the Greco-Roman Empire, who were proud of their Hellenistic culture, and resented the existence of the Jewish island of resistance.

One way of combating Jewish intransigence was simply to deny the validity of Judaism and the Jewish pretensions to being the people of God. But another, and more insidious, way was to infiltrate Judaism, seize and occupy its citadels, and oust the Jews themselves from them as unworthy to remain in them. This is analogous to the invaders of a land, who by no means minimise the desirability of the land itself, but regard themselves as somehow more entitled to benefit from it than its original inhabitants. Where scorn predominated, Jewish pretensions were denied; where envy predominated, schemes were developed for annexing the Jewish role.

The earliest attempt of this kind, as briefly mentioned earlier, was that of the Gnostics. This, however, was a mixture of scorn and envy, and therefore constituted an imperfect take-over bid. The

Gnostics, who engaged in an encounter with Judaism, developed a kind of Hellenistic antisemitism that was half-admiring and half-contemptuous. The admiration is shown by the use made by these Gnostics of the Hebrew Bible, especially the early chapters of Genesis. This Scripture is treated as authoritative in the sense that it gives unique information about the creation of the world. On the other hand, it is unauthoritative and open to criticism because it comes not from the High God whom the Gnostics worship, but from an inferior god, the Demiurge, who is the Creator of this evil world, the author of the Torah, and the evil inspiration of the uncomprehending Jews, who do not understand his limitations.[1]

The Gnostics are thus certainly intending to oust the Jews from the position of the people of God, but the invasion is only partial, because the Gnostics do not wholly prize the territory which the Jews occupy. The true people of God are indeed to be found in the Hebrew Bible, but not where the Jews find them. The book of Genesis is indeed to be read as Gnostic scripture, but only when reinterpreted and transvalued. The Hebrew Bible contains a spiritual genealogy, in which the credentials of the Jews as people of God are traced. In the pre-Flood period, the line of Seth is preferred to that of Cain, so that Seth's descendant Noah is saved, while all Cainites perish in the Flood. Out of all the families of humans descended from Noah, Abraham is chosen, then Isaac (in preference to Ishmael) and Jacob (in preference to Esau). Among the progeny of Jacob are found the priestly line of Aaron, the kingly line of David, and also the irregular line of prophets, marked out by personal charisma, not genealogy, but still within the Israelite covenant and tribal confederation. Outside these genealogical lines, some revered figures are to be found: Melchizedek is a priest of the most high, though not an Aaronite; Balaam is a prophet, though not an Israelite; Cyrus is a messiah, though a Persian; but these are exceptional figures who do not affect the main line of authority and inspiration which is traced through Israel.

The Gnostics reject this main line and focus on the periphery. Thus Seth, the son of Adam, who in the Hebrew Bible is merely a precursor of Noah and thus of Abraham, is regarded by certain Gnostic sects as a true adherent of the High God, the founder of a line of enlightened ones who bypass the Israelite tradition and render it subordinate and unspiritual. On the other hand, some Gnostics went even further in transvaluation by electing Cain as the enlightened one, rejecting the preferred status of Seth, ancestor of Noah and Abraham, as a by-product of the unenlightened prejudice of the Jewish editors of the Hebrew Bible.

The Gnostics are thus usurpers of Israel only in a limited sense. They do indeed take over Jewish tradition for their own ends by adopting features of Jewish scriptures. A great part of the apparatus of Gnostic mythology is appropriated from the Bible. But the usurpation may be likened to an invasion of raiders, rather than of settlers. The Gnostics enter the Jewish tradition, look round for items that appeal to them, and make off with them, leaving the rest behind in contempt. The exercise does reduce the status of the Jews, but not to the condition of pariahs, rather to that of an amusedly despised bourgeoisie, incapable of aristocratic unworldliness, the guardians of pearls which they do not appreciate, and which would shine more brightly in other hands.

The tone of the Gnostic usurpation may be seen in the following extract from Gnostic writings:

And Abraham and Isaac and Jacob were a laughingstock, since they, the counterfeit fathers, were given a name by the Hebdomad, as if he had become stronger than I and my brothers. We are innocent with respect to him, since we have not sinned. David was a laughingstock in that his son was named the Son of Man, having been influenced by the Hebdomad, as if he had become stronger than I and the fellow-members of my race. But we are innocent with respect to him; we have not sinned. Solomon was a laughing-stock, since he thought that he was the Christ, having become vain through the Hebdomad, as if he had become stronger than I and my brothers. But we are innocent with respect to him. I have not sinned. The twelve prophets were laughingstocks, since they have come forth as imitations of the true prophets. They came into being as counterfeits through the Hebdomad, as if he had become stronger than I and my brothers. But we are innocent with respect to him, since we have not sinned. Moses, a faithful servant, was a laughingstock, having been named 'the Friend', since they perversely bore witness concerning him who never knew me. Neither he nor those before him, from Adam to Moses and John the Baptist, none of them knew me nor my brothers.

For they had a doctrine of angels to observe dietary laws and bitter slavery, since they never knew truth, nor will they know it. For there is a great deception upon their soul making it impossible for them ever to find a Nous of freedom in order to know him, until they come to know the Son of Man. Now concerning my Father, I am he whom the world did not know, and because of this, it (the world) rose up against me and my brothers. But we are innocent with respect to him; we have not sinned.

For the Archon was a laughingstock because he said, 'I am God, and there is none greater than I. I alone am the Father, the Lord, and there is no other beside me. I am a jealous God, who brings the sins of the fathers upon the children for three and four generations.' As if he had become stronger than I and my brothers! But we are innocent with respect to him, in that we have not sinned, since we mastered his teaching. Thus he was an empty glory. And he does not agree with our Father. And thus through our fellowship we grasped his teaching, since he was vain in an empty glory. And he does not agree with our Father, for he was a laughingstock and judgment and false prophecy.

O those who do not see, you do not see your blindness, i.e. this which was not known, nor has it ever been known, nor has it been known about him. They did not listen to firm obedience. Therefore they proceeded in a judgment of error, and they raised their defiled and murderous hands against him as if they were beating the air. And the senseless and blind ones are always senseless, being slaves of law and earthly fear.

(*The Second Treatise of the Great Seth* VII, 2, 62–64)

This is an important text for studying the transition between the Gnostic raid on Judaism, and the Christian expropriation of the status of 'the true Israel'.

The Gnostics are not interested in being 'the true Israel'. Consequently, they do not have the problem of fitting the Jews, as a demoted and subordinate class, into their Gnostic scheme of community.

Indeed, the Gnostics do not really have a scheme of community, for whereas they have taken over some cosmological ideas from Judaism, they entirely lack Judaism's interest in history. In so far as they see a historical scheme in their succession of enlightened ones (whom they do not even name, apart from some figures derived from the Hebrew Bible), this is supplied only by the continued opposition and false pretensions of the Jewish succession of kings and prophets.

The above Gnostic text, then, is concerned to combat the Jewish pretension to supply a chain of authority persisting through history. The text itself, as it stands, is a Christian Gnostic text, not an expression of pure pre-Christian Gnosticism. But Christianity has been absorbed in a characteristically Gnostic way. Jesus (who is the speaker), instead of being the unique Saviour, is simply the leader of a band of 'brothers', who by achieving enlightenment, have freed themselves from the chains of this evil world and from the domination of its creator and ruler, the Demiurge, here called the Hebdomad (because of his residence in the Seventh Heaven) and also the Archon (meaning 'Ruler').

The Jewish chain of authority is denied, not with hate but with laughter. All the authority figures of patriarchy and prophecy (Abraham, Isaac, Jacob, Moses, the twelve prophets), and of the Jewish monarchy (David, Solomon) are declared to be a 'laughingstock'. The Demiurge himself is finally declared to be a 'laughingstock' because of his self-delusion in thinking himself to be the true High God.

On the other hand, the Jewish chain of authority, and even the Demiurge its inspirer, are not entirely dismissed as evil. They are regarded as having a certain limited validity. This is shown by the admission that the Gnostics have learnt something from them ('. . . we mastered his teaching'). Also, the assertion 'we are innocent with respect to him' repeated in connection with each authority figure, shows a need to vindicate the Gnostics from the charge of disrespect. The point is not that the Jewish tradition and its God are evil, but that they are limited. The Gnostics have transcended them by reaching a realm of spirituality that is beyond the understanding of those who worship the Demiurge and revere his revelation, the Hebrew Bible.

Even the alleged murder of Jesus by the Jews arouses no feeling of hatred in the Gnostics, but rather amused contempt – '. . . they raised their defiled and murderous hands against him as if they were beating the air.' Since the Gnostics did not believe in the reality of the body or of this physical world, death had no terrors for them. It was simply a transition to a higher spiritual plane. Those who thought that they were depriving Jesus of life were comically deluded, for all that they could attack was his unimportant body. Thus Gnosticism, the earliest form of cosmic antisemitism, the first doctrine to apportion to the Jews a role as devotees of a power in some way opposed to God, did not contain the potentiality for hatred found in orthodox Christianity, in which the alleged attack on the body of Jesus was a Satan-inspired attempt to annihilate the Incarnate God.

Though Gnosticism, being anti-political, did not contain the possibility of a Jewish pariahdom in the sociological or political sense, there is in fact inherent in Gnosticism a form of categorisation of mankind that can be thought of as a kind of caste-system. This is the division of humanity into three grades, of which the highest is that of the enlightened Gnostics themselves, the 'pneumatics' (from the Greek *pneuma*, 'spirit'). The other two grades were the 'psychics' (from *psyche*, here meaning 'animal life') and the 'hylics' (from *hyle*, 'matter'). In the more tolerant forms of Gnosticism, each grade was assigned a function in the scheme of things. The middle grade, the psychics, to which the Jews and their tradition were assigned, had the job of keeping this mundane world going by developing and administering a code of law, and it was even acknowledged, at times at least, that the ordered world provided by these useful if unspiritual people was of some help to the pneumatics in sustaining their physical being during the stages of their transition to a better world.

Some Gnostic systems, including the ancient Valentinians and the medieval Cathars, did achieve a political or social form, and in these the theoretical classification of human types was embodied in a societal structure. In Catharism there was a two-fold structure, consisting of 'the Perfect' (pneumatics) and the Believers (psychics). The hylics, however, were not represented within the Cathar community, but only in the unregenerate non-Cathar world. The Perfect led a totally unworldly life, separated from sex, and meat eating (prohibited as sexually begotten rather than for humanitarian reasons), and functioning as a priesthood for the Believers.

The categorisation of humanity into types thus arises from the Gnostic dualism of matter and spirit, which requires some kind of compromise in which spirit is served by matter. This leads to division of mankind to enable the more noble spirits to escape from the demands of earthly living through the subordination and enslavement of inferior types. In Hinduism, the broad division of humanity into Priests, Warriors, Merchants and Slaves (the *varnas*, within which the castes, or *jatis*, are located) was validated by a myth in which these four types derived from the dismemberment of a primeval god, so that every human being was allotted by fate or predestination to his earthly lot. The idea of predestination has always been bound up with the goal of an unworldly spirituality, since it is clear that such a goal can be attained only by an élite. Thus we see that in the thought of Nietzsche, the concept of a spiritual élite gives rise to ideas of predestination.

Thus in the study of caste, however refined into religious schemes of spirituality, the basic denial of equality often arises from a very simple and crude human situation, that of the conquerors and the conquered. The conqueror has at his disposal a mass of humanity whom he can use to free himself of the chores of everyday living. To this end, he develops a myth of his own innate superiority, which entitles him to god-like leisure and the pursuit of higher cultural interests. He may also develop a myth of the conquered people's inferiority, either innate, or acquired through the guilt of historical sins which need to be expiated through service to the innocent.

The demotion of the Jews by the Gnostics to a caste of animal-like psychics, doomed to perform unspiritual chores in the form of 'good works', is thus a step in the downward progress of the Jews in the caste system, but is certainly less drastic than the later Christian relegation of the Jews to the status of sin-ridden pariahs, doomed to perform taboo acts that are of benefit to the Christian community. In both cases, the demotion begins as an expression of envy, a dislodgment of the Jews from their self-designated position as the people of God. In the case of the Gnostics, this dislodgment remains notional. In the case of Christianity, which attained the power to translate its fantasies into social reality, the Jews became indeed a pariah class in Christendom, with all the sufferings entailed by that status.

As mentioned earlier, there is an interesting parallel between the Gnostic attitude to the Jews and the 19th-century Romantic attitude to the bourgeoisie. The rise of a middle class with a conventional code of morality, a work ethic that discounted spirituality in favour of profitable applications of scientific knowledge, and a self-importance that threatened aristocratic privilege, produced the Romantic reaction. In this, the gradual, calculating life-plan of careerism was jettisoned and a cult of youth took its place, recklessly courting early death. Poets cultivated aristocratic values, sometimes naturally, as in the case of Byron and Shelley, sometimes unnaturally, as by Keats, the apothecary's assistant, who apostrophised the night-ingale as the symbol of a higher world of poesy beyond 'the weariness, the fever and the fret'. The poet and artist, previously the lackeys of the aristocracy, became themselves an aristocracy of the spirit, like the pneumatics of old, regarding with disdain those who accepted and manipulated the limitations of this world. The Romantic move-ment even produced its own political movements, especially Marxism, which equated the mundane 'huckster' values of the bourgeoisie with Judaism; and Nazism with its own Jew-bourgeoisie equation. Yet at the same time, Marxism unconsciously paid tribute to the idealism inherent in the Jewish embrace of this world's potentialities by its messianic longings for a classless society of prosperity and peace, echoing the aspirations of the Jewish prophets of the Kingdom of God on earth.

Judaism indeed, by its emphasis on this world and humanity, is the projector of schemes of equality, as opposed to other-worldly doctrines which inevitably give rise to the idealisation of inequality (since only a privileged few can aspire to god-like status). In the Egypt from which the Israelites escaped, Pharaoh was worshipped as a god and a cult of immortality flourished, through which a rigid stratifi-cation of society was maintained, first by confining the assurance of immortality to the upper classes, and later by promising it to all on condition that they acquiesce in the earthly status quo. In Israel, immortality is no longer an aim, and therefore this-worldly equality cannot be denied to the people. Even when a king is appointed, against the wishes of the prophet Samuel, he is no divine figure, reducing his subjects to lower caste status, but a *primus inter pares*, who must take care that 'his heart be not lifted up above his brethren' (Deut. 17:20).

CHAPTER 6

CASTE IN JUDAISM

It may be asked, however, to what extent Judaism itself contains a caste system. It has already been mentioned that the invasion of the Israelites led to the enslavement of the Canaanites, who then formed an inferior group, very much in the same way (it may be thought) that the invading Aryans in India (after an initial period of attempted genocide) incorporated the conquered Dravidians into a caste system as the Sudras, or fourth *varna*, who functioned as slaves or servants to the three Aryan castes, the Brahmins, the Kshatriya, and the Vaisya. Further, it could be argued that the claim of the Israelites to be the people of God is itself a caste concept, relegating all non-Israelites, even those dwelling outside the area of conquest, to inferior status.

To take the second point first, it may be said with little hesitation that the Israelite doctrine of chosenness is not a caste concept. Far from basing their election on their superior nature and merits, the Bible continually stresses the unworthiness of the Israelites, their backslidings and failures, and the patience which God has to exercise not to reject them. It is true that a kind of aristocracy is claimed for them in their descent from Abraham, Isaac and Jacob, but this descent is used most often as a stick to beat them with, since the emphasis is that on their own merits they would not have been chosen. When we compare this with the Hindu glorification of the Brahmins as racially superior and spiritually even higher than the gods, we see a world of difference.

Moreover, the barriers of caste are not present in Israelite religion, for the 'nation of priests' is open to recruitment from the peoples of

74

the world by conversion to Judaism, as is seen in the Bible by the addition of a 'mixed multitude' of Egyptians at the time of the Exodus and by the individual conversions by Jethro, Naaman, Ruth, and many others incidentally mentioned (such as Uriah the Hittite and Doeg the Edomite). Pride in descent from Abraham, Isaac and Jacob is no bar to such recruitment by conversion, since converts, by inter-marrying with those of native stock, produce children who can at once claim Abrahamic descent. At a later period, whole nations became added to the Jewish stock by conversion (Idumaea, Adiabene, Khazaria), as well as countless individuals, many of them black (since colour prejudice plays no part in Judaism in strong contrast to Hinduism), and there was never any feeling that this was a breach of caste. It is true that, unlike the case of Christianity, the conversion of the whole world to Judaism is not envisaged, conversion being regarded as a matter of priestly vocation rather than of salvation. But a priesthood is not, in itself, a caste, unless it isolates itself by prohibitions against intermarriage or recruitment. That is why, for example, the Roman Catholic priesthood is not a caste: it is not hereditary, being celibate, and it is open to all the talents, though preserving its élite character as a vocation.

While the relation between Israel and the outside world is not one of caste, it is possible to discern something of a caste system within Israel itself. The hereditary Aaronite priesthood undoubtedly forms a caste, since all recruitment is barred from outside its ranks. Like the Brahmin priesthood, it is not barred from intermarriage with the non-priestly ranks, the child following the status of the male parent, i.e. only the sons of Aaronite fathers are Aaronites, or Kohanim. The privileges and authority of the Kohanim are by no means as great as those of the Brahmins, for the Kohanim are limited Temple function-aries rather than spiritual leaders. The teaching function belongs not to them but to the Prophet, and later to the successors of the Prophets, the Rabbis, who are not priests (though a priest, if qualified by inspi-ration or training, could also be a prophet or rabbi). So the existence of a priestly caste is far less important in Israelite than in Hindu religion, where it is all-important, since in Hinduism the Brahmin performs the function of priest, prophet and rabbi combined, and even sometimes that of god.

At the other end of the social scale, the Israelite community contained further caste elements. These were those who were barred from 'entering the community of the Lord' (Deut. 23:1–3). Contrary to common supposition, this did not mean that such people were barred from being Israelites, but it did mean that they were subject to marriage restrictions within the Israelite (later Jewish) community. These categories were three: the *mamzerim*, i.e. those born from incestuous or adulterous unions; those derived from certain nations (Ammonites, Moabites, Edomites, Egyptians) who were stigmatised in the Torah for their hostility to early Israel; and the slaves. These low castes might marry among themselves, but not with ordinary Israelites or with priests.

It is important to notice, however, that these low castes are not excluded from any religious or social privilege other than that of marriage. They could all offer sacrifices in the Temple, and all castes could eat together without difficulty. Very significantly (as Mary Douglas has pointed out[1]), the castes were not distinguished in relation to purity laws. The lower castes did not have to be avoided by the upper castes (as in Hinduism) as unclean, since ritual purity laws applied to all castes alike, and a priest, when suffering from impurity (caused, say, by touching a corpse) would be just as much a source of impurity as his fellow-Israelite the *mamzer* who had touched a corpse – and just as easily purified by the prescribed ablutions. Neither a *mamzer* nor any other low-caste person was unclean in himself, but only through incurring one of the objectively-listed forms of impurity, each of which had its remedy.

The Israelite caste-system did not arise out of the heart of Israelite religion, and therefore it shows a continual process of attrition, by which it eventually became virtually abolished. It arose not out of any philosophy of human categorisation or racialism, but simply out of certain verses in the Bible which forbade unlimited connubium to certain categories of community members. The tendency of Judaism is to find, in the course of time, a way to accommodate biblical injunctions which are felt to contradict the central drive of the religion. Thus the injunction forbidding connubium (whether 'for ever' or for a limited number of generations) to Ammonites, Moabites, Edomites and Egyptians was nullified by the formulation that

Sennacherib, the Assyrian emperor of the 8th century BCE who had adopted a policy of population shifting, had mixed up all the nations so that it was no longer possible to determine who was an Ammonite, a Moabite, an Edomite or an Egyptian.[2] The ban against connubium with a slave had the simple remedy of freeing the slave, which turned him into a freedman, who had no marriage restrictions.

The ban against connubium with a *mamzer* has been harder to deal with. Attempts were made to abolish it, but did not gain majority consent, so it was softened instead. A legal fiction was adopted that undetected *mamzerim* died young, so that anyone presenting himself for marriage did not need any search to establish his legitimate credentials.[3] Ways were discovered by which the children of a *mamzer*, if not the *mamzer* himself, could escape from *mamzer* status. Much was achieved to render this form of low-caste status inoperative, but the situation remains unsatisfactory to this day. It should be pointed out that 'illegitimacy' in the sense of being born simply of unmarried parents never carried any legal stigma in Judaism. Only the children of incestuous or adulterous unions were stigmatised as illegitimate, and this was a moral advance on the practice of other ancient nations of exposing or killing such offspring.

In the case of the low-caste marriage status of *mamzerim*, or Ammonites, Moabites, Edomites and Egyptians in the Jewish community, we cannot attribute the motivation previously discussed, namely, usurpation of a conquered community. Ammonites, Moabites and Egyptians were never subjugated by the Israelites, but continued to be independent nations. Their low-caste status on entering the Jewish community as converts was due to an historical memory of past hostility, given authority by Holy Writ. The low-caste status of the *mamzerim* arose from horror of the offspring of taboo forms of sexual behaviour, a horror again authorised and given legal form by Scripture. It was natural that these motivations should become weakened in the course of time, as ancient animosities receded, and primitive horror abated.

The case of the slaves, however, is different, and needs further discussion. After an initial period of slaughter of the Canaanites, the Israelites began to accept the defeated people into their own ranks, but in the capacity of slaves or menials. An example is the Gibeonite tribe, who were spared at an early stage, but only to become 'hewers of wood and drawers of water' for the Temple (Joshua 9:23). This group retained its separate caste identity for many centuries, being known as the Nethinim, or Temple servitors, though their attachment to the Temple gave them a certain cultic status. They were forbidden to marry ordinary Israelites, but might marry into any of the other lower castes. Of similar servile but cultic status was the group known as 'the slaves of Solomon', who were the descendants of the Canaanite slaves assembled by King Solomon to do the heavy work of the building of the Temple. But there were also individual slaves, not belonging to any recognised group but serving as slaves in households. These were originally only Canaanites, but later included slaves bought from other non-Israelite nations, who, however, were also designated in Jewish law as 'Canaanite slaves'. All persons of slave status, however, formed a caste, in that they were not allowed to marry ordinary Israelites, so long as they remained slaves.

The 'Canaanite slaves' were distinguished from the 'Hebrew slaves', who were Israelite-born, and had sold themselves into slavery, being bankrupt, to pay their debts. The 'Hebrew slave' was really a bondman, who had to be released by his master after a limited number of years of service, unless he voluntarily chose to remain (Exodus 21:2). He was therefore not subject to any caste marriage restrictions.

It should be stressed, however, that even the Canaanite slaves belonged to the community, and despite their foreign origin, were regarded as Israelites or Jews, with many of the same rights and privileges as free Israelites. In fact, a Canaanite slave was regarded as a special kind of convert to Judaism. He had the same religious duties as Israelite women, and the same rights to rest on Sabbaths and festival days. His master was not allowed to mistreat him, and if he did, for example by knocking out his tooth, he had the right to freedom and full Israelite status. It is doubtful, therefore, whether even the Canaanite slave was really a slave in the sense understood generally in the ancient world. In Rome, for example, a master could kill his slave with impunity, whereas in Israelite law the killing of a slave was treated as murder. The right of the slave to buy his freedom, or to be freed by permission of his master, was a feature of slavery everywhere, though the freedman did not automatically become a full citizen elsewhere as in the Israelite community.

Nevertheless, it is clear that the Canaanite slaves formed a caste in Judaism that derived from the fact of conquest. Only this caste had a 'usurpation myth' attached to it, designed to explain and excuse its members' subjection to the conquerors of their ancestors, the original occupants of the land. In these respects, the position of the Canaanite slaves is similar to that of the Dasyu and Dravidian inhabitants of India who were reduced to slave-caste status – the lowest of the four *varnas*, the Sudras – by their Aryan conquerors. These were not represented as primitives, and were treated with some respect, though not included in the 'twice-born', i.e. initiated class. The Sudras were not Untouchables – the 'fifth *varna*' – but correspond, in Western history, to the Saxons, who were subjected to the conquering Normans and confined to menial vocations. The Untouchables, however, comprising such castes as the Chandalas, Parayas and Nishadas, were regarded as primitive. These classes were already depressed and disprivileged before the Aryan invasion, and represent an indigenous population even earlier than the Dravidians. Even more despised were the hill-tribes, which continued to live by hunting, and were regarded as outside the caste system altogether. In the course of time, much shifting of status took place, since a caste could improve its status by adopting the purity-laws of a higher caste. Such upgrading, however, took several generations to accomplish. Even some hill-tribes moved into the caste system, but hardly improved their status, since they were accepted only at the Untouchable level (see also Chapter 15).

There are some important differences, however, between the Hindu experience of caste and that of Israelite religion. Perhaps the most important of all is that the Israelite caste system was never involved in colour prejudice. The Hindu system, on the other hand, was riddled with colour prejudice. The word *varna*, which designates the main broad divisions of the caste system, actually means 'colour'. The castes in Hinduism have always been distinguished by their whiteness or blackness, and it is the great pride of the highest caste, the Brahmins, that they have preserved their relative whiteness. This aspect of caste makes the gradual wearing away of the caste system very difficult.

In Israelite religion, there was never the slightest hint of colour prejudice. The Canaanites were never stigmatised as of darker colour than the invading Israelites. There has been some misapprehension of this point, because certain modern racialists have mistakenly tried to base their doctrines on the authority of the Hebrew Bible. Some Boer writers who supported apartheid, being of fundamentalist religious belief, tried to draw proofs of the God-given subordination of the black races from the story of Noah's curse against Ham. Jewish tradition has never made this deduction. Noah's curse of future slavery was directed not against Ham himself, but against his son Canaan. It is true that Ham was regarded in ancient times as the ancestor of the blacks, but only through his other son, Cush, regarded as the ancestor of the Ethiopians. The curse against Canaan did not apply to Cush, whose descendants, the black Ethiopians, are always regarded with honour in the biblical writings. We are told that Moses, the founder of Judaism, married an Ethiopian wife (Numbers 12:1), and that his brother Aaron and sister Miriam reproved him for this. We are not told whether their reproof was based on colour prejudice, but in any case they were punished by God for their presumption, and Miriam was even made to suffer leprosy, as if to tell her that whiteness is not necessarily good. Jewish tradition does not even mention colour prejudice as the motive actuating Aaron and Miriam in this matter, saying that they were concerned only about the slight to Moses' first wife, Zipporah, or that Zipporah was herself the 'Ethiopian wife', and that Moses had been neglecting her because of his God-given mission.

The Canaanites, who suffered from Noah's curse by becoming the slaves of the Israelites, were a white people. The attempt of the Boer writers to foist colour prejudice on the Bible authors was thus based on ignorance and misreading.

The Canaanite slaves were not distinguished in any cultic way from the rest of the worshipping community. They were not, for example, regarded as more subject to ritual impurity than others, and they were not excluded from offering sacrifices in the Temple. Here they differ from the lowest Hindu castes, which convey impurity to the higher castes by touch or even proximity, merely by virtue of their caste status, and are not allowed to sacrifice or assist in sacrifice. In the course of time, the Canaanite slaves disappeared from the Jewish scene as they attained freedman status and intermarried with the general Jewish community.

The Canaanite slaves never became a demonised or even a denigrated group among the Israelites. Their low-caste status was regarded as their misfortune, not as evidence of their depravity. The legend of their ancestors' sins, which caused God to eject them from rule over the Holy Land, was not extrapolated into a myth of their continuing depravity and inborn wickedness. Nor did they become the subjects of a myth that gave them a permanent role as opponents of God, or as acolytes of the Devil, who indeed played no important part in Jewish thinking.

Most important and indeed decisive, was that the Canaanite slaves were not required to perform any tasks that were regarded as taboo for other members of the community. Hewing wood and drawing water were not taboo activities, merely laborious. Indeed, when the hewing and drawing was done as part of the work of the Temple, it even took on an aura of holiness, so that the Nethinim and 'slaves of Solomon' were regarded as Temple ministers, hardly inferior to the Levites who were involved in the upkeep and removal of the Temple furniture and fabric, itself a physically arduous task. Since Judaism was a non-dualistic religion, it did not give rise to notions of what has been called 'transgressional sacralism'[4], i.e. the belief that certain acts were wrong and yet religiously and socially essential. All necessary acts, however unpleasant, were permitted, and could be performed by the highest and most saintly members of society. The idea of an act that is both necessary and wrong is foreign to Jewish thinking, and therefore there is no need for an accursed subset of people to incur damnation for the sake of the community. This is the basic reason why in Judaism a pariah group could have no permanent place, and the low-caste groups that did arise, for one reason or another, eventually disappeared.

CHAPTER 7

PAUL AND THE FORMATION
OF THE USURPATION MYTH

The first attempt to supplant Judaism, relegating it to the status of an obsolete or subordinate religion while utilising its material, was, as we have seen, that of Gnosticism. The general tone of the Gnostic dismissal of Judaism and the Jews was condescending and contemptuous rather than savagely hostile. For example, in the extract from Gnostic writings quoted earlier, the criticism offered against Judaism and the Jews is: '. . . they had a doctrine of angels to observe dietary laws and bitter slavery.' This may be paraphrased as follows: 'They (the Jews) have restrictive food laws that were given to them not by the High God, but by lower powers (angels). They have thus lost their freedom and potentiality for god-like status and have become slaves to the Torah.'

This attitude towards Judaism as limited and unspiritual rather than evil is found in Christianity too, though only as one dimension of Christian antisemitism. It is found particularly in the writings of Paul, who had not yet developed the aspects of Christian antisemitism relating to the charge of deicide. Instead, Paul adopts a form of opposition to Judaism that is hardly distinguishable from that of Gnosticism. It was he, in fact, who first alleged that the Torah was given not by God, but by angels. This was Paul's own version of the earlier Gnostic theory that the Torah was given by the Demiurge, the self-deluded Creator of this imperfect world, who imagined himself to be the High God. In the course of time, many Gnostics became converted to Christianity, and formed their own sects of Gnostic Christianity. In these, the original Gnostic thesis that the Torah was

82

given by the Demiurge became Christianised, or Paulinised, in the form that the Torah was given by angels, as is said in the Christianised Gnostic work quoted above.

The difference is that angels, while limited supernatural beings, are not in opposition to God, like the Demiurge, but working under His supervision. Thus, unlike the Gnostics, Paul was not setting up a rival system to Judaism, based on a different god, but was taking over Judaism from within, claiming that his new system had been intended by God to be the fulfilment of Judaism from the start, and He had only sent an interim message to the Jews through the agency of his inferior servants the angels.[1] Thus, unlike the Gnostics, Paul did not impugn the prophetic status of the line of Hebrew Prophets beginning with Moses. On the contrary, Paul confirmed that they were all true prophets; but he interpreted their message in such a way that they all became proto-Paulinists. Moreover, he interpreted them as prophesying their own eventual obsolescence on the advent of their destined supersessor, Christ, in the light of whose teaching (as explicated by Paul) and salvific immolation, their own teachings would be revealed as temporary only.

The question now for Paul was what to do with the Jews. For the Jews, or the vast majority of them, did not accept their own obsolescence. They continued stubbornly to think of their founding prophet Moses and the succeeding prophets as the purveyors of an eternal covenant. They thought of Jesus not as the founder of a new covenant superseding that of Sinai, but as a messiah-figure who had mistakenly thought himself the herald of the kingdom of God prophesied by Isaiah, Zechariah and other Hebrew prophets, and whose death on a Roman cross as a rebel proved him to be one more tragic messianic failure, like Judas of Galilee, Theudas, Athronges, Bar Kokhba, and many others.

Paul's ideas on what would happen to the Jews in a Christian world are explained in his Epistle to the Romans, chapter 11:

For I would not brethren that ye should be ignorant of this mystery, lest ye should be wise in your own conceits; that blindness in part is happened to Israel, until the fulness of the Gentiles be come in. And so all Israel shall be saved: as it is written, There shall come

out of Sion the Deliverer and shall turn away ungodliness from
Jacob:
For this is my covenant unto them, when I shall take away their
sins.
As concerning the gospel, they are enemies for your sakes: but as
touching the election, they are beloved for the fathers' sakes.

(Romans 11:25–28)

The key phrase here is '. . . blindness in part is happened to Israel,
until the fulness of the Gentiles be come in.' This is called a 'mystery',
which means that the 'blindness' of the Jews is part of God's plan. The
rejection of Jesus by the Jews has been instrumental in the salvation of
the Gentiles. It is necessary for the Jews to remain 'blind' until the
whole Gentile world has been converted; and then the Jews themselves
will be converted. Here we have the first adumbration of the idea,
so fateful for the future of the Jews in Christendom, that the stubborn
rejection of Christ by the Jews is somehow instrumental in the salvation of Gentile Christians.

There are some difficulties in Paul's thought in this passage. In what
way, according to Paul, do the Jews contribute to Gentile salvation by
refusing salvation for themselves? Are we to think that if the Jews
had accepted Christ, salvation would have stopped with them, and
would never have reached the Gentiles?

Part of the idea seems to be that the Jews were entitled, as the
people of God, the descendants of the Patriarchs, Abraham, Isaac
and Jacob, and the recipients of the Sinai covenant and the messages
of the Prophets, to first refusal, so to speak, of the new covenant
offered by Jesus. By their refusal, they opened the way to the Gentiles
to become the holy people in their stead, while they themselves
became a secondary group, who were, however, not entirely abandoned, but were assured that one day, in recognition of their former
status, they would be included in God's favour too. From primary
status, they had sunk to secondary status; they had in fact
exchanged status with the Gentiles, who now became the primary
vehicle of God's grace. If, however, the Jews had accepted Christ, they
would have retained their primary status; the centre of the Christian
Church would have remained in Jerusalem, instead of moving to

84

Rome (though this geographical aspect was not yet apparent to Paul, for whom Rome was still the centre of a pagan Empire), and the Jews, residing in the land of Israel (instead of being ejected as exiles for their sin of refusal) would have functioned as a priest-nation, ministering to the Gentiles of the world-wide Christian Church.

The topic receives further and less tolerant treatment in the Gospel of Matthew, which was written about 20 years later than Paul's Epistle to the Romans:

> When Jesus heard it, he marvelled, and said to them that followed, Verily I say unto you, I have not found so great faith, no, not in Israel.
> And I say unto you, That many shall come from the east and west, and shall sit down with Abraham, and Isaac, and Jacob, in the kingdom of heaven.
> But the children of the kingdom shall be cast out into outer darkness: there shall be weeping and gnashing of teeth.
> And Jesus said unto the centurion, Go thy way: and as thou has believed, so be it done unto thee.
>
> (Matthew 8:10–13)

This and other Gospel passages express the supplanting of the Jews ('the children of the kingdom') by the Gentiles, but here there is no mere exchanging of primary for secondary status, but outright expulsion into 'outer darkness', without any vision of a time when the Jews will be received back into the fold. Between Paul and the Gospels, the Christian attitude has hardened towards the Jews.

Paul's policy of relegation, rather than expulsion, of the Jews contains an interesting echo of Jewish tradition itself. A Midrashic story, no doubt stemming from a period earlier than the birth of Christianity, tells how the Torah came to be accepted by the Israelites at Mount Sinai:

> 'The Lord came from Sinai' (Deut. 33:2). Hence we learn that God went about from nation to nation to see whether they would receive the Torah, and they would not receive it.
>
> (Pesikta de-Rav Kahana, 199b)

This rejection of the Torah by the nations, however, is not a rejection of salvation, for that could be obtained by Gentiles without acceptance of the Sinai covenant by adherence to the Noachic covenant, but only a rejection of the special role of priest-nation conferred on Israel.[2] The purpose of the story is not to consign the Gentiles to damnation, or even to a limbo of suspended animation pending their eventual conversion, but only to fend off any criticisms that God showed favouritism to Israel by conferring the election on them without giving other nations a similar opportunity for special distinction. Individual Gentiles can still join the priest-nation by conversion, but there is now only one nation that can claim the position of priest-nation; whereas, before Sinai, other nations, according to this story, might have claimed the same position. Thus the situation does not give rise to any stratification into castes. Gentile nations remain sovereign nations, (since Judaism never had any aim of world conquest), and are subordinate to Israel only in the sense of lacking priest-nation status.

Paul's solution of the problem of what to do with the Jews also does not imply, at least directly, pariah status for the Jews. Paul does not really envisage the situation that later developed; namely, a Europe-wide Christendom, with Jews included as landless exiles. As far as Paul knew, the Jews would continue to occupy their own land, though under Roman suzerainty, and Christians, however successful in missionary activities, would constitute only one element in a largely pagan Roman Empire. Paul saw the Jews as a continuing force that would stand against the process of Christianisation, which would eventually achieve success not by political conquest of the Roman Empire, but by the advent of the new kingdom of the spirit. His campaign of conversion of the Gentiles, which took him over a large part of the Roman Empire, should not be seen in the light of what happened much later. He was not trying to convert the Roman Empire to Christianity, but to save as many Gentiles as possible before the coming of the eschatological day when it would be too late for conversion. He was not envisaging this as due to happen in the very near future, for such immediate expectancy would have left no time for planning an extended missionary campaign; nor would it have left time for a historical scheme in which the Jews would be suspended in disbelief 'until the fullness of the Gentiles be come in'. But his historical scheme did not include so daring a political vision as the hope of dominance over the Roman Empire – a vision that is already beginning to enter the minds of the writers of the Gospels twenty years later.

Nevertheless, some features in Paul's scheme for the Jews do point in the direction of pariahship as a distinct possibility, if Jews should ever find themselves under Christian rule. In particular, the Jews are given a *function* in Christian society. Moreover, this function is directly related to their disbelief. Just because they are disbelievers, they contribute to the well-being of the Christian community. This kind of service through sin is what constitutes a pariah caste.

If Paul's type of Christianity had come to power in the Roman Empire, rather than the Gospel type based on the dramatic and violent Passion story with its portrayal of the Jews as deicides, the Jews would possibly have had a position similar to their status later in Islam: they would have constituted a *dhimmi* of second-class citizens, despised and disprivileged, but not loathed or demonised. But this was not a likely outcome, once Paul had sown the seed of the necessary sin (a concept lacking in the Islamic concept of *dhimmi*). Paul's notion that the disbelief of the Jews had a God-given purpose lent itself to easy extension. If the Jews had been blinded by God (thus being rendered incapable of recognising the divinity of Jesus), might not this blindness have been the cause of hostile acts against Jesus, culminating in responsibility for the Crucifixion? In such a scenario Paul's idea of a people designated by God to reject Jesus is completed: the Jews are designated by God (just as Judas Iscariot was designated by Jesus) to perform an act of treachery which at the same time was indispensable and God-given for the salvation of mankind. Thus finally the Jews would assume full mythic, demonic status as the performers of destined and necessary evil, rather than as mere blind, deluded and unspiritual persons.

There is indeed one passage in Paul's writings that seems to initiate the myth of deicide:

You have fared like the congregations in Judaea, God's people in Christ Jesus. You have been treated by your countrymen as they are treated by the Jews, who killed the Lord Jesus and the prophets and drove us out, the Jews who are heedless of God's will and enemies of their fellow-men, hindering us from speaking to the Gentiles to lead them to salvation. All this time they have been making up the full measure of their guilt, and now retribution has overtaken them for good and all.

(I Thess. 14–16)

This, in itself, is as openly antisemitic as any passage in the Gospels, having verbal links with, for example, Matthew 23:34. The accusation that the Jews killed their own prophets, so that their alleged murder of Jesus was the culmination of a long national career of crime and rebellion against God, forms part of a portrayal of the Jews as an innately wicked people, who were destined from the first to play the role of deicides. The accusation that the Jews are 'enemies of their fellow-men' is part of the vocabulary of Hellenistic antisemitism, which saw the refusal of the Jews to share in polytheistic worship as evidence of misanthropy and unsociability. It was this very accusation that led the Syrian-Greek commander, Antiochus Sidetes, to contemplate seriously, in 133 BCE, the annihilation of the whole Jewish nation.[3]

Even more damaging, in Jewish terms, is the accusation, 'All this time they have been making up the full measure of their guilt', for this expression relates the Jews to the Canaanites as a doomed and guilty nation ejected from God's favour. The allusion is to Genesis 15:16: 'For the iniquity of the Amorites is not yet full.' The Amorites were the leading nation among the Canaanites, and here Genesis is looking forward to the fuller expression of Leviticus:

Defile not ye yourselves in any of these things: for in all these the nations are defiled which I cast out before you:
And the land is defiled: therefore I do visit the iniquity thereof upon it, and the land itself vomiteth out her inhabitants . . .
For all these abominations have the men of the land done, which were before you, and the land is defiled;
That the land spew not you out also, when ye defile it, as it spewed out the nations that were before you.

(Leviticus 18:24–28)

88

By deliberately recalling these passages, I Thessalonians speaks the language of usurpation and pariahship. The Jews, like the Canaanites, are to be expelled from their heritage because of their polluting sins, and the Gentile Christians are to inherit the blessings given to Abraham. The Jews are to become exiles from their land, and to occupy the position of Canaanite slaves in the Christian community; foreshadowed is the Church definition of the Jews as *servi*. This terrible passage is very different from the picture in Romans 11 of a Jewish people continuing in their land in parallel with the Christian community outside, until such time as the veil is lifted from Jewish eyes. Instead of a picture of a people with a long and noble record who had unaccountably (or providentially) failed at the last hurdle by rejecting the divine Messiah, we have the picture of a congenitally wicked people, soiled by a continuous record of murder and disobedience, who have finally caused God to run out of patience.

Fortunately, there is good reason to suppose that Paul was not the author of this passage, but that it was inserted by some later hand into the text of I Thessalonians. The hinted references to the destruction of the Temple and the subsequent Jewish sufferings and exile ('. . . now retribution has overtaken them', and the parallel to the Canaanites) are sufficient to make it probable that this passage was inserted into I Thessalonians at least fifteen years after its composition by Paul. Although in fact the destruction of the Temple was not followed by the exile of the Jewish people as a whole, who continued to form the majority of the population of the land for another six hundred years, until the upheavals connected with the Arab conquest, there was a considerable movement of Jews after the destruction to other lands, either as fugitives or as captives. This may have been interpreted by the author of this passage as a fulfilment of the prophecy that the Jews, if disobedient, would suffer the same fate as the Canaanites. That Paul foresaw, with prophetic power, the destruction of the Temple, is hardly likely, and the tone of virulent antisemitism is not in accordance with his attitude elsewhere in his writings.

The date of the insertion of this passage in the text must therefore be shortly after 70 CE, as indicated by the use of the word 'now' in the expression 'now retribution has overtaken them'. The passage thus indicates that in the short period of about fifteen years, a marked deterioration had taken place in the Christian Gentile attitude towards the Jews. Instead of Paul's pained surprise about the lack of response among the Jews to his new preaching of the divine Christ, we have an actively hostile and denigrating attitude that denies the Jews their status as the people of God and declares them accursed. The mythological faculty has been at work to provide an explanation for the exclusion of the Jews from salvation and their suppression by the Christian Church. We have here the earliest adumbration of the deicide myth which reaches full elaboration in the Gospels. We note too how the author of the passage dissociates himself from the Jews to the extent that he relates to them as if to a foreign nation. Paul, in writing about the Jews elsewhere, never uses this distancing tone, but rather is at pains to stress his own Jewishness – which is so important to him, indeed, that his stress on it seems at times strident. Here no distinction is made between the Jewish leaders, such as the High Priest, and 'the Jews' in general; indeed the use of the blanket term 'the Jews' reminds us of its use as a term of opprobrium in the Gospel of John.

We may conclude, then, that though this antisemitic passage cannot be attributed with any confidence to Paul, it represents the swift and inevitable transition from Paul's conception of Jewish unbelief as providential to the idea that it was the destiny of the Jews, as proved by their whole wicked history, to act as the betrayers of Jesus. Whereas Paul sought to explain why the Jews were unresponsive to his message, the emphasis shifted in the immediately following generation to the responsibility of the Jews for the death of Jesus.

In the period between the composition of Paul's Epistles and the appearance of the Gospels, there was rapid development of the mythological aspects of the death of Jesus. The story of the Virgin Birth and the birth narrative of the manger, the star and the three Magi can all be traced to this period. All were unknown to Paul; yet they were the outcome of Paul's mythicisation of Jesus as a descending and ascending deity, who came to earth for the express purpose of dying on the Cross, so that others, by symbolically sharing in his death and resurrection, might achieve immortality. Once Jesus had been turned into a salvation deity in this way, it was inevitable that narrative elements characteristic of other salvation deities, such as Osiris, Adonis, Attis and Dionysus, should be attached to him.

At the same time, the growing Pauline Gentile Church was becoming strongly aware, during this interim period, of the need to adopt a positive and reconciling stance towards the power of Rome. The Jews had become notorious, during this very period, for their rebelliousness. This had burst out into the open insurrection of the Jewish War of 66–70 CE, in a bold attempt to take advantage of Roman disunity. The problem for Pauline Christians was that while they had no interest in Jewish struggles for independence, being of non-Jewish stock and having a religious belief that was totally non-political and other-worldly, they tended to be identified with the Jews, since they worshipped a human-divine deity known to have been of Jewish origin. Consequently, the story of Jesus' death began to be told in such a way as to exonerate the Romans and totally blame the Jews. Already in the inserted passage quoted above in I Thessalonians, the responsibility of the Romans for the crucifixion of Jesus has been obliterated, and instead we have the unqualified expression, relating to the Jews, '. . . who killed the Lord Jesus'. Even the Gospels do not go as far as this. Being based on authentic traditions of the Jerusalem Church, of which they are highly-edited versions, they cannot deny that Jesus was executed by the Romans, but only attempt to cast blame on the Jews indirectly, by claiming that they brought influence and blackmail to bear on the well-meaning Roman governor, Pilate (who in historical fact was brutal and corrupt, and would not have hesitated to execute anyone claiming to be 'King of the Jews'). Only the Gospel of John, by an equivocal expression, suggests that it was the Jews themselves who crucified Jesus, and, as a result, in the course of later time, the assertion that 'the Jews crucified Jesus' has become a commonplace of Christian polemics. But this distortion is already foreshadowed in the passage added to Paul's epistle.

Yet even this openly antisemitic passage, containing an accusation that is lacking in three, at least, of the Gospels, falls short of the full antisemitic myth which the Gospels promulgate. For both Paul, and whatever disciple appended this passage, are unaware of the Judas Iscariot myth, which symbolically marks out the Jews as collectively representing the dark betrayer found in other myths of human-divine sacrifice, such as those of Osiris, Baal, Dionysus and Balder. Paul never mentions Judas Iscariot, and he actually makes a statement which shows that he knew nothing about the alleged betrayal by one of the twelve disciples. He says (I Cor. 15:5) that after the Crucifixion, the resurrected Jesus appeared to all twelve disciples, at a time, when, according to the Gospels, there were only eleven disciples, Judas having defected. The Gospels themselves, in contrast, are very precise in numbering the disciples as 'eleven' at this point, see Matthew 28:16, Mark 16:14, Luke 24:33. The contradiction between Paul's Epistles and the Gospels shows that the Judas Iscariot legend arose in the period of fertile myth making between 60 and 70 CE, when the death of Jesus was fully developed into a mystery-religion narrative.[4]

Paul created a new religion by an inspired act of conflation, by which he brought together three separate religious traditions: Judaism, Gnosticism and mystery-religion. In this new amalgam, Judaism provided the historical sweep, from Adam to the Endtime, that was lacking in Gnosticism (which was so anti-world and anti-sex that it provided no principle of organised historical continuity). Mystery-religion, on the other hand, provided a sacrificial element that was also lacking in Gnosticism: the sacrament of blood, the excitement of violence, the drama of initiation. Mystery-religion itself, however, as practised in the Hellenistic world, lacked universalism, being local in character – Osiris in Egypt, Attis in Asia Minor, Adonis in Syria, Dionysus in Greece. Paul's new synthesis provided a religion of unlimited appeal; but also, in its relation to Judaism and the Jews, it set up the possibilities for a usurpation myth of unprecedented virulence and potentiality for pariahship.

CHAPTER 8

THE DEVELOPMENT OF THE
CHRISTIAN USURPATION MYTH

The factors leading to the development of a Christian usurpation myth ousting the Jews from election were complex. In addition to the trauma arising from Jewish refusal to accept the divinity of Jesus with its consequences in schism and displacement, there was the problem of disassociation from Jewish rebelliousness against Rome. But there was also an important factor arising from the conflict between the two early forms of Christianity, the Pauline and the Petrine.

The Jerusalem Church, led by James, the brother of Jesus, and by Peter, designated by Jesus as 'the Rock on whom I build my Church', came into conflict with Paul in a way that has long been a subject of heated discussion. According to orthodox Christian belief, the conflict was wholly resolved, so that Paul and Peter became allies in the foundation of the Western Church, both suffering martyrdom in Rome, which then became sanctified as the centre of Christendom. This concept is a little too convenient for the claims of the Church of Rome to be beyond suspicion. In fact, there is no reliable evidence that Peter ever went to Rome, or that he ever ceased to be associated with Jerusalem, the centre of Jewish Christianity. The story of how Peter slowly, and with much obtuseness, became reconciled to Pauline ideas is told in the book of Acts, and is at variance with the story of irreconcilable conflict between Peter and Paul told in Galatians.

The work of F. C. Baur and the Tübingen school, showing that the conflict between the Jerusalem Church and the Pauline Church was never resolved (contrary to the story given in Acts) was unpalatable to Christian scholars, and was declared on various specious or irrelevant grounds go be unsound. Recently, however, the Tübingen view of the history of early Christianity has been coming back into favour.[1] It has begun to be realised how much in the Gospel accounts derives from the rivalry between the two Churches; particularly the picture given of the immediate disciples of Jesus as stupid, weak people who failed to understand Jesus' teaching, kept thinking mistakenly that he had political ends in view, and in the event even proved less than loyal to him. This Gospel polemic against the disciples is really a polemic against the Jerusalem Church, in which these very disciples were the leaders. The contention of the Gospels and Acts that the disciples did not understand Jesus' motives, and had to be educated in these matters by Paul, who never met Jesus in the flesh, but received superior information through visions of the heavenly Jesus, should at least be regarded as open to question, rather than accepted uncritically in the manner usual even in modern New Testament scholarship.

The unfavourable picture of the disciples given in the Gospels reaches its peak in the character of Judas Iscariot, the disciple who went so far in incomprehension and disloyalty that he betrayed Jesus to his death. Careful examination of the Gospel accounts, in which the character of Judas Iscariot receives progressive development in the snowballing fashion of legend accretion, shows that in the earliest negative portrayal of Judas, he was not a traitor but a political activist. In this role, he represented the political activism of the Jerusalem Church, which was unacceptable to the anti-political other-worldliness of the Pauline Church for which the Gospels were written. The Jerusalem Church consisted of Jews who were loyal to the Torah which they observed piously, and who were also patriotic Jews who hoped for the liberation of Judaea from Roman rule and the restoration of the Jewish monarchy. Jesus himself they regarded quite literally as 'King of the Jews', and they expected him to return, following his miraculous resurrection, to resume his mission of liberation and take his place in Jerusalem as rightful King, on the throne of his ancestors, David and Solomon. Meanwhile, his brother James, his nearest relative, acted in his stead as Prince Regent, with Peter as his Chief Minister.[2]

Later, the negative picture of Judas Iscariot as an activist ringleader was taken over in Pauline anti-Jerusalem propaganda by Peter. It was then that Judas Iscariot was cast for a more baleful role, that of representative of the allegedly treacherous Jewish people, who did not merely misunderstand Jesus, like the Jerusalem Church, or merely show weakness of loyalty to him, but, allegedly, actively betrayed him to his enemies. So the double war that was being waged by the Pauline Church against the authority of the Jerusalem Church, who believed in Jesus but in Jewish terms as a human, kingly figure, and against the authority of the Jews themselves, who saw Jesus as a failed messiah, achieved crystallisation in the symbolic role of Judas Iscariot, a figure of the utmost significance for the pariah role of the Jews in later Christendom.

For the development of Jesus by Paul in the direction of a human-divine saviour-god, dying a savage death on behalf of his community, had awakened many resonances in the minds of the converts who had come to Paulinism from a pagan background. It was these converts who welcomed such accretions as the birth in the manger, adapted from the birth of Horus, or in a cave (an alternative version found in an apocryphal Gospel), adapted from the birth of Mithras, or the visit of the Magi, again from Mithraism, or the Virgin Birth, adapted from many legends of virgin goddesses (such as Diana) and the births of heroes, such as Hercules, whose mothers were impregnated by gods. These converts again responded to the familiar figure of the Betrayer, so essential to any narrative of the sacrificial death of a saviour-god. Osiris had been betrayed to his salvific death by his wicked brother Set, Dionysus had been dismembered, to the advantage of all those partaking in the Dionysiac mysteries, by the wicked Titans. In other mystery cults probably not known to Paul's converts, yet throwing comparative light on the matter for modern investigators, Baal, the Syrian salvation-god was betrayed by his brother Mot, and Balder, the Scandinavian mystery-god by his evil fellow-god Loki. The pattern of salvation became complete with the election of Judas Iscariot to the vacant role of Betrayer of Jesus.

The reason why the figure of the Betrayer is so essential to mystery-cults is that he relieves the initiates of what would otherwise be an unbearable load of guilt. In any salvation religion in which the initiate achieves immortality through participating in the cruel death and miraculous resurrection of the human-divine sacrifice, the moral difficulty is that the initiate is actually glad that the salvific death takes place, since without it he would forgo salvation. This gladness, however, must at all costs be disguised, since it cannot be admitted that the initiate, and the community to which he belongs, actually share responsibility for the cruel death by their strong desire and gratitude for it. Consequently, some dark figure of a Betrayer must be provided, on whom the deed of blood can be blamed. In prehistoric times, no doubt, the Betrayer, or Sacred Executioner, played a ritual role in the drama of human sacrifice. We can see, under various disguises, the existence of such a ritual figure in legends and myths of the historical period: Cain, for example, portrayed as a murderer in the Hebrew Bible, but showing his original traits as Sacred Executioner of a human foundation sacrifice in his banishment and protection from capital punishment.[3] In the myths of Osiris and Balder, the Betrayer or Executioner is disguised by the elevation of the events to a supernatural level: the story is told of gods, though it was played out originally in human society. Yet in the case of Osiris and others, the societal aspect is retained by the memory of the human beginnings of the sacrifice: Osiris was a human king of Egypt before he became a god, just as Jesus was a human king of Israel before his ascension to heaven.

When Jesus was made by Paul into a human-divine sacrifice bringing salvation to those initiated by baptism, the associations of such salvific sacrifices came flooding back, negating the long effort of Judaism to build a religion in which sacrifice was a meal of meat or vegetables shared with God, and the concept of human-divine sacrifice was outlawed. Among the features that now became necessary was the Betrayer or Executioner, who would bear the burden of guilt associated with the sacrifice, so that the community of initiates could display only grief at the death of the Saviour, and wash its hands, like Pilate, of all complicity. Primitive narrative elements made their return in this atavistic relapse into prehistoric religion, notably the idea of the double nature of salvation, which required two saviours – one, the White Christ, to die on behalf of the community, the other, the Black Christ, to assume the guilt of the sacrifice itself – one to sacrifice his body for the community, and the other his soul, one to die, the other to endure excommunication and banishment. This double nature of salvation is no doubt symbolised in the Day of Atonement ceremony of the two goats, one of which dies, while the other, the Scapegoat, is banished. It was also this double nature of salvation that led to the common feature in human-sacrificial legend that the Executioner was the brother, even the twin, of the Executed – for example, Cain and Abel, Romulus and Remus. This close relationship emphasises the kinship of the two roles, and their twin necessity for salvation. Sometimes the two roles are even combined, as in the Scandinavian myth of the self-immolation of Odin.

In the Christian myth, the part of the Betrayer, or Loki, is played by Judas Iscariot, who as a member of the band of Apostles, has the required closeness and affinity to the human-divine sacrifice, Jesus. There are even hints that Judas was Jesus' brother, since Jesus did indeed have a brother called Judas; or even his twin, since a memory is retained of a disciple called Judas Thomas, or Judas the Twin (described in apocryphal literature as being Jesus' double). But these hints of brotherly relationship were suppressed at some point in the development of the legend because of the need to stress the perpetual virginity of Mary, so that Jesus could not be allowed to have a brother, and also the need to deny Jesus' close affinity with his family, which would have allowed too much to the claims of the Jerusalem Church to be led by members of Jesus' royal family.

On the other hand, the role of Betrayer is also played in the Christian myth by the Jewish people as a whole, especially when they call for the crucifixion of Jesus when they could have saved him through the alleged *privilegium paschale*, yet called for the release of the bandit Barabbas instead. This communal, rather than individual, responsibility for the guilt of the salvific sacrifice is probably unique in myth.[4] The myth of the Christian mystery-cult is unique in combining an initiation myth with a usurpation myth. The mystery-cults of Osiris, Attis and Adonis were not endeavouring to supplant a previous religion, much less to incorporate its scriptures, in re-interpreted form, in their own mysteries. Consequently, their Betrayer could be an individual, who disappears from the story once his mission of salvific murder has been accomplished.

In the Christian myth, there is indeed an individual Betrayer who disappears from the story by his remorseful suicide (according to Matthew's version) or by his horrifying death by the hand of God (in the version of Acts). Yet even this individual Betrayer is not without communal aspects. In several ways, he is made to be representative of the Jewish people as a whole. The chief means to this end, of course, is his name. Of all the disciples, the one who was chosen by the myth makers of the seventh decade to be the Betrayer was the one who bore the name of the Jewish people. In historical reality, there was no Betrayer.[5] Jesus went to his death, as many messiah-figures did before and after him, as a victim of Roman imperialist occupation of a conquered land. But as a salvation-god, he had to have a Betrayer, and the most suitable one was the disciple who could function, by his name, as representative of the people whose religion was supplanted and annexed by the new cult. Judas, a name of honour in Judaism, became a name of horrified opprobrium in the successor-religion, Christianity.[6]

In the Christian myth, the real Betrayer is the Jewish people, of which Judas Iscariot is merely the symbol. In a series of excoriating scenes, the Jews are portrayed as not only rejecting Jesus, both as a teacher and as divine visitant, but also as working for his death. Jesus is portrayed as a figure of perfect innocence who is hated by all sections of Jewish society, except the small band of his followers (and even they, as we have seen are not wholehearted in their loyalty, a feature aimed at the Jerusalem Church rather than the Jews as a whole). Nothing could be more strikingly dramatic than the image we receive from the Gospels of Jesus, a centre of light, borne down by the dark satanic forces of malice, stupidity and envy, all represented by the Jews, for the non-Jews in the story, on the contrary, are all shown sympathetically.

The groups of Jews shown arrayed against Jesus are the priests, the Pharisees, the Sadducees, the Herodians and the people. These groups are not clearly delineated, for their differences from each other are far less important in the story than their common hatred of Jesus. The priests are the most active in seeking Jesus' arrest and death; the Pharisees in opposing his teaching on the Sabbath; the Sadducees in opposing his teaching on resurrection; and the people, after an initial period of partial support, in demanding his death to save Barabbas, and deriding his sufferings on the cross. Thus no section of the Jews is excluded from blame. In the latest composed of the Gospels, that of John, we no longer find Jesus' opponents named as 'Pharisees', 'priests', 'Sadducees', 'Herodians', or 'people', but simply as 'Jews', so that this most influential of the Gospels – known as 'the Gospel of the Church' because of its total embodiment of emphases important in later Christianity – has the most powerful antisemitic impact of all.

We are also left in no doubt that, as a result of their betrayal of Jesus, the Jews are now under a continuing curse. This is stated plainly in the non-Pauline passage in I Thessalonians quoted above, 'now retribution has overtaken them for good and all' (the Greek is *eis telos*, which means both 'completely' and 'for ever'). Paul's hope that the Jews would eventually be saved is lacking here. It is also absent in the Gospels, which nowhere hold out hope for the eventual salvation of the Jews, but on the contrary expect their everlasting damnation, as in the Barabbas scene, where the Jews themselves call a curse on themselves: 'His blood be on us, and on our children' (a scene constantly quoted through history by Christians to explain the sufferings of the Jews, as graphically recorded by Claude Lanzmann in his filming of Polish peasants' reactions to the Holocaust in *Shoah*). The fate held out for the Jews in the Gospels is 'weeping and gnashing of teeth' (Matthew 8:12, Luke 13:28), an expression associated with 'darkness' and 'raging fire', and evidently signifying eternal punishment in Hell.

In historical fact, the life and death of Jesus are impossible to understand unless one is aware of the deep divisions within the Jewish people, which are glossed over by the Gospels in their concern to implicate all sections of the Jews equally in his death. There are two sections of the Jews who are likely, historically, to have been implicated in the betrayal of Jesus to the Romans and his subsequent execution: the Herodians and the High Priest with his entourage. These were the politically powerful elements of the Jews who were hand-in-glove with the Roman occupation, from which they entirely derived their power. The Herodians were led by Herod Antipas, the ruler of Galilee, son of Herod the Wicked, appointee and pawn of the Romans. Herod Antipas was ostensibly an independent ruler, but only in the same sense as Pétain ruled Vichy France. The High Priest was also an appointee of the Romans. He was essentially a native police chief, keeping order among the Jews on behalf of the Roman occupation. He had no standing among the Jews as a spiritual leader. The teaching authority among the Jews lay with the Pharisee sages, who at this time were led by Gamaliel, to whom even the New Testament pays tribute as 'a teacher of the Law held in high regard by all the people' (Acts 5:34).

The implication of the Pharisees in the death of Jesus is one of the most artificial and unhistorical features of the Gospels. The sympathetic stance of Gamaliel towards Peter and his companions shortly after the Crucifixion of Jesus is in glaring contradiction to the alleged bitter opposition to Jesus during his lifetime. Even the Gospels do not allege any complicity of the Pharisees in the Sanhedrin trial of Jesus; in fact, the disappearance of the Pharisees from this scene is significant, since if they had been present they would no doubt have adopted the same attitude as did Gamaliel in the Sanhedrin trial of Peter. The absence of the Pharisees is one more indication that the Sanhedrin trial is fictitious. If the Pharisees had really hounded Jesus, 'desiring his death', for healing people on the Sabbath, why were these charges not raised at his Sanhedrin trial by the Pharisees who, in fact, formed the majority of the Sanhedrin? At the trial of Peter, the Pharisee majority was vocal enough, through its leader Gamaliel, and the same thing happened at the later trial of Paul. Only in the alleged trial of Jesus is the Pharisee majority totally silent. It is the Gospel of John that reveals the truth of the matter by omitting the Sanhedrin trial altogether, and describing instead an interrogation of Jesus by the High Priest in his own house, leading to the handing over of Jesus to the Romans as a fomenter of sedition against the Roman occupation.

Of course, it is not quite clear from the account in Acts that Gamaliel was the leader of the Pharisees. It could be taken rather that he is acting alone, and is an unrepresentative Pharisee, and this is how Christian commentators have usually explained his surprising intervention, even arguing at times that he must have been a secret Christian. But this leaves unexplained his influence on the whole Pharisee party, who joined him in voting for the release of Peter. In fact, we have ample evidence in the rabbinic literature that Gamaliel was the leading representative of Pharisaism in his day, being the grandson of Hillel, the ancestor of Gamaliel the Second and Judah the Prince, and an honoured figure in the Jewish religious establishment.

This being so, it seems most unlikely that the Pharisees who regarded Gamaliel, the defender of Peter, as their leader would have been the implacable enemies of Jesus only a few years before. On examination, we find that indeed the stories of Pharisee opposition to Jesus are highly implausible. They mostly turn on questions of Sabbath observance, especially the issue of healing on the Sabbath. It is because Jesus healed on the Sabbath that the Pharisees are alleged to have sought his death. In fact, however, the Pharisees did not disapprove of healing on the Sabbath.[7] Where there was no breach of Sabbath laws such as building a fire, or grinding medicines, any healing could be performed, for they did not regard healing itself as an infringement of the Sabbath. Jesus healed not by any method that infringed the Sabbath, but by faith healing, which was totally allowed even where the illness treated was slight. In the case of serious life-threatening illnesses, the Pharisees permitted treatment even when this involved direct breach of Sabbath laws, such as building a fire for some-one suffering from hypothermia; just as they permitted the eating of normally forbidden foods, as medicines or to combat starvation, if life was endangered. All the stories alleging that the Pharisees sought Jesus' death because he healed on the Sabbath are inventions, in the light of our knowledge of actual Pharisee teaching. Even Jesus' supposedly original aphorism on Sabbath-healing, 'The Sabbath was made for man, not man for the Sabbath', was a saying current in the Pharisee movement, with the same connotation in which Jesus used it, that urgent human needs took precedence over Sabbath observance.

The blackening of the Pharisees in the Gospels, therefore, is a phenomenon demanding explanation. Modern scholars, both non-Jewish and Jewish, have seen the denigration of the Pharisees as a problem, and have laboured to show that the Pharisees, far from being the hypocrites and cruel legalists depicted in the Gospels, formed one of the greatest and most enlightened movements in the history of religion. They were a movement in which discussion took the place of dogma, decisions were made not by supernatural claims but by vote, reforms were made by the application of rational and sensitive moral insights, and the ruling emotions were compassion for the poor and oppressed and courage in withstanding oppression. The works of Travers Herford, George Foot Moore, E. P. Sanders, Ephraim Urbach, Claude Montefiore, Israel Abrahams, among others, should be consulted. The upshot of such study is that all the allegedly new and revolutionary teaching of Jesus in the Gospels was current Pharisee teaching. The final surprising conclusion is that Jesus himself was a Pharisee.

How, then, and with what motive on the part of the editors, does Jesus become the castigator of the Pharisees in the Gospels? Many explanations have been put forward by modern scholars who wish to avoid acknowledging that the editors of the Gospels are engaged in a campaign against the Pharisees for religio-political reasons. The most far-reaching explanation is that the Pharisees should be regarded as quite unconnected with the rabbinical movement, from whose post-Destruction writings we learn about the (purported) teachings of Pharisees such as Hillel and Gamaliel. According to this theory, such teachings are pseudepigraphic, and their ascription to pre-Destruction Pharisees is part of a campaign of post-Destruction rabbis to give themselves spurious authority by claiming continuity with earlier times. This theory has been seized on by Christian scholars looking for support for traditional belief, for it enables them to retain faith in the reliability of the Gospel accounts. For the Pharisees of the Gospels are not to be assessed, according to this theory, in the light of rabbinic writings which idealise the Pharisees by endowing them with (admittedly enlightened) late rabbinic doctrines. The Pharisees may have been just as hateful as the Gospels present them, after all. Welcome as this theory is to believing Christian academics (such as James Dunn), it has also been furthered by some Jewish scholars, such as Jacob Neusner.

Fortunately, the inherent improbability of lack of continuity between the Pharisees and the Rabbis has halted the progress of this attractive way of reasserting the historical authenticity of the Gospels. Recently, the work of Martin Hengel, Geza Vermes and others has pointed to obvious evidence from Josephus, the New Testament, the Dead Sea Scrolls and the intertestamentary literature to show that the Pharisees and the Rabbis formed one movement – the change of nomenclature being due only to the disappearance of the opposing Sadducees after the Destruction, whereby a sectarian name for the Sages or Rabbis was no longer needed.

Many other theories have been used, however, to explain the negative Gospel picture of the Pharisees and their alleged hostility to Jesus. One method has been to divide the Pharisees into conflicting groups, only one of which, it is argued, was hostile to Jesus. This preserves both the positive view of the Pharisees deriving from the rabbinic writings and the negative view present in the Gospels. Thus the existence of two factions among the Pharisees, the House of Hillel and the House of Shammai, may be found useful. According to rabbinic tradition, the House of Shammai was usually more severe in its decisions than the House of Hillel. The Pharisees who persecuted Jesus, then, were Shammaiites. This line, however, does not have many adherents today, since it has become clear that the differences between the two Houses were on small points, not on general outlook. If anything, Jesus ought to be regarded as being aligned to the severer section of the Pharisees, because his views on divorce correspond closely to those of the House of Shammai.

Another strategy is to point to the division among the Pharisees between 'legalists' and 'charismatics'. The latter are the so-called *hasidim*, or saints, who led a life of supererogatory virtue, and were credited with gifts of supernatural healing and rain-making; examples are Hanina ben Dosa and Honi the Circlemaker. The theory is that the opponents of Jesus were the 'legalists', while the *hasidim* did not oppose him, and in fact had much in common with him. Geza Vermes at first espoused this theory, but in his recent writings seems to have lost enthusiasm for it. The trouble is that there is no evidence of any serious conflict between legalists and charismatics in the Pharisee movement. Both existed happily side by side, and sometimes both types were combined in one person. Adherence to the law did not rule out saintliness, nor did saintliness involve opposition to the law.

Many other attempts have been made to discover what it was about Jesus' teaching that offended against Pharisee thinking. One writer even suggested that Jesus offended because he preached in the open air, instead of indoors! This theory evinces some degree of desperation, and founders on the fact that Pharisee preachers often preached in the open air. Their preaching was also very like that of Jesus: they were fond of using parables, for example, and parallels to Jesus' parables are to be found in the rabbinic literature. Some scholars (e.g. Joachim Jeremias) have attempted to counter such evidence by arguing that the rabbis copied their style of preaching, including their use of parables, from Jesus. That rabbis of the post-Destruction period, when Pauline Christianity had become a dangerous rival to Judaism, should turn to the Church's recently composed annals for models for their preaching, is too unlikely to be seriously considered. Before this period, the Jerusalem Church actually formed part of the Jewish community, whose traditions of liturgy and teaching styles it followed, rather than creating new models for other Jews to follow. The teaching of Jesus, recorded in the Gospels, actually provides valuable evidence from a source outside rabbinic tradition that rabbinic modes of thought and teaching existed in the pre-Destruction period. Jesus in the Synoptic Gospels is a rabbinic figure; though in the Fourth Gospel, this rabbinic style has disappeared, and he has become a Hellenistic mystagogue. Hellenised styles of expression have taken over, in this latest Gospel, from the rabbinic modes still preserved in the Synoptic Gospels. If Jesus (according to Jeremias) had such an influence on rabbinic modes, it is surprising that he had so little influence on his own followers. Far more likely is the hypothesis that Jesus spoke out of his own Jewish tradition, which continued in the rabbinic movement but was lost in the Gentile Church.

The difficulty that Jesus preached in such a rabbinic way (a difficulty, that is to say for those seeking a reason why the Pharisees should have been hostile to him) has been tackled in a very different way. This is to deny that Jesus *did* preach in a rabbinic way. The characteristically rabbinic views and expressions were put into his mouth by 'Judaising' editors at the time of the composition of the Gospels. On this theory, the communities for which the Synoptic Gospels (especially Matthew) were composed had weakly reverted from the radical views of Jesus to more traditional Jewish ways of thinking, and the speeches put into Jesus' mouth at this period are the outcome of this 're-Judaisation' process. This theory formed part of the 'form criticism' of the Gospels, in which these documents were regarded as written to serve the doctrinal and liturgical purposes of specific Christian communities, rather than as historical records based on authentic traditions. Thus scepticism was employed to preserve faith in the Jesus of the Church: a rejection of the authenticity of Gospel material showing the Jewishness of Jesus preserved the image of a Jesus who opposed the Judaism of his day. The paradoxical result was that belief in the historical validity of the Jewish Jesus portrayed in the Synoptic Gospels was, for a time, largely confined to Jewish New Testament scholars, who were criticised for their failure to apply the highly scientific principles of form criticism.

Again, this sophisticated ploy has ceased, recently, to carry conviction with a growing number of New Testament scholars, prominent among whom is E. P. Sanders. The so-called 'Jewish Christian' community of Matthew has come to seem a figment, and the more common-sense view has asserted itself that Jesus is portrayed in the earlier Gospels as a very Jewish figure because these Gospels, though hostile to the Pharisees, still retain authentic Jerusalem Church traditions of the kind of things that Jesus said and thought; traditions which, in the light of comparative study of rabbinic literature, place Jesus firmly in a rabbinic and Pharisaic setting.

CHAPTER 9

THE PHARISEES IN THE
USURPATION MYTH

The more one studies the teaching of Jesus, the more the gap between him and the Pharisees diminishes, until it almost becomes invisible. Any differences arise from one factor: that Jesus was preaching the imminent coming of the Last Days. Thus when he says, 'Sell all thou hast and give it to the poor', this is in contrast with the Pharisee or rabbinic teaching that a person should not give away more than a fifth of his income in charity, lest he add one more to the ranks of the poor. But this Pharisee teaching is intended for a settled community, making the best of an imperfect world, and resigned to the thought that the messianic kingdom of God is probably a long way off. Yet Jesus' apocalyptic and eschatological ethic is by no means absent from Judaism. It exists there not only as a feature of messianic thinking, as in Jesus' case, but also as a counsel of perfection for rare souls of unusual spiritual stature even in non-messianic days. For example, parallel to Jesus' adjuration, 'Take no thought for the morrow', is the saying of Rabbi Eliezer, 'Anyone who has food for today, but is concerned about food for tomorrow is a person of little faith' – to which the rabbinic comment is 'Many tried to follow this precept, but only a few succeeded.'

A question that ought to be put about Jesus' moral teaching, however, is, 'What is the function of this teaching in the Gospel story?' There seem to be two Jesuses in the story. One is the divine sacrifice, who descends into the world from his place on high in order to die an agonising death on the Cross for the sake of mankind. This is the Jesus in whom Paul is interested; Paul indeed hardly mentions Jesus' moral teaching. The other is Jesus the reforming teacher, preaching an ethic of love as opposed to the legalistic following of rules. One may ask why this teaching was necessary. If Jesus had been merely a teacher, would he thereby have fulfilled his mission? If he had spent his lifetime in teaching, finally dying of old age, his mission in the world would have been totally unperformed according to the Pauline doctrine that gave rise to Christianity as a world religion. In this doctrine, Jesus' death was far more important than his life, for it was his death that gave meaning to his existence on earth. By his death, he functioned as an atoning sacrifice for mankind, giving them hope of eternal life.

The answer seems to be that in the Gospels as we have them, the teaching of Jesus does perform a function in the drama of salvation by sacrifice. The point is precisely that Jesus is preaching an ethic that is impossible to put into practice, at least on any societal scale. The effect of Jesus' ethic is to induce moral despair in any ordinary person, not envisaging a life of continual self-sacrifice and abnegation. To give away all one's possessions to the poor, to take no thought for the morrow, to make no resistance to evil, to give up a law-suit before it has started – these are demands which will evoke the response, 'If this is what I have to do to be saved, then I am lost.' This is just the frame of mind necessary for the acceptance of salvation through the vicarious suffering of a sacrificial figure. In other words, the impossible morality preached by Jesus is the other side of the coin of the doctrine of Original Sin, as expounded by Paul: the doctrine that we are all desperately wicked and incapable of achieving goodness.

Thus we find modern writers such as Enoch Powell telling us that Jesus preached a morality that he never intended to be put into practice. Its precepts are there just to provide a saintly standard in the light of which we can assess our own shortcomings. Meanwhile, Powell argues, real-life behaviour, in politics for example, must ignore such impractical teachings and find its own level of expediency, which cannot properly be regarded as in the sphere of morality at all. Some few saints can reach Jesus' standards, but only at the cost of cutting themselves off from the business of the world, which must proceed on very different principles.

A superficially similar double standard exists in rabbinic Judaism too, as explained above; but it is in reality very different. In rabbinic thinking, the saint (known as the *hasid*) is admired, but is not regarded as the exemplar of morality. He is a virtuoso, but his performance is not at the centre of religion. That is occupied by the morality of the ordinary person, who struggles to make his way in the world for himself and his family. This kind of morality is what engages the attention of the rabbis in their strenuous communal effort of ethical thought, enshrined in the Mishnah, Talmuds and other rabbinic writings. It is not what can be achieved in the way of individual performances that is important, but what can be achieved in and by society as a whole, and that means that the ordinary person is the focus of morality.

The part of Jesus' teaching that is appropriate only for saints is thus not foreign to rabbinic Judaism, but has been given a perspective in the Gospels that is in keeping with the Pauline doctrines of Original Sin and salvation by vicarious suffering. Jesus himself never held such doctrines. The doctrine of Original Sin is not to be found in his teaching, and he had no intention of dying an atoning death on a Roman cross.[1] He advocated supererogatory virtue both because he was temperamentally a *hasid* and because he believed the Kingdom of God to be at hand. People should therefore abandon their ordinary concerns and careful preparations for the future, which in normal circumstances would constitute their duty.

Jesus' preaching of repentance was again part of rabbinic teaching, but he carried it to lengths that were appropriate to the Endtime. Thus there was nothing new in saying that the repentant sinner was more beloved by God than he who had never sinned, as in the parable of the Prodigal Son. This was a commonplace of rabbinic thinking. But Jesus' campaign of repentance, taking him into the company of abandoned sinners, went beyond ordinary practice of the rabbis and was appropriate to apocalypticism.

Those areas of Jesus' teaching that went beyond ordinary morality have the function in the Gospels (though not in the historical reality) of making him seem an unearthly, angelic being, marked out for destruction by the prosaic, banal establishment. Jesus' messianic aim of bringing about the Kingdom of God on earth is eliminated, and instead he is represented as wanting to bring about a heavenly kingdom of immortality, a kingdom that is not of this earth. To this end, he must endure the incomprehension and hostility of earthly powers and finally undergo an agonising death, which will be the prelude to a new spiritual world.

But somewhat at variance with this picture is the image of Jesus as a religious reformer, which also plays a large part in the Gospel narrative. For Jesus as a protester against the alleged harshness of the Sabbath rules, or the law of 'an eye for an eye', is portrayed as a legislator, seeking not to transcend the law altogether, but to make it milder and more civilised. In this role, Jesus comes into conflict with the Pharisees, shown as rigid and severe in their interpretation of the laws. It is this Jesus who has inspired liberal thinkers of modern times, seeking to temper antiquated laws, but far from wishing to retire from the world and do without laws altogether.

The two images together, however – Jesus as the abolisher of the law, and Jesus as the reformer of the law – work together to present his alleged opponents, the Pharisees as, on the one hand, opponents of the new spiritual order heralded by Jesus' descent to earth from heaven, and on the other hand, as cruel, severe administrators of a law to which Jesus gives a more loving interpretation. The Pharisees thus become terrifying father-figures, the representatives of a religion that has gone wrong.

In Christian eyes this image has attached itself to the Jewish religious leadership ever since. The visual propaganda of Christian antisemitism, from the art of the medieval Church to the caricatures of Nazi newspapers has focused on the bearded rabbi-figure, presenting a learned, condemning pose, yet inwardly corrupt and self-serving. The Nazis delighted in stripping these figures of their composed dignity; shaving off their beards, those symbols of authority, making them perform menial tasks, finally stripping them even of their clothes as they were marched naked to the gas-chambers. This was the final protest against the lofty pretensions of the Pharisees to be the teachers of mankind.

It is remarkable that those very same beards, and the very same air of moral peace and composure, are found attractive in communities other than that of the Pharisees or of Orthodox Jews. The Amish

communities of America, for example, are regarded as charming tourist attractions, though their outward appearance is very similar to
that of Jewish Chasidic communities. Also like the Chasidic communities, they adhere to a code of rules which preserves their way of life
in the face of the attractions of modern media, entertainments and
technology. Their air of peace is not construed as self-righteousness,
nor is their dedicated isolation condemned as misanthropy. The
Chasidic communities are regarded quite differently. No one has ever
thought of treating the Chasidic communities as a tourist attraction.
They evoke rather a shuddering distaste, combined with a willingness
to believe evil of them. This is because they, more than Westernised
Jews wearing 'ordinary' clothes, evoke the image of the Pharisees
who, allegedly, hounded Jesus to death. Their idiosyncratic, sober
style of dress (actually derived from 18th-century Polish styles) is
construed as ostentation, and their separateness as hatred of mankind.
In a recently published school textbook for religious classes, a chapter
on the alleged hypocrisy and inflated pretensions of the Pharisees is
illustrated by a photograph of a New York Chasid in his long coat
and caftan, with the caption, 'Jesus rebuked the ostentation of the
Pharisees, saying, "They enlarge the borders of their garments".'
Strangely, it did not occur to the editor to illustrate the theme of
religious ostentation by a photograph of, say, a Christian archbishop
in full ceremonial dress, to which, from the point of flamboyant glory,
nothing corresponds in Judaism.

Jesus as reforming legislator is hardly reconcilable with Jesus the
divine sacrifice. For, as divine sacrifice, Jesus takes the place of the
law altogether, becoming a new means of salvation by faith, instead
of by works. No longer is the worshipper to accumulate good deeds,
of if he does, this is irrelevant to salvation. Consequently, to reform
the law is beside the point; such reform would imply that the law
is still a valid means to salvation, but simply requires some
improvement.

Jesus as reforming legislator is also a most implausible figure,
because his reforms had already been made by the Pharisees, who
were a movement who had precisely the flexible, dynamic view of
the Torah as a developing process attributed to Jesus. The Sabbath
reforms advocated by Jesus, the reinterpretation of the 'eye for an eye'

injunction, the Golden Rule of behaviour, the lenient interpretation of penal laws – all these were already established features of Pharisee teaching.

Why then is Jesus portrayed as a reformer? The reason is that it was imperative to portray Jesus as a rebel against the Jewish religion of his time. It was not sufficient to show Jesus as allegedly offending the High Priest by a blasphemous claim to be the Messiah. The High Priest as a centre of religious authority, and the Messianic claim as blasphemous, were not sufficient distortions of the Jewish religious scene. It was impossible to conceal the fact that the real religious authority lay with the Pharisees, who 'sat in Moses's seat', rather than with the High Priest, the ceremonial descendant of Aaron. In the Synoptic Gospels, at any rate, the Pharisees are still portrayed as teachers of the people, who have to be shown as being in unsuccessful debate with Jesus (in the Fourth Gospel, however, the Pharisees are no longer teachers, but simply coalesce with the 'priests' as figures of oppressive power, in the phrase 'the pharisees and the priests').

In order to usurp a culture that is not primitive but equipped with a sophisticated literature and learning system, it is necessary to discredit in particular the bearers of this culture, who act as its teachers, judges and authorities. These, in the Jewish culture, were particularly the Pharisees, and there is thus, in the Gospels, a campaign to deprive them of their claims to dignity and authority. This campaign was so successful that the name 'Pharisees' has been totally divested, in Western civilisation, of the awe which once adhered to it. It has come to mean simply 'hypocrites' or 'pedants'. In fact, as the Gospels themselves show when read carefully, the Pharisees were regarded with both love and reverence by the masses of the Jewish people. A measure of the respect in which they were held is the care with which Paul insists on his own Pharisee credentials. While denying that Pharisee authority continues to hold, he knows that he cannot better uphold his own claim to have knitted together the old dispensation with the new than to claim that he has mastered the Pharisee learning. Here we discern an echo of the Gnostic claim to have 'mastered' the teaching of the Demiurge. There is thus a dissonance between Paul's claim to continuity with the Pharisees, and the Gospels' contemptuous dismissal of them. This is hardly a contradiction, however, because the very prestige of the Pharisees is the reason for the need to dismiss them; and the Gospels witness to this prestige in the act of demolishing it.

There is thus a threefold attack, in the New Testament, on the Jews as the people of God. The attack is directed against their sacerdotal hierarchy, their teaching élite, and the people themselves. This three-fold attack was necessary to reverse the status of the Jews. Instead of being the people of God, they were to be rejected and hated by God. This drastic reversal prepared the Jews for their later status in Christian society as a pariah class, serving to promote Christian truth by their degradation.

The attack on the priestly hierarchy would hardly be damaging in itself, if it were ever acknowledged that the priests had no teaching authority. But instead, the priests are systematically confused with the Pharisees, so that the average reader of the Gospels is hardly aware that there is a difference between the two categories. In historical fact, as shown above, the High Priest and his immediate entourage (but not the rank and file of the priests) probably did act as opponents of Jesus, just as they opposed other messianic claimants who threatened the Roman power which had appointed the High Priests as their henchmen. But the New Testament absurdly represents the High Priest at the chief guardian of Jewish orthodox belief, rending his garments at the heretical claims of Jesus.

When, in an earlier book, I pointed out that the High Priest was a person of no teaching authority in the eyes of the masses, I was rebuked by one scholar, James Dunn, as showing too little respect to the High Priest, and even reviving ancient squabbles between the Pharisees and the Sadducees. I was touched by this solicitude by a modern scholar for the dignity of the Jewish High Priest, but could not help wondering whether the attempted rehabilitation of the High Priest as chief representative of Jewish religion had anything to do with the need for such a person to carry the burden of Jewish religious guilt. A High Priest who was unrepresentative of the Jewish people and the Jewish religion would never be able to play the significant part in the story of the betrayal of Jesus that the Gospel account requires. Consequently, conservative scholars have recently seized on every possible argument to show that the Pharisees did not in fact have the central role in Jewish education to which even the Gospels, and certainly Josephus, as well as the rabbinic writings, testify. Even E. P. Sanders, to whom no such conservative motivation can be attributed, has contributed to the revival of the conception that the teaching role of the priests, contrary to the evidence of the New Testament, Josephus and the rabbinic writings, continued throughout the 1st century.[2]

In any case, the treatment of the New Testament caused the roles of Pharisees and priests to coalesce in the eyes of Christian readers, so that a composite figure, the Pharisee-priest, became the religious persecutor of Jesus. The rabbis were the heirs of this composite image. In the Middle Ages, the Jewish rabbis, in the eyes of the Christian populace, were the visible successors of the Pharisees who allegedly persecuted Jesus; and since the distinction between priest and rabbi, so important in Judaism, did not exist in Christianity, it was hardly surprising that the populace saddled the rabbis with the guilt of the High Priest too. In historical fact, there was no High Priest in Judaism after 70 CE, and the priests in general had only a vestigial role; but the ignorance of both Christian clergy and laity enabled them to regard any prominent rabbi as a very Caiaphas.

Thus the New Testament portrayal of the Pharisees, together with its blurring of the distinction between Sage and priest, influenced greatly the pariah-status of the Jews in Christendom. The Jewish religious leaders of the Middle Ages, including such figures as Maimonides, Ibn Ezra, Rashi and Nachmanides, worthy to rank among the world's intellectual élite, were branded with the stigma of deicide. Even so, Jewish intellectual achievement could not help impressing Christians of genuine stature. Thomas Aquinas quoted Maimonides on philosophy, the Christian humanists quoted Ibn Ezra and Rashi on Hebrew grammar and the rational interpretation of Scripture. The Jewish philosopher Ibn Gabirol even became a classic in Christian circles, though under the misapprehension that he was a Christian writer called Avicebron. But the stigma remained, attached particularly to the Jewish leadership. In the early Middle Ages, the Jewish leadership, possessing the charisma of ancient learning and a long tradition of public service, was regarded with respect by Christian common folk, who even asked the rabbis to bless their fields. But as the vilifying propaganda of the lower clergy increasingly took effect, this respect for the rabbis waned and turned into hate.

The vilifying campaign of the New Testament against the Jews is indeed three-pronged: against the priests, the Pharisees and the people. The first two targets coalesce, as shown; but the third target remains distinct, the Jewish people itself. The particular loci of this blackening are the crowd scenes, particularly the Barabbas scene; and the direction of blame to the Jewish people at large is complicated by an element of treachery. For the crowd is shown at times as supporting Jesus, so that the priests fear to proceed against him because of this popular support. Thus the final turning against Jesus by the crowd makes them share in the treachery of Judas. Even here, however, the deeper blame of the Jewish clergy is emphasised, for they are constantly portrayed as inciting the crowd to turn against Jesus.

There is, however, another ingenious mode adopted by modern scholars to deflect the balefulness of the New Testament campaign against the Jewish religious leadership. This is the argument that the vituperation against the Pharisees is simply part of normal sectarian argument, and should not be assessed in the light of the antisemitic purposes to which it was later put. According to this argument, vituperation was quite normal in intra-Jewish disputation, and the tone of the anti-Pharisee passages in the New Testament is no stronger than can be found in, for example, the Dead Sea Scrolls when fulminating against Jewish opponents.

This argument omits to take note of the narrative elements in the New Testament onslaught against the Pharisees. No other sectarian invective has this narrative element. In the New Testament, the Pharisees are not merely denounced as having wrong views and inadequate morals. They are made participants in a drama of cosmic proportions: a divine figure invested with infinite pathos, a visitant from outer space, is being hounded and done to death by cosmic forces of evil led by Satan. All the forces of good and evil are ranged against each other throughout the universe; and the Pharisees, with their alleged allies the priests, are foremost in the ranks of evil on earth. The blackening of the Pharisees is thus on an entirely different plane from intra-Jewish sectarian squabbles.

The role of cosmic antagonist might have been taken by the Romans, who in historical reality were chiefly responsible for the death of Jesus. In one New Testament book, Revelation, we do see the Romans as the representatives of evil; for this book retains the standpoint (though overlaid by later editing) of the Jerusalem Church, which regarded Rome as the enemy. But as the Church was taken over by Pauline ideas, this anti-Roman stance could not survive. For to oppose Rome would have been to align Christianity with Jewish hopes of this-worldly revolution; to abjure a purely 'spiritual' other-worldly stance and face the realities of imperialism and oppression. Instead it was much easier to put the Jews into the role of villains. Starting with the nucleus of the collaboration of the High Priest with Roman oppression, the Jewish religious establishment was substituted entirely for the imperial establishment of Rome. Indeed, Rome itself was absolved, being pictured as innocently succumbing to inexorable Jewish pressure. Romans such as Pilate and the centurion are shown expressing appreciation and adoration of Jesus, in resonance with the shift of the Church to Gentile membership. The conditions were set up by which Christianity could become a Roman religion, with its centre at Rome instead of at Jerusalem.

The Jerusalem Church, even though it regarded Rome as the enemy, did not diabolise Rome to the extent to which the Pauline Church diabolised the Jews. For Rome remained on a par with previous empires who had deprived the Jews of independence, Babylonia, Persia and Greece. There was no impetus in Jewish-Christianity, or in Judaism itself, to set up a sacrificial drama with a demonic Executioner or Betrayer. The issue was not the salvation of the individual soul from Satan, but the liberation of the Jewish community and nation from occupation and slavery. But the Pauline Church, with its influences from mystery-religion and Gnosticism, had a much more lurid scenario, and a much more baleful role for those elected to play the villains. Those chosen for this essential role were also being marked out for a pariah position in the universal supra-national society to which Pauline Christianity aspired.

CHAPTER 10

SACRIFICE IN THE NEW TESTAMENT

The opprobrious position occupied by the Jews in the Christian mind of the Middle Ages and after was not simply caused by the myth that the Jews were responsible for the death of Jesus. After all, the Athenians were held responsible for the judicial killing of Socrates, without incurring any such perennial stigma. If, however, Socrates, after his death, had become the central divine figure of a religion in which his death functioned sacrificially as the means of salvation for initiates, and if this religion had spread chiefly among non-Athenians, a mythic role of god-killers might well have become attached to the Athenians; especially if Athenians were actually visible as a depressed class in the Socrates-worshipping society. For nothing is more convenient to those whose salvation depends on a deed of blood than to have in visible proximity a whole class of people to whom the blame for the deed can be attributed, so that the community of the saved can transform their secret satisfaction about the means of their salvation into a ritualised, horrified condemnation of identifiable scapegoats.

If Jesus, then, had been regarded as a martyr in the cause of a doctrine of love and equality, or a Martin Luther King falling victim to discriminatory prejudice, or a reformer destroyed by the forces of reaction, there would have been no Christian Church, and the Jews would never have been made into a pariah people. These modern descriptions of Jesus are inconsistent with earlier christology. What caused the Christian Church to arise and become successful was Jesus as Saviour, not as role model for the liberation of societies from tyranny or discrimination. On the contrary, belief in Jesus ran counter to liberation-hopes, for the initiate in the Pauline Church (though not the Jerusalem Church) was indifferent to the political betterment of this world. Instead he or she had hopes of attaining immortality and leaving this world, with all its imperfections, behind.

Since this matter has been much obscured in recent times, it will be useful to recall in some detail the place of Jesus' death in the thinking of the early Pauline Church.

Paul himself makes it clear that he does not regard the death of Jesus as a martyrdom in the cause of political reform. He has no plans to alter the political status quo, declaring roundly, 'The powers that be are ordained of heaven.' (Romans 13:1). His attitude to slavery is shown in his exhortation to Titus: 'Tell slaves to respect their masters' authority in everything, and to comply with their demands without answering back.' (Titus 2:9).

The death of Jesus was rather to liberate the soul from the trammels of the sinful body into eternal life. It therefore acted as a sacrifice that atoned for sin and thus enabled the believer to escape the consequences of his sin, namely death or damnation. Paul states this clearly enough: 'For all alike have sinned, and are deprived of the divine splendour, and all are justified by God's free grace alone, through his act of liberation in the person of Christ Jesus. For God designed him to be the means of expiating sin by his sacrificial death, effective through faith.' (Romans 3:23–25). In plain words, the death of Jesus, a wholly innocent person, wipes away the sins of guilty persons, so long as they place their faith in the efficacy of the sacrifice. God Himself, the Father, devised this means to save mankind from damnation. Knowing that by their own efforts they could do nothing to avoid the damnation owing to them, he sent his own divine Son into the world to suffer torture and death on their behalf. 'He that spared not his own Son, but delivered him up for us all, how shall he not with him also freely give us all things?' (Romans 8:32).

Modern liberal Christians have found this explanation of the saving force of Jesus' death nothing short of appalling. For if the innocent dies for the guilty, then Christianity is based on the most ancient form of atonement, human sacrifice. To escape this understanding of the atoning power of the Cross, ingenious reinterpretations of Paul's expressions have been introduced, and many Christians have convinced themselves that Paul never meant to advocate a doctrine of vicarious atonement. Meanwhile, evangelical Christians of traditional stamp continue to preach the doctrine in its most unregenerate form, oblivious of the pain they are causing to their liberal brethren.

Liberal Christian scholars, however, have expressed their discomfort with the traditional doctrine of atonement by sacrifice on the Cross not so much by arguing against it as by ignoring it. Though hymns and carols continue to proclaim the doctrine in unmistakable fashion, and popular preaching promulgates it as if it has never been questioned, learned articles in theological journals and academic books generally fail even to mention it. One can search, for example, James D. G. Dunn's *Christology in the Making* from cover to cover without finding any reference to the doctrine of atonement through the death of Jesus on the Cross. Similarly, Christopher Rowland, in his *Christian Origins* (subtitled 'An Account of the Setting and Character of the most Important Messianic Sect of Judaism') does not consider worthy of inclusion any discussion of the central Christian doctrine, by which Christianity has defined itself through all ages except the present (and even in the present except in academic literature), that Christians are saved through the death of Christ.

This is an extraordinary state of affairs. One explanation of it is implied in the subtitle of Christopher Rowland's book. It is very much a concern of recent scholarship to deny any Hellenistic influence on Pauline Christianity, and to assert that Christianity is indeed a 'Messianic sect of Judaism'. Thus all the obvious influences on Christianity from Gnosticism and mystery-religion are discounted, and arguments are marshalled to show that Pauline dualism comes from the Dead Sea Scrolls, the deification of Jesus from the personification of wisdom in the Proverbs, and so on. The idea of the atoning death of a human-divine figure, taking away the burden of human sin, is too difficult to find in Jewish sources, though some have tried. The heroic course has been taken, therefore, of denying that it exists in the Christian sources.

What cannot be denied is that the atonement of the Cross permeates

Christian thinking after the closure of the New Testament canon until the modern era. The writings of the early fathers and of medieval Christian theologians and commentators continually press home the 'ransom' by which Jesus Christ paid for the sins of mankind by his blood. This dominant sacrificial theme set the tone for the attitude of Christians towards Jews. The death of Christ was a sacrifice, and therefore the Jews were not merely murderers, or betrayers (when the Roman execution was remembered), but sacrificers, unwittingly bringing atonement while working on the side of Satan. This dimension of paradox added an eerie mythic quality to Jew-hatred that was all-important for medieval developments.

Yet, in fact, this predictably cruel and oppressive outcome of a myth of blood was not a post-New Testament phenomenon, but is firmly rooted in the New Testament itself.

The book of the New Testament that outlines the sacrificial theory of the death of Jesus most clearly and exhaustively is the Epistle to the Hebrews. This book was attributed to Paul, but modern scholarship has shown that it was not actually written by Paul. Its canonisation, however, and the belief that it was written by someone of such high Christian authority as Paul, has made it one of the chief sources of Christian belief on the meaning of the Cross.

The Epistle to the Hebrews has no compunction in claiming that the death of Jesus was a sacrifice which atones vicariously for the sins of mankind. Jesus was both the High Priest and the sacrifice: 'Such a high priest does indeed fit our condition – devout, guileless, undefiled, separated from sinners, raised high above the heavens. He has no need to offer sacrifices daily, as the high priests do, first for his own sins and then for those of the people; for this he did once and for all when he offered up himself.' (Hebrews 7:26–27). Continuing the theme: 'The blood of his sacrifice is his own blood, not the blood of goats and calves; and thus he has entered the sanctuary once and for all and secured an eternal deliverance. For if the blood of goats and bulls and the sprinkled ashes of a heifer have power to hallow those who have been defiled and restore their external purity, how much greater is the power of the blood of Christ; he offered himself without blemish to God, a spiritual and eternal sacrifice; and his blood will cleanse our conscience from the deadness of our former ways and fit us for the service of the living God.' (Hebrews 9:12–14).

Further:

'Indeed, according to the Law, it might almost be said, everything is cleansed by blood and without the shedding of blood there is no forgiveness. If then these sacrifices cleanse the copies of heavenly things, those heavenly things themselves require better sacrifices to cleanse them. For Christ has entered, not that sanctuary made by men's hands which is only a symbol of the reality, but heaven itself, to appear now before God on our behalf. Nor is he there to offer himself again and again, as the high priest enters the sanctuary year by year with blood not his own. If that were so, he would have had to suffer many times since the world was made. But as it is, he has appeared once and for all at the climax of history to abolish sin by the sacrifice of himself. And as it is the lot of men to die once, and after death comes judgement, so Christ was offered once to bear the burden of men's sins, and will appear a second time, sin done away, to bring salvation to those who are watching for him.'

(Hebrews 9:22–28)

'But Christ offered for all time one sacrifice for sins, and took his seat at the right hand of God, where he waits henceforth until his enemies are made his footstool.'

(Hebrews 10:12)

Note that here neither Judas Iscariot nor the Jews generally are blamed for the death of Jesus, who, indeed, is made responsible for his own death by his voluntary decision to die on the Cross. When the Jews are obliquely referred to in this work, it is in the role of unbelievers, not of Christ-killers:

'The fact remains that someone must enter it, and since those who first heard the good news failed to enter through unbelief, God fixes another day . . . Let us then make every effort to enter that rest, so that no one may fall by following this evil example of unbelief.'

(Hebrews 4:6, 11)

Clearly, at the time this Epistle was written, the Jews had not yet been chosen for the role of Betrayers, nor had the character of Judas Iscariot been created. Even if not written by Paul himself, the Epistle shares this attitude with Paul, and must have been written by a close disciple of Paul in the pre-Gospel era. Yet the development of the myth of Jesus' death as sacrificial is here manifest (though the care with which it is explained shows it to be novel at this time), and potentialities are broached for a process of scapegoating, by which the responsibility for the sacrifice will be shifted from Jesus himself to the Jews.

The concept of Jesus as a High Priest who officiates at his own immolation is unique in the New Testament. It is not quite unique in the history of religions, for we find in Norse mythology the story of the self-immolation of Odin. The identity of the sacrificer and the sacrificed is also hinted at in the occurrence of myths in which sacrificer and sacrificed are twins (e.g. Romulus and Remus). These mythic trends arise from a need, in all sacrifice whether of humans or of animals, to incorporate in the ritual a willingness on the part of the victim to die. Walter Burkert has shown how this ritual need was incorporated in the procedure of Greek animal sacrifice.[1] In Aztec ritual of human sacrifice, the willingness and even joy of the victim (arising from the deeply-held conviction that death would result in deification) altogether removed the guilt of the sacrifice from the sacrificer. Consequently, human sacrifices were carried out by ordained priests, who retained their sense of innocence and purity, however many bloody sacrifices they performed. This state of the human-sacrificial myth of Jesus is preserved in this extraordinary work, the Epistle to the Hebrews, which has proved such an embarrassment to modern commentators because of its unashamed promulgation of a doctrine of human sacrifice. Yet it is able to be so forthright because of its relative innocence, knowing nothing of the furtive guilt through which responsibility for human sacrifice is shunted to others by those benefiting from the deed of blood.

121

In the later narrative of the Gospels, the willingness of Jesus to die as a sacrifice is still featured, as in his admonitions to his dismayed disciples that he is going to Jerusalem, not to assume the throne of David and Solomon, but to die, and that this is something necessary and fated. But this aspect of acceptance and willingness is not stressed as much as in Hebrews. Much less is Jesus given any active role as sacrificer, taking responsibility for his own death. Instead, there is a scenario of evil powers, combining to bring about the death of an innocent, passive victim. The willingness of the victim only adds to his pathetic helplessness, which in turn adds to the malice of his persecutors. The atmosphere is that of a Passion Play of unbearable melodrama, evoking emotions of pity, sorrow and bitter anger. Nothing could be more different from the atmosphere of the Epistle to the Hebrews, where, despite the subject matter of a bloody sacrifice, the tone is calm and exalted, the death a matter of high ceremony, as in the Temple, rather than drama.

The contention of Hebrews is that the death of Jesus is the culmination of the Jewish sacrificial system of the Temple, providing both its climax and its supersession. Whereas the Temple sacrifices required continual renewal, the sacrifice of Jesus was once and for all. Yet in the theory of Hebrews, the sacrifice of Jesus was the logical outcome and continuation of the Temple sacrifices, in their function as atonements for sin. Just as in the Temple sacrifices, there was no atonement without blood, so the cancellation of the sins of mankind could be procured only through the shedding of the blood of a sacrifice without blemish – that of Jesus, who, being divine, could effect a permanent, instead of a temporary, atonement.

The claimed continuity between the sacrifice of Jesus and the animal sacrifices of the Temple is an early example of the characteristic striving of Christianity to find sources for its doctrines in Judaism. Paul himself, whose ideas lie behind the Epistle to the Hebrews, constantly strives to link his doctrines with Judaism, so that the prestige of Judaism can be annexed by a system of belief which, in reality, owes far more to Gnosticism and mystery-religion. The same link between the sacrifice of Jesus and the Jewish animal sacrifices is asserted by Paul in various places, e.g. 'a propitiation through faith in his blood' (Romans 3:25). Here the word *hilasterion*, 'propitiation',

translates the Hebrew *kaporet*, or 'mercy-seat', on which the High
Priest sprinkled the blood of expiatory sacrifices on the Day of Atonement. Similarly, in the Fourth Gospel, Jesus is referred to as '... the
Lamb of God; it is he who takes away the sins of the world' (John
1:29).

In reality, however, the link between the sacrifice of Jesus and the
animal sacrifices of the Temple is tenuous. If Jesus was a sacrifice,
then he represents a return to human–divine sacrifice, against which
the Hebrew Bible continually protests; e.g. Jeremiah 7:31: 'They have
built the high places of Topheth, which is in the valley of Hinnom,
to burn their sons and their daughters in the fire; which I commanded
not, neither came it into My mind.' The story of the Akedah, or
'binding' of Isaac marks the point of departure of Israelite religion
from the concept of human sacrifice, and the substitution of animal
sacrifice – a substitution that led to a profound change in the concept
of sacrifice itself. Long before the beginning of the Christian era,
sacrifice was interpreted in Judaism in a non-vicarious sense; i.e. the
animal was not thought to be taking the place of the offerer of the
sacrifice, suffering punishment in his place. Indeed, at least half of
the sacrifices offered were not sin-offerings at all, but celebratory
offerings, known as thank-offerings or peace-offerings, and these
did not even have to be animal sacrifices, but could be vegetable
offerings. Such offerings could not possibly be understood vicariously; they were celebratory meals shared with God, in thanksgiving for some favour or rescue. The sin-offerings too had long
been understood in the same way: as meals of reconciliation shared
with God. The sin-offerings did not atone for sin in any primary
way, for the only atonement for deliberate sin was repentance and,
where appropriate, reparation. It was only after this primary work
of repentance had been completed that the sin-offering was brought.
The rabbis pointed out that in the Hebrew Bible, sin-offerings
are prescribed only for unintentional sins, never for intentional
sins. But they interpreted certain verses to mean that repentance
turns intentional into unintentional sins, and therefore, once repentance has taken place, a sin-offering can be brought to mark
the final reconciliation (*kapparah*). Unintentional sins carried no
penalty in law, but brought grief to their performer and a sense of dis-

tance from God which was removed by the sacrifice of reconciliation.

Certainly there remain traces in the Hebrew Bible of an earlier theory of sacrifice in which it had substitutionary or vicarious efficacy. For example, the impressive ceremonial of the scapegoat on the Day of Atonement bears this character, especially in view of the words: 'He shall lay both hands on its head and confess over it all the iniquities of the Israelites and all their acts of rebellion, that is all their sins; he shall lay them on the head of the goat and send it away into the wilderness in charge of a man who is waiting ready. The goat shall carry all their iniquities upon itself into some barren waste and the man shall let it go, there in the wilderness.' (Leviticus 16:21–22).

As against this, however, we have the saying of the Mishnah: 'He who says, "I will sin, and the Day of Atonement will atone"; the Day of Atonement does not atone.' (M. Yoma 8:9). This saying is directed against any theory of the magical efficacy of the Day of Atonement to wipe away sins in the absence of repentance. Thus even the awesome ritual of the scapegoat was not taken as a literal absolution, but only as a symbol of repentance.[2]

Ritual, it is clear, was a spur to repentance, but did not take its place. Thus despite the apparently unambiguous statement of the Torah: 'It is the blood, that is the life, that makes expiation' (Leviticus 17:11), this was taken to mean only that the shedding of the blood of the sacrifice was the final step in an expiatory process that began, and chiefly consisted of, repentance and reparation. In consequence, when the Temple services ceased, this was not the end of Judaism (as might have been expected if sin-offerings were so essential to atonement), but only the appearance of a ceremonial lacuna in the expiatory process, which could be filled by prayer or acts of charity.

In Christianity, however, beginning with Paul, the shedding of blood had a much more mystical and substantive meaning. The violent death of Jesus was alleged to have taken over the expiatory function of the Temple sacrifices, but in a literal sense that the Temple service no longer had for Jewish minds. The blood of Jesus atoned for mankind because Jesus had offered himself as a substitute for sinful mankind, suffering the death that they deserved, and thus vicariously removing their burden of guilt. This was a throwback not merely to the more primitive meaning of animal sacrifice, but to its predecessor, human sacrifice.

To this, the reply is often made by modern apologists that the sacrifice of Jesus cannot be regarded as a sacrificial guilt-offering, because another aspect of it is stressed more prominently: the efficacy of Jesus' death in procuring immortality for his faith-community. This is often referred to as the 'participationist' aim of the doctrine of the Crucifixion. By participating in Jesus' death, believers can also participate in his Resurrection into eternal life, and this positive aim far outweighs the negative aim of escaping from guilt. We all die, but Jesus, by voluntarily undergoing the common fate of mankind, enabled them to share in his own conquest over death.

Paul, it is argued in particular, holds a participatory rather than a substitutional theory of atonement. This is argued for example by D. E. H. Whitely in his *The Theology of St Paul*, writing, 'Christ shared our life in order that we might share his.' Whitely quotes such texts as the following: 'but the truth is, Christ was raised to life – the firstfruits of the harvest of the dead. For since it was a man who brought death into the world, a man also brought resurrection of the dead.' (I Cor. 15:20–21); 'He died for us so that we, awake or asleep, might live in company with him.' (Thess. 5:10). Whitely admits that many other Pauline texts appear to have a substitutionary sense (e.g. Romans 8:3–4, Cor. 5:21, Gal. 3:13), but argues that such an interpretation is not entirely necessary, and in the light of the clearly participatory texts, all texts should be interpreted in a participatory sense.

The participatory interpretation of New Testament texts would be much more convincing if Jesus had died of old age. Then indeed one could plausibly argue that he came to the world to share human experience and so enable mankind to share his own experience of resurrection. As it is, the participationists ask us to believe that the violence of Jesus' death has no significance in the theory of atonement and salvation. If the violence can be ignored, then the sacrificial aspect of Jesus' death can be discounted, despite its centrality in classical Christian belief. In so far as the violence is admitted at all into the consciousness of liberal theologians, it is regarded as an instance of martyrdom, not sacrifice, and as irrelevant to soteriology.

In point of fact, the violence of Jesus' death has never been irrelevant to its saving power. In the constant attempts to relate Jesus' death to the Jewish sacrificial system (however much based on a misreading of that system) we see that the Crucifixion has saving efficacy precisely because it is a sacrifice. This relates the death of Jesus (as interpreted by Christians from Paul onwards) to the violent deaths central in other mystery-religions, those of Osiris, Attis, Adonis and Dionysus. Why these man-god figures had to die such grisly deaths, and how the salvation brought by them is related to the grisliness of their deaths, can be explained only through investigation of the meaning of sacrifice itself. But for the moment it need only be pointed out that the figure of the tortured, dying Jesus on the Cross, pictured in countless Christian representations and a central feature of every church, cannot be discounted in the bland way employed by so many liberal Christian apologists. Much more honest, and truer to the Christian record and tradition, is the attitude of the poet T. S. Eliot, who accepted that the grisly, violent death was the essence of Christianity, and did not balk at the idea that this put Christianity in the category of mystery-religion. To Eliot, the violence of the Christian myth was the index of its profundity. In the choruses of *Murder in the Cathedral*, he relates the death of Christ to a world 'red in tooth and claw', in which all beings live by eating others, the nightmare world of tearing and rending that Christ came to redeem by his own sacrificial suffering, which transmuted the cruel biting teeth into a spiritual world of mutual incorporation. In 'Gerontion', he refers to 'Christ the tiger', who comes to eat and be eaten; in 'Ash Wednesday', the leopard symbolises the violence of the Christian life of *imitatio Christi*. Eliot would have regarded present-day Christian liberalism as a namby-pamby bowdlerisation of a religion that takes the violence of the world into its heart, and thus maintains the romance of the violent dying young God in the face of calculating compromise with the values of old age.

But in any case, the 'participationist' theory cannot do the task for which it is intended. To say that for Paul, the purpose of Jesus' death was not so much to suffer vicariously for others' sins as to enable them to participate in eternal life, is by no means equivalent to saying that the violence of Jesus' death was unnecessary to salvation. For 'participation' has always been an important feature of sacrificial religion that has been indissolubly linked to violence. The mystery-religions, indeed, were primarily participatory. The aim of the initiate in the mysteries of Osiris, Attis, Adonis or Dionysus was precisely that asserted of Pauline Christianity: to attain eternal life, and thus become god-like. But this did not mean that the death of the god concerned could be anything less than violent. It was the violence of the death that enabled the initiate to participate. This was simply because the mystery-religions were spiritualised versions of very ancient rites of human sacrifice, which built on the efficacy of the killing of the chosen victim, sometimes complicated by prolonged torture in order to increase the efficacy of the magic. For part, at least, of the aim of sacrifice is to make use of the life-force of the victim, and one way to make full use of the life-force is to milk it slowly and painstakingly so that none of it is dissipated in a quick and useless leakage. The use of sacrificial torture is well exemplified in the human-sacrificial rituals of the Apache Indians.

In the Hellenistic mystery-religions, participation was paramount, since the notion of atonement for sin formed hardly any part in the theory of the saving efficacy of the death of the man-god. In Pauline Christianity, the stress on atonement for sin is greatest in Hebrews, and is undoubtedly present as an important theme in the genuine Pauline epistles, but is subordinate there to the chief theme of attainment of immortality. Yet Paul does not thereby subordinate the theme of the violent suffering of Jesus on the Cross. On the contrary, he stresses this as the core of his faith. 'We proclaim Christ – yes, Christ nailed to the cross' (I Cor. 1:23); 'I am crucified with Christ; nevertheless I live; yet not I but Christ liveth in me' (Gal. 2:20). Participation and crucifixion are uttered in the same breath. Atonement for sin is certainly part of the efficacy of Jesus' death on the Cross, but sin is regarded as chiefly an impediment to immortality. Thus the attempt to divide atonement from participation is ill-conceived; they are part of the same pattern of divinisation of humanity. If only mankind could get rid of the stain of Adam's sin, it could become immortal and therefore divine. The Gnostic yearning for divinity is impeded by a Jewish consciousness of sin, and the Gnostic belief in transcendence by *gnosis* alone has disappeared, leaving only the hope in vicarious sacrifice. Whereas in Judaism, sin is regarded as an impediment to the life of good works on earth, and therefore has to be tackled piecemeal by repentance and struggle with the 'evil inclination', in Pauline Christianity sin is an impediment to escape from this world into deity, and therefore must be eradicated by a once-for-all sacrifice of cosmic proportions.

In Paul, however, the divine sacrifice comes about through evil forces. He states: 'The powers that rule the world have never known it [i.e. God's secret purpose]; if they had, they would not have crucified the Lord of glory.' (I Cor. 2:8). Here we have the germ of the doctrine that produced Christian antisemitism. Unlike the myth of Hebrews (in which Christ crucifies himself) here we have the more characteristic Christian myth that gives evil a holy task: to bring about salvation unwittingly, while purposing only evil. Paul himself does not identify the powers of evil with the Jews. He appears to be referring here to cosmic powers of evil, and his kinship with the dualism of Gnosticism is manifest. But it was not long before the move was made to identify the Jews as the earthly representatives of cosmic evil, and this move was made in the Gospels.

CHAPTER 11

THE STIGMA OF DEICIDE

The sacrificial myth that Paul wove around the death of the Jewish messiah-figure Jesus attained its full narrative potential in the Gospels, where the Jews begin to be cast for a demonic role. Before examining these Passion narratives, however, it is advisable to consider another transition document, the extraordinary Epistle to the Colossians. The consensus of scholarly opinion is that this was not written by Paul, to whose authorship the Epistle itself lays repeated claim. The arguments are not so overwhelming as in the case of Hebrews (which itself makes no claim to Paul's authorship), and the possibility remains that this Epistle was, after all, written by Paul from prison, as it claims to be. At any rate, it undoubtedly bears the stamp of Pauline ideas, and at the least was written by a close disciple of Paul.

The sacrificial theme is announced early: 'Through him God chose to reconcile the whole universe to himself, making peace through the shedding of his blood upon the cross – to reconcile all things, whether on earth or in heaven, through him alone. Formerly you were yourselves estranged from God; you were his enemies in heart and mind, and your deeds were evil. But now by Christ's death in his body of flesh and blood God has reconciled you to himself, so that he present you before himself as dedicated men, without blemish and innocent in his sight.' (Col. 1:20–22). Here the accent is on the remission of sins through Jesus' sacrifice, not on participation in immortality. The link between remission of sins and immortality is asserted later: 'And although you were dead because of your sins and because you were morally uncircumcised, he has made you alive with Christ. For he has forgiven us all our sins; he has cancelled the bond which pledged us to the decrees of the law. It stood against us, but he has set it aside, nailing it to the cross. On that cross he discarded the cosmic powers and authorities like a garment; he made a public spectacle of them and led them as captives in his triumphal procession.' (Col. 2:13–15). The evil powers here are not the Jews but cosmic forces opposed to Jesus, who has conquered them and reduced them to figures of ridicule in his triumph. This has been accomplished through his suffering on the Cross. The note of exultant scorn of the 'cosmic powers' reminds us of the Gnostic dismissal of the Demiurge and his followers as a 'laughingstock'.[1] Yet the theme of redemption through divine sacrifice is foreign to Gnosticism, as is the emphasis on 'Christ's death in his body of flesh and blood'. In Christianity, the sacrifice must be a real one, and the suffering on the Cross must involve real pain and shedding of blood; otherwise there is no redemption. Here in Colossians we see clearly displayed the unique blend of Gnostic dualism with mystery-religion sacrificial themes that defines Christianity. So clear is this indeed that the 'participationists' and other exegetes of non-sacrificial Christianity have never attempted to reinterpret Colossians in their cause, thinking that the widely-held view of Colossians as spurious relieves them from the mental acrobatics they have applied to the accepted Pauline Epistles.[2]

It is in the Gospels that the evil supernatural powers earlier held responsible for the death of Jesus come to be identified with the Jews as their earthly representatives. Thus the Jews become marked out for pariah status in any political context where Christianity has been adopted as the official religion.

The Gospels construct a narrative of the birth, life and death of Jesus, setting him in a context of Jewish and Roman religious and political history. Figures such as Pontius Pilate, Caiaphas, Herod Antipas, John the Baptist, and movements such as the Pharisees and the Sadducees (as playing any part in the life of Jesus), are unmentioned in the earliest composed documents of the New Testament, the writings of Paul and his disciples. What motivated the composition of the Gospels as narratives, as opposed to the writing of hortatory and theological compositions treating Jesus as a cosmic, rather than historical, figure?

The striking difference between the Epistles and the Gospels has given rise, at times, to theories of the totally mythical nature of the character of Jesus. Georg Brandes, and more recently G. A. Wells, have argued that Jesus never really existed, and that the apparently historically grounded Gospels are attempts to historicise a myth.

Such theories would be persuasive if the only Gospel extant were that of John, but the authentically Jewish material in the Synoptic Gospels makes it impossible to regard Jesus as merely mythical. The reason why the Gospel authors felt the need for historical narrative is that the expectation of an immediate eschatological event had become eroded, and the followers of Jesus were forming an established community needing institutions. The Jerusalem Church, being firmly anchored in Judaism, probably needed only a collection of Jesus' sayings, such as has been discerned in the Q document embedded in the Gospels, but the oral tradition of the Jerusalem Church preserved much of a historical and biographical character. But those followers of Jesus who had severed links with Judaism, and felt the Jerusalem Church as a rival threatening their own version of Jesus' mission, could not do without a canonical account of what Jesus was aiming at, and how he met his end. Many Gospels were written to provide the needed narrative, four of which managed to survive the vicissitudes of early church disagreement and become canonised. These Gospels all used material derived from the oral tradition of the Jerusalem Church, shaped and edited to conform to Pauline ideas of Jesus' mission.

The great event that occurred between Paul's writings and the Gospels was the destruction of the Jewish Temple. This is what determines the huge difference in tone between the earlier and later writings. When Paul was writing, the Jewish state was still in being; racked by the misfortunes of corrupt Roman administration and Jewish resistance, but still preserving religious and political structures from the days of self-rule. By the time the Gospels were written, all this had gone. The massive trauma of the destruction of the Temple, combined with military defeat and the departure of many thousands of the population into slavery, comprised an event of apocalyptic proportions. Certain trends of Jewish belief, including Sadducaism and the Dead Sea Scroll sect, never recovered from the blow. Only

Pharisaism, because of its relatively detached attitude towards the Temple and the priesthood, was able to survive the crisis.

Even in modern times, we have seen how a striking event such as the Six Day War can give rise to apocalyptic interpretations, both among Jews and Christians. Among the Jews, the destruction of the Temple recalled the previous destruction by the Babylonians, which was followed seventy years later by the return and the rebuilding of the Temple. It was probably this pattern that determined the timing of the Bar Kokhba revolt seventy years after the destruction of the Temple by Titus.

We do not know how the Jewish Christians of the Jerusalem Church interpreted the destruction of the Temple. They fought along-side their Jewish brethren in the war against Rome[3], and were left a crippled organisation. Later they refused to take part in the Bar Kokhba insurrection, since they regarded Jesus, not Bar Kokhba, as the Messiah. One might guess that the Jewish Christians saw the destruction of the Temple as part of an apocalyptic pattern leading up to the triumphant return of Jesus, who would rebuild the Temple.

For Pauline Christians, however, the destruction of the Temple was an event of far greater theological meaning. It meant that God had decided to end the covenant of Sinai and replace it by the new coven-ant of the blood of Jesus. This is the symbolism of the rending of the Temple 'veil' at the time of the Crucifixion, as recorded in the three Synoptic Gospels (Matthew 27:51, Mark 15:38, Luke 23:45). 'And Jesus cried with a loud voice, and gave up the ghost. And the veil of the Temple was rent in twain from the top to the bottom.' (Luke however makes the rending of the veil precede the final cry of Jesus.[4]) The 'veil' of the Temple was the curtain that stood before the Holy of Holies. It was passed only once a year, by the High Priest on the Day of Atonement. It represented, therefore, the ultimate means of atonement or salvation afforded by Judaism. The rending of the 'veil', therefore, presaged the destruction of the Temple, and marked the cessation of Judaism as a means of salvation. As a prophetic event, it is, of course, legend, and its presence in the Gospels shows that they were written after, and in the light of, the historical destruction of the Temple.

The destruction of the Temple was thus a welcome and liberating event for the Pauline Church, which had broken away from Judaism and severed all ties with Jewish patriotism as well as with the Jewish claim to be the people of God. To think of the Gospels as written out of a surge of confidence and confirmation is to understand their extraordinary brio and mythopoeic drive. The break with Jewish authority (both in the form of Judaism itself and of the awesome charisma of the Jerusalem Church) was attended by misgivings and trepidation; now however, it had been proved right. The Jews had been smitten by the wrath of God. Their bold attempt to break free from the power of Rome had proved a delusion, or even a trap set for them by the God who had rejected them. Worse still, the suffering they now underwent was on such a scale that they must have been guilty of a terrible crime. What could this be except the greatest of all possible crimes, the murder of Christ? Whereas up to this point the blame for the death of Jesus had been largely attributed to evil cosmic powers (the Pauline and pseudo-Pauline Epistles), aided and abetted by the pagan oppressors the Romans (Revelation), it now became clear that the true villains were the Jews.

In recent times, New Testament commentators have sought to explain the Gospels in terms of the social and religious needs of the communities for which they were written. This has involved much research into the historical circumstances of the early Christian communities in Alexandria, Antioch and Rome and other places. Strangely, however, with a few exceptions (notably S. G. F. Brandon), scholars have failed to consider the impact of the most startling contemporary event, the destruction of the Temple, on the aims and content of the Gospels.

Combining with the need of the Pauline Church to define itself as non-Jewish because of the general unpopularity in the Roman world of the rebellious Jews, the disaster that had befallen the Jews provided the sign from heaven that was required to institute a full anti-Jewish campaign. The disaster was traumatic enough; but the resilience of the Jews was such that they were able to recover from the blow and launch an even more damaging rebellion against Rome after a surprisingly short interval. It is possible to argue that the effect of the destruction on the Pauline Church, by which the Jews were allotted the role of justly punished deicides, was, in the long run, more harmful to the Jews than the destruction itself.

The Gospels are skilfully and dramatically constructed to emphasise Jewish guilt. At the same time, the Gospels also emphasise the inevitability of Jesus' death as the means of salvation for the world. Taken together these two factors give the Jews the role of Sacred Executioners, doomed to bring about salvation through their own damnation.

Jewish guilt is conveyed in countless subtle ways. As we have seen, the figure of Judas Iscariot functions symbolically to represent the treachery of the Jews generally to one of their own. 'He came unto his own, and his own received him not' (John 1:11). All sections of the Jewish people are shown as hostile to Jesus, and when they temporarily support him (as on Palm Sunday) this only adds to their guilt, since their subsequent withdrawal of support adds an element of treachery. Some Jews, of course, do support Jesus, his closest disciples, the Apostles. But even they show lack of loyalty and understanding, since they represent the Jerusalem Church, which, however, is finally shown as succumbing to the superior vision of Paul. As we have seen, the denigration of the Pharisees completes the disgrace of the Jewish people and their tradition. Sometimes the Jews are portrayed as merely blind and stupid, rather than malicious. This attitude is the legacy of Gnosticism, with its view of the Jews and Judaism as earthly and unspiritual. More often the note struck is one of vicious, mindless desire to strike down Jesus out of satanic hatred of the good.

The excuse is often put forward that the Gospels are not specifically aimed against the Jews, but only against human evil, of which the Jews happened to be representative at the time. In words often used, 'If we had been there, we would have done the same.' This contention is wrong for many reasons. The very fact that the earlier literature of the New Testament does not blame the Jews shows that the anti-Jewish orientation of the Gospels was a conscious decision. Instead of blaming the Romans, who actually carried out the crucifixion of Jesus (and of thousands of other Jews regarded as subversive), the understandable, if cowardly decision was made to put the entire blame on the Jews, a people at this time in the depths of defeat and misery. It was a safe decision, because no retaliation could be expected from a helpless people. The Romans, on the other hand, were not a safe object to blame, and Pauline Christians rightly feared that any hint of blame cast on Rome would put them in the same rebellious camp as the Jews in Roman eyes. Yet it is really remarkable how the Gospels manage to exonerate the Romans from all blame, in the face of the remnants of historical fact which even they were unable to obliterate.

The Book of Revelation does blame the Romans, and even foretells the fall of Rome as punishment for their crime, but only under the disguise of 'Babylon'. The Pauline and pseudo-Pauline Epistles do not blame any earthly authority – apart from the pseudo-Pauline addition to I Thessalonians, which anticipates the Gospel strategy of antisemitism. But even the policy of blaming cosmic powers is really a veiled way of blaming the Romans, who, as a superpower, the 'powers-that-be', could easily be identified with the 'prince of this world', Satan. A circumspection about mentioning Rome, even under the disguise of an earthly pseudonym, is already apparent in the Epistles, but it has not yet developed into exoneration.

In the Gospels, however, Rome is carefully exonerated. Pilate, the Roman Governor, is portrayed as most unwilling to execute Jesus. He is even shown as unaware that there is anything threatening to Rome in Jesus' claim to be King of the Jews. On the contrary, in the Gospel of John (21:12–15), he presents Jesus to the Jewish crowd, saying, 'Behold your King!' He has to be told by the Jews, 'If thou let this man go, thou art not Caesar's friend; whosoever maketh himself a king speaketh against Caesar,' as if a Roman Prefect needs to be told that a claimant to the Jewish throne is liable to crucifixion for rebellion. The Jews call out, 'Away with him, away with him, crucify him,' upon which ensues the following incredible dialogue: 'Pilate saith unto them, Shall I crucify your King? The chief priests answered, We have no king but Caesar.' The picture of Pilate (known from other sources to be a butcher) as a political innocent is only exceeded by the unlikelihood that Pilate, unlike the crass, worldly Jews, appreciates that when Jesus calls himself King, he means that his kingship is not of this world. Previously in the same scene, when Pilate has declared: 'I find no fault in him,' the Jews (the scene alternates between 'the Jews' and 'the chief priests' in such a way as to implicate all Jewry from the highest to the lowest) have revealed their allegedly real reason for wanting to do away with Jesus: 'We have a law, and by our law he ought to die, because he made himself the Son of God.' Thus the full scenario is: the Jews wish to kill Jesus for religious reasons, because his claim to divinity is 'blasphemous'; they therefore manufacture a *political* reason for denouncing him to the Romans, knowing full well that Jesus has no political aims. Pilate, knowing that Jesus is non-political, has to bow to the Jewish false charge that Jesus is a political threat, while awed by the conviction that Jesus is indeed the Son of God.[5] This whole scenario manipulates the historical facts, which are simply that Jesus was indeed a threat to the Roman occupation, being a claimant to the Jewish throne, and that the Romans, together with a few Jewish quislings, therefore eliminated him by their usual punishment for subversion, crucifixion. The total result of the Gospel manipulation is that the Romans are innocent victims of Jewish subterfuge. No more unlikely perversion of historical facts could be imagined.

In addition to the whitewashing of Pilate, the Romans are consistently shown in a good light. The first person to acknowledge the divinity of Jesus is the Roman centurion who seeing him die, says, 'Truly this was the Son of God.' (Matthew 27:54, Mark 15:39, but in Luke 23:47, the centurion only says, 'Certainly this was a righteous man'; Luke apparently balks at the crudeness of the transfer of religious insight and authority to the Romans from the Jews). The very person who superintends the crucifixion is exonerated from blame because of his worship of the crucified. Nowhere in the Gospels do we see the Romans as cruel oppressors of a brutally subjected and exploited people.

Thus the claim that the Jews merely represent human evil is contradicted by the fact that the Gospels are engaged in a deliberate transfer of guilt from the real executioners of Jesus, the Romans, to the Jews. The claim itself is intended as a kind of comfort or consolation extended to Jews who feel dismayed at being portrayed as the villains of the Gospel story: 'We don't really blame you, because anyone else would have done the same.' This forgiveness echoes Jesus' alleged cry on the Cross (known only to Luke), 'Father, forgive them, for they know not what they do.' (Luke 23:34). One is reminded of Father

Kolbe (canonised by the Roman Catholic Church), who believed every foul charge made against the Jews, including the blood libel, but forgave them for everything. Such saintliness is hardly welcome to victims of slander. False accusations are not improved by forgiveness; nor can forgiveness take the place of enquiry into whether the defendant is actually guilty.

Some commentators suggest that even if the charge of deicide made against the Jews is not true, the Jews should not mind, because the charge is only symbolic. 'The Jews' who continually appear in John's narrative should not be identified with any actual Jews, since the term is meant only to stand for human sinners in general, who, in any or every historical epoch, deny Christ, and who may therefore be regarded as spiritually responsible for his death. I wonder what the response would be if the term 'the blacks' were substituted for 'the Jews'. I think it might then appear obvious that the use of *any* human group as symbolic of evil is unacceptable. The effect of such use is the exact opposite of the effect proposed: instead of influencing readers to apply the blame for evil to themselves, it invariably influences them to attach full blame to the group held up in the narrative for obloquy. A double-dyed villain, such as Iago, paraded in all his villainy on the stage, is hissed by the audience, not used as a spur to self-castigation and identification with villainy. Even Iago is not so melodramatic a villain as Judas Iscariot (who indeed inspired all the motiveless, satanic villains in Western literature), and if the 'we-are-all-guilty' argument is not applied to Judas (as it does not seem to be) it should not be regarded as relevant to the collective Judas, the Jewish people. If the Gospels really aim to induce readers to blame themselves, they have adopted the least effective artistic method to this end.

Even more important for the demonisation of the Jews, and their eventual role as a pariah caste in Christendom, is the elevation of their crime of deicide to the status of a saving event. This may seem surprising and paradoxical. Many Jews (including Disraeli) have wondered why the Jews are not regarded with gratitude, instead of hate, by Christians, since their alleged killing of Jesus was the direct cause of Christian salvation. But the matter ceases to be surprising when one compares the Christian narrative of salvation to similar narratives, such the myths of Osiris, Balder, and others. The attitude of the initiates towards the death of their saviour must be one of pure grief and mourning. There must be no admixture of satisfaction or delight at the thought that this terrible death brings salvation, a thought which is banished from the mind at the time of mourning. When the good news is broken that the resurrection has taken place, an amazed delight supervenes, all the greater because salvation is totally unexpected. The phenomenology of salvation-by-sacrifice is thus one of dissociated states of mind, which must be kept separate, or the whole saving scenario will dissolve. The initiates will become aware that, far from being the recipients of unexpected salvation, they have engineered the whole drama themselves.

This syndrome of dissociation may provide a better explanation of the birth of tragedy than the various and conflicting explanations hitherto offered. The starkness of the tragic plays of the Athenian dramatists has been attributed to a profound understanding of the inexorable process of fate, against which human attempts at self-assertion constitute *hubris*. This may indeed be the artistic consummation of Athenian tragedy, but its origins, which were undoubtedly religious, may lie in the dissociation characteristic of rites of human sacrifice. The same religious festivals that contained performances of tragedy were occasions also for the performance of comedy, but the two could not be mixed. The tragedy derives from the mourning of the man-god sacrifice, which must be unadulterated by hope, the comedy from the blaze of unexpected joy at the resurrection of the sacrificed hero. A similar dissociation can be seen in the earliest version of the Gospel of Mark, which ended with the death of Jesus and contained no account of the Resurrection.

It is this tragic dissociation that explains the special hatred directed against the Jews. Where the sacrificial victim is brought to his death by man, not by God, it is all-important that the initiates should have clean hands. It is therefore necessary to have a person, or class of persons, on whom the deed of blood can be blamed. The more this person, or class of persons, is rejected with horror, the more the initiate can disclaim responsibility for the horrifying murder which brings him salvation. Thus hatred becomes ritualised. The hatred itself becomes part of the process of salvation.

In actual rites of human sacrifice, as practised in primitive times and sporadically in historical times up to the present day, there was a ritual figure who performed the sacrifice, and was then cursed by the tribe and banished into the desert. In the Hellenistic world this ancient ritual of salvation had become spiritualised into cults of initiation, in which the sacrifice was symbolic, being embodied in a narrative or myth of the violent death of a man-god, betrayed by an evil, sometimes supernatural, figure. In Christianity, the death was that of an historical figure, the Jewish messiah-claimant Jesus, whose death at the hands of the Romans had been mysticised into a sacrificial death. The role of Sacred Executioner therefore devolved on historical figures, too, the Jews, elected to this role because Pauline Christianity had defected from the Jewish struggle against Rome.[6]

It requires to be shown, however, what has sometimes been denied, that the death of Jesus in the Gospels is portrayed as a sacrifice.

It is true that, in the Gospels, there is a certain reticence about the sacrificial nature of the death which forms the culmination of the story. While there are occasional explicit statements that Jesus had to die for the salvation of mankind, there is no extended theological discussion of how his death atones, as in the Epistles; no exposition, for example, of Original Sin, or explanation of how Jesus expunges the sin of Adam. The Gospels function as Passion narratives, almost as Passion Plays, in which the hero progresses towards his inevitable death, surrounded by incomprehension, even from his closest followers. Even though only one Gospel (Mark, in its earlier form) suppressed the Resurrection, all the Gospels do so in a way, by the brevity and cryptic quality of their reference to it. The artistic effect of all the Gospels is that they end in mourning and puzzlement for an inexplicable death, with a few intimations that there is more to come.

Allowing for their function as Passion narratives, rather than as complete statements of Christian belief, the Gospels nevertheless do state or indicate the sacrificial nature of Jesus' death. Examples are the following:

'And he said unto them, This is my blood of the new testament, which is shed for many.' (Mark 14:24) (cf Exodus 24:8 'the blood of the covenant', sprinkled by Moses from the sacrifices marking the covenant of Sinai.)

'Even as the Son of Man came not to be ministered unto, but to minister, and to give his life a ransom for many.' (Matthew 20:28) (Mark 10:45)

'For this is my blood of the new testament, which is shed for many for the remission of sins.' (Matthew 26:28)

Such statements are explicit enough, but far more effective in setting the mood of voluntary sacrifice are the narrative devices of the Gospels which emphasise that the death of Jesus as a destined and necessary event which Jesus undertakes willingly, makes no attempt to avoid, and even deliberately refuses to avoid. For example, Jesus says to Pilate, 'Thou couldest have no power at all against me, except it were given thee from above: therefore he that delivered me unto thee hath the greater sin.' (John 19:11). Here we have not only the God-given nature of Jesus' death, but the paradox of the Betrayer, who takes the blame away from everybody, including Pilate and even God, who otherwise might be held chiefly responsible, since it is by His decree that Jesus dies. The voluntary nature of Jesus' death is emphasised even further in Jesus' alleged saying, on his arrest, 'Thinkest thou that I cannot now pray to my Father, and he shall presently give me more than twelve legions of angels? But how then shall the scriptures be fulfilled, that thus it must be?' (Matthew 26:53–54). A similar atmosphere of destiny is displayed in the Last Supper scene, where Jesus actually designates Judas as his Betrayer, telling him, 'That thou doest, do quickly.' (John 13:27). Judas is playing a destined role, but this does not in any way absolve him from blame and obloquy, because it is precisely his role to take the blame for the performance of the sacrifice. The whole destined situation is summed up in Jesus' alleged saying: 'The Son of Man indeed goeth as it is written of him: but woe to that man by whom the Son of Man is betrayed! good were it for that man if he had never been born.' (Mark 14:21, Matthew 26:24, Luke 22:22), a perfect summary of the shifting of responsibility and the ritualisation of blame in the institution of human sacrifice; it could act as the motto of the relegation of the Jews to a pariah status in which they undoubtedly often wished that they had never been born.

This destined and voluntary nature of Jesus' death marks it as a sacrifice, not as a martyrdom. A martyr does not seek death. He follows a cause that brings him into danger of death, and the cause is so dear to him that he is willing to suffer death for it. In Jesus' case, he is not represented as risking death for a cause, but rather as seeking death itself as his main purpose. Though at times Jesus is represented as espousing liberal causes against the reactionary Pharisees, in the end this portrayal fades away, and he emerges as one who submits to a destined and necessary death as a 'ransom' or as one whose blood must be shed to inaugurate a new covenant.

The idea that Jesus dies to inaugurate a new covenant has sometimes been cited to show that his death is not a sacrifice.[7] Again, this line of argument arises from the misapprehension that only one kind of sacrifice exists, namely the atoning sacrifice. In reality, many kinds of sacrifice exist, though it may be possible to see a common factor in all the varieties. One kind of sacrifice is what has been called the 'foundation sacrifice', which is performed when some great new thing is inaugurated – the founding of a city, or of a tribe, or a temple. To say that Jesus' death marked the end of an era (or 'aeon') and the beginning of a new one, the Christian era, is not to deny it the status of a sacrifice, but only to transfer it from the status of an atonement sacrifice to that of a foundation sacrifice. In reality, however, the sacrifice of Jesus, in Pauline theory, was multivalent, and this is true of sacrifice in general. What persists in almost all sacrifice, however, is the feeling of guilt involved, because of the violence both desired and deplored, and the need to shift this guilt to some person or community that can be made the object of ritualised blame.

CHAPTER 12

THE MEANING OF SACRIFICE

One approach to the death of Jesus, as presented in the narrative of the Gospels, is to say that it is indeed a sacrifice, but is a sacrifice to end all sacrifices. One could say that the first writer to propose this view was the author of the Epistle to the Hebrews; for he argues that the sacrifice of Jesus, being the culmination and fulfilment of the Temple sacrifices, rendered obsolete the Jewish institution of animal sacrifice. It is possible to argue that only by instituting a once-for-all symbolic sacrifice could the whole institution of animal sacrifice, so important in all religions of the ancient world, be brought to an end. Among modern writers, René Girard has promulgated something like this view.

On the other hand, one could argue that the symbolic sacrifice as found in Christianity, continually rehearsed in canonical story and Church art, and also embodied in the sacramental ritual of the Eucharist (where the blood and body of the sacrifice is ingested by the worshipper), makes sacrifice far more central in religion than the bodily animal sacrifices of the Jewish Temple. One can argue, in fact, that in Christianity sacrifice is far more important than it ever was in Judaism; that the attempt to abolish sacrifice only succeeded in making it more important, while also entailing an increase in guilt that required an outlet in the diabolisation of the Jews.

Here one may ask the question, 'What is the meaning of sacrifice?' Why was it so important that only its intensification on a symbolic level could bring about its physical demise?

René Girard has made a very interesting and important contribution towards answering this question in his book *Violence and the Sacred*. He criticised the work of Henri Hubert and Marcel Mauss, in their book *Sacrifice: Its Nature and Functions* (often regarded as the classic treatment of the subject) as failing to understand the importance of the aspect of violence in sacrifice. Interestingly, Girard argues that the work on sacrifice of structuralist anthropologists, such as Claude Lévi-Strauss, suffers from the same defect, since sacrifice is treated as a gift to the god rather than as a mode of coping with the problem of violence in society. Consequently, Hubert and Mauss and Lévi-Strauss, just as much as their much-criticised predecessor Sir James Frazer, relegate sacrifice to the limbo of outmoded superstition, instead of appreciating its urgent relevance to all forms of society including our own.

We have already seen how reluctant New Testament scholars are to acknowledge that the violence of Jesus' death has anything to do with its efficacy as an atonement, or a foundation event, or a means of participation in immortality – however its efficacy may be defined. Their explanations, it has been pointed out, would fit the circumstances just as well, or better, if Jesus had died of old age. In general, scholars have shied away from the violence of religious practice of the ancient world, with the sole exception of the violence against animals in the Jewish Temple, which, we are often told, 'reeked like an abattoir' from the blood of the sacrificed animals. The fact is that Judaism confined this violence to animals, and that the Temple indeed functioned as an abattoir, since most of the animals sacrificed were eaten; the practice of meat slaughtering (universally practised but hidden away from sight in the modern world) was thus given societal sanction and divested of guilt. In other ancient cultures, however, including that of Greece, human sacrifice was practised as well as animal sacrifice; a fact denied or discounted by scholars, especially in their own area of special study, at least before the work of Sir James Frazer, Jane Harrison, Walter Burkert and others.

Girard's theory is that sacrifice performed an essential function in society in the ancient world because it canalised the violence that would otherwise be turned against society itself. Communities that were only precariously based on institutions of co-operation and peace, feared above everything a relapse into chaos in which every man's hand would be against his neighbour. Society itself, according to Girard, began when a state of primitive violent anarchy was resolved into order by the discovery that human beings could be united by shared violence against one of their number.

Sacrifice, in Girard's view, becomes unnecessary only when society develops a strong judiciary system backed by central government power. This ends the situation of chaos in which private revenge rules; instead of the ever-spreading vendetta, we have a central power of justice, which is in fact the sole wielder of revenge. By having only one wielder of revenge, the situation of uncontrolled revenge, producing chaos, is ended. 'Vengeance is Mine, saith the Lord.'

Primitive societies have no central judiciary backed by irresistible power. Yet they manage to control chaos and prevent the chain reaction of revenge by the institution of sacrifice, as well as by other methods, such as bargaining about compensation for injuries or murders. We know about sacrifice chiefly through documents surviving from societies which have already grown beyond sacrifice because of their development of a judiciary, so that the evidence comes from societies in which sacrifice, while still practised, is becoming obsolete. But we can extrapolate from the available evidence to more primitive societies in which sacrifice was an urgent practical necessity to hold society together.

Girard's theory of sacrifice provides a more comprehensive explanation of sacrifice than any previously offered. It explains why sacrifice ceased to be practised as a central institution in later societies, without resorting to condescending assessments of earlier societies as superstitious or ignorant.

A society without powerful central authority and a judiciary enforcing law lives in a state of constant tension, contrasting with the informality and easy-going behaviour of a society with central power and the rule of law. Consequently, every change of state in a lawless society threatens chaos: transition from childhood to adulthood, for example. Every transition, therefore, must be marked by the canalising of fear and rage into the killing of a victim, which however must be ritualised (i.e. performed according to strict rules), for one wrong step could nullify the effect. The killing of the victim unites the community by diverting its fear and rage from each other against a victim specially chosen to be (a) one of themselves; (b) without avenging connections. This theory then explains why sacrifice seems, bewilderingly, to take so many forms: initiatory, expiatory, foundational, etc.

Indeed, other theories of sacrifice may be regarded as taking some particular aspect of sacrifice and making it paramount, explaining the other aspects in terms of the selected one. Thus, Hubert and Mauss concentrate on the aspect of mediation between man and god, as the root conception underlying all sacrifice. Jane Harrison, on the other hand, selects the aspect of initiation, marked by rites of passage, and tries to explain all the variations in the occasions for sacrifice in these terms. Walter Burkert finds yet another way of unifying the phenomena of sacrifice: all derive from the hunting period of humanity, when the guilt and fear aroused by killing animals had to be allayed. Girard, again, sees the effect of sacrifice in smoothing the conflicts of society, by unifying it in violence against a victim, as paramount.

Without attempting to arbitrate between these various theories, we may ask to what extent Girard's theory throws light on the topic of this book, namely the effect of sacrificial ideas on the making of a pariah person or caste through the shifting of the guilt of sacrifice from the community to a scapegoat.

Girard hardly seems aware of the existence in most sacrificial systems of a secondary scapegoat, the Sacred Executioner, who is blamed for the performance of the sacrifice. Instead, he stresses the double nature of the victim, who is regarded as both good and bad, or as sometimes good, sometimes bad (since he has to be blamed in order to be justified in the role of victim, but as good in that he brings the salvation of the community from chaos). This is a valid perception, but he overlooks the fact that the double nature of the victim often lends itself to a splitting into two separate mythic individuals, one as the 'White Christ', the other as the 'Black Christ' (who brings about the death of the 'White Christ'), so as to cope with the guilt involved in the sacrifice itself.

A writer who is aware, to some extent, of this dimension of sacrifice is Walter Burkert. Since he traces all sacrifice to the hunting period of man's development, he sees animal sacrifice as primary, human sacrifice as secondary. In prehistoric times, animals, though they provided the chief source of food, were regarded as divine, so that killing them aroused more guilt and fear than killing human beings. The eating of animals was a sacramental act, by which not merely physical but also spiritual, or divine, nourishment was ingested. Consequently, the hunting and eating of animals was surrounded with ritual, chief of which was the sacrifice, which gave all animal killing the sanction of divine approval. The sacrificial animal was treated with reverence, and its soul became a tutelary spirit, defending the tribe and supporting its hunting activities. The killing of the sacrifice was attended by rites of propitiation, by which the forgiveness of the animal was sought and the aggression of the tribe excused.

The advantages of Burkert's theory are many. He provides a plausible explanation of the universal existence of sacrificial rites in the ancient world, as a survival of the hunting period, which was a universal earlier stage of humanity's development. He also concentrates on the aura of guilt that surrounds the act of sacrifice, an aspect ignored by the earlier theorists Frazer, Hubert and Mauss, and Harrison. He shows, for example, that Greek sacrifice was attended by a 'comedy of innocence', by which responsibility for the sacrifice was shifted from the sacrificers. A bizarre instance of this is the well-known Bouphonia sacrifice at Athens, in which responsibility for the sacrifice is attributed to the sacrificial knife, which is formally tried, found guilty and then thrown into the river. It is easily understandable, on the basis of Burkert's emphases, how responsibility for the sacrifice can sometimes be attached to a human evil Sacrificer or Betrayer, who is banished, or killed, or reduced to pariah status.

Yet the analyses of both Girard and Burkert are, in a way, too profound for the purposes of our present enquiry. Both offer an explanation of the origins of sacrifice that go back to prehistory and treat sacrifice as a survival into historic times. Both, for example, regard the distinction between animal and human sacrifice as theoretically unimportant. This, however, is to ignore a development in human culture that was very important in systems of sacrifice, and of symbolic sacrifice, in historic times. At a certain point of history, the killing of humans took on the aspect of a horrific crime, while the killing of animals became divested of its aura of deicide. This development is illustrated, for example, in the Hebrew Bible, where Adam is created 'in the image of God', whereas animals are relegated to serve human purposes, including sacrifice and food. Even as late as the Hebrew Bible, however, this distinction is not entirely clear-cut. Animals were allowed for sacrifice, but not for food, in the pre-Diluvian period. Only after the Flood, in God's revelation to Noah, were animals sufficiently desacralised to be allowed for food. Even so, the eating of meat was allowed to the Israelites at first only through partaking in a sacrifice; non-sacrificial meat was not permitted until the writing of Deuteronomy. Moreover, the ingestion of the blood of an animal was forbidden, since 'the blood is the life'. Only when the animal had been reduced to lifeless desacralised meat could it be eaten; any suggestion of a transfer of vital force from the animal to humans had to be avoided.

The more that animals were desacralised, the greater became the gap between the killing of animals and the killing of humans. In place of the prehistoric situation, in which killing and eating an animal was a sacramental act, in which the divine spirit of the animal was absorbed thus endowing humans with a secondary divinity, animals now became a source of calories for humans, mere nourishing meat – and as such a fit present either to humans or to gods. This stage is marked by Jeremiah's fulminations against human sacrifice, though the primitive religion which pre-dated Israelite religion may have included human sacrifices in the form of killing of the first-born. Animal sacrifices became, in Israelite religion, a substitute for human sacrifice. In the revulsion against the latter, animal sacrifice became invested with a glow of virtue, rather than with guilt. Thus the evidences of guilt discerned by Burkert in relation to Greek animal sacrifice are absent from the biblical sacrificial prescriptions.

In other cultures of this period we can discern the same horror of human sacrifice, combined with the official confinement of sacrifice to animals. Yet in these cultures, human sacrifice continued, but in an unacknowledged and occasional form. The desacralisation of animals made human sacrifices, in contrast, seem immeasurably more potent in their magical effect. Thus, though officially proscribed and denied, they became a remedy of last resort, when more civilised procedures had failed. The highly-civilised republic of Athens, at the height of its sophistication in the time of Themistocles, resorted to human sacrifice in the extremity of the Persian threat. Moreover, Athens retained the institution of the *pharmakos*, or human scapegoat, who, in times of plague or famine, would be flogged through the streets, struck by the populace and whipped on his genitals, and finally ejected from the city, or even at times killed. Human sacrifice was deprecated as savage, but still regarded as potent, and therefore occasionally practised. The guilt involved is shown by the secrecy employed, and by the disguised form in which the practice is described in myths and legends.

It was guilt about human sacrifice, requiring 'distancing' devices of many kinds, that gave rise to the pre-eminent way of avoiding guilt, the introduction of the figure of the Betrayer or Sacred Executioner. The exegesis of myths, especially those related to mystery-cults, cannot be carried out successfully without awareness of this figure. Girard's interpretation of myths is handicapped by this lacuna in his thought. It means that he is often struggling to accommodate a myth, or adaptation of a myth in the form of tragedy, to a state of mankind far more primitive than is appropriate for the material.

An example is the story of Oedipus, which has been the focus and testing-ground of so many wide-ranging theories, including those of Freud and Lévi-Strauss. Girard rightly criticises Freud's theory as too narrowly psychological to cope with the societal issues involved, and Lévi-Strauss's theory as missing the essential element of violence. But Girard himself finds great difficulty in fitting Oedipus into his scenario of the 'surrogate victim', who absorbs the violence of the community, thus saving it from its own crisis of indiscriminate violence. For if this explanation were correct, we would expect Oedipus to be killed by the Theban populace, not expelled to become a wanderer. Expulsion and wandering are characteristic not of the sacrificial victim, but of the dark figure who brings about the death of the victim, either by betrayal or murder. The populace, or community, thus obtains the saving sacrificial death, but without incurring responsibility for it, and indeed, by piously washing its hands and expelling the murderer, preserves its innocence entirely. It is this dark figure, embodied in the person of Judas Iscariot, symbolising a whole people which eventually became a pariah caste, that engendered the phenomenon of anti-semitism.

In the story of Oedipus, the sacrificial victim is not Oedipus, who survives, but Laius, whom Oedipus kills. The crisis which this sacrifice is intended to solve is not the plague (which comes at a later point in the story) but the depredations of the Sphinx, the monster who is terrorising the community of Thebes. The killing of the King, Laius, is in line with the sacrificial role of kings, of which Jesus is one more instance in his role as 'King of the Jews' (i.e. in the Hellenistic mythologising version of his Jewish status as a claimant to the Jewish throne). The killing is disguised as a quarrel, a frequent distancing device, as in the case of the sacrificial killing of Remus by his brother Romulus, the foundation-sacrifice of Rome. Yet the sacrificial nature of the death of Laius is clear in the manner of his death, for he is dragged by horses, a form of sacrifice paralleled in the deaths of Hippolytus, Oenomaus, Abderus and others.[1] The later plague is caused by the failure of the community to expel the Sacred Executioner, Oedipus, and is allayed when he is duly sent away to wander, like other Sacred Executioners, such as Cain, and the Wandering Jew (who is emblematic of the exiled Jews as a whole). Sophocles, in his tragedy, chose to focus his attention on the killer of the sacrifice, rather than the sacrificial figure of Laius, and he followed this by another drama in which he described the fortunes of the exiled Oedipus, who, in his wanderings, exemplified the positive features of the Sacred Executioner as bringer of salvation (cf. the positive version of the Wandering Jew, who repents of his crime, accepts his suffering as deserved, and is a force for good in his wanderings – a Christian image of how the Jews should embrace their status as pariahs in Christendom). The unwitting crimes of Oedipus – killing his father and marrying his mother – are, as Girard rightly argues, not the central part of the story (as Freud thought), but part of the blackening of the character of the Betrayer; indeed these same crimes play a similar role in the medieval embroiderings of Judas Iscariot's story in *The Golden Legend*.

Another way in which the potency of human sacrifice was exploited, while the attendant guilt was appeased, was in the mystery-cults, in which human sacrifice was central, but only in symbolic or mythical form. In the mystery-cults of Dionysus, Orpheus, Osiris, Attis and Adonis, no actual sacrifice took place. Instead a story was recited and enacted; the story of the violent death and resurrection of the god. Even the story was to some extent disguised, for the death of the god was not described as a sacrifice, but as a death caused by hostile forces. Yet the beneficent consequences of the death show it to be a sacrifice, for without it there would be no salvation. The chief good aimed at by the mysteries was immortality. So the evil warded off by the sacrifice is no less than death. Yet in one way the mysteries are very different from the actual human sacrifices which they echo and replace: the salvation aimed at is individual, not communal. Instead of warding off some evil that threatens the whole community – plague, or military defeat – the sacrifice which the initiate mimics gives him a means of escape from the human lot. For immortality meant divinity; the aim was to become a god. This aim shows a decline of public life in the Greco-Roman empire, where the tightly-knit human community had given way, to a large extent, to member-ship of an impersonal and vast political machine.

There is, on the face of it, a striking parallel between the mystery-cults and Pauline Christianity. There is the same horrific suffering and resurrection of a man-god figure, the same hopes of immortality through initiation ceremonies evoking the story of the suffering of the god. The parallel was so striking indeed, that it aroused the attention of early Christians themselves, and of their opponents, who pointed out that Christianity was just another mystery religion. An early Christian apologist, Tertullian, took note of these allegations. He acknowledged fully the similarity between Christianity and the mystery-cults, but explained it by saying that they had been adum-brations of divine truth, foreshadowing the appearance of the true and final mystery, Christianity. Modern Christian apologists, how-ever, have not followed Tertullian's line. Tertullian was not embar-rassed, as modern Christian apologists are, by the idea that Christianity has at its centre a man-god sacrifice. Modern writers, however, are fully aware of the primitive nature of such a sacrificial scheme, and therefore seek to play down all aspects of the death of Jesus that have been given a sacrificial connotation in the past. The similarities between Christianity and the mystery-cults have been dismissed as mere superficial coincidences. Another line is to attack the historicity of the mystery-cults themselves, arguing that the evidence for them is late. Consequently, similarities can be explained by the influence of Christianity on the mystery-cults, rather that the other way round. It has been argued that while the mystery-cults do show evidence of a suffering god, there is much less evidence that they contained the idea of a resurrected god. In general, the existence of mystery-cults contemporaneous with Christianity has proved so embarrassing that there has been great impetus to deny Hellenistic influences on Christianity, and to stress its links with Judaism, often in a very implausible way.

One of the most remarkable instances of a reluctance to apply normal anthropological standards of comparison to Christianity is to be found in the work of Girard. Here is a writer who has displayed the greatest perspicacity in relation to the topic of sacrificial religion, showing how its adherents habitually conceal its sacrificial nature from themselves, and that indeed this concealment is essential for the efficacy of religion as a mode of social unity and cohesion. Yet he himself is a prime example of such blindness to the sacrificial nature of the religion which he professes. Instead, he declares that the death of Jesus which lies at the heart of Christianity is so far from being sacrificial in nature that it is the negation of sacrifice. He freely admits, however, that ever since the foundation of Christianity, the death of Jesus has usually been 'misunderstood' as sacrificial, and that this misunderstanding has been the cause of many unfortunate oppressive features of historical Christianity, including its antisemitism. This concept of a religion which means one thing, but has always been misunderstood to mean another, is not uncommon among Christian apologists, whose motto is, 'Christianity has not been tried and found wanting; it has never been tried.' Girard subscribes enthusiastically to this school of thought. Against it, one might remark that a religion is not so easily separated from its manifestations. Such a separation might be construed as a failure to accept responsibility for the failures of one's tradition. A saying of Jesus is very relevant here: 'Ye shall know them by their fruits.' The real test of a religion, or any other ideology, is the way it works out in practice; and the fact that its protestations of love always seem to turn into manifestations of hate may be due, not to misunderstanding of a difficult doctrine, but to hidden flaws in the doctrine itself. We have seen this in relation to Communism, which also presented itself as a doctrine of love, and whose adherents have also commonly resorted to the plea that 'true' Communism has yet to be practised.

As it happens, the Passion story of the Gospels fits Girard's theory of the origin of sacrifice better than any of the other myths which he, sometimes unconvincingly, analyses. According to Girard, sacrifice is essentially a deed arising from mob violence. The archetypal setting of sacrifice is a scene of indiscriminate hostility, suspicion and mutual violence in which peace is achieved by the fixation of the mob on one victim; their unanimity in turning their violence against this victim becomes the basis for a peaceful, ordered society. The institution of sacrifice then becomes the ritualisation of this primal act of unifying violence. Girard himself points out that the Gospel story exemplifies this scenario. 'Jesus is presented to us as the innocent victim of a group in crisis, which, for a time at least, is united against him. All the sub-groups and indeed all the individuals who are concerned with the life of and trial of Jesus end up by giving their explicit or implicit assent to his death: the crowd in Jerusalem, the Jewish religious authorities, and even the disciples, since those who do not betray or deny Jesus actively take flight or remain passive.'[2] One may doubt one of these remarks, that Jewish society is portrayed as 'a group in crisis'. Historically, it was indeed a society with many rival parties, in which Pharisees, Sadducees, Herodians, Samaritans, Zealots and other groups strove for supremacy; but the Gospels actually disguise this fragmentation in order to display the Jews as unanimously opposed to Jesus. Certainly, however, Girard is right in saying that the Gospels give a picture of a hostile society united in bringing the innocent Jesus to his death. It would also be true to say that the death thus brought about results in salvation, in the opinion of the Gospel authors. To conclude, therefore, as Girard does, that the Gospel authors do not regard Jesus' death as sacrificial is perverse. On his principles, he should have regarded it as a prime example of a sacrificial death.

Girard's argument, essentially, is that since Jesus abjured all violence, he could not have regarded his own death as a sacrifice, since sacrifice is based on the saving efficacy of violence. Jesus did bring about salvation, but only by non-violent means; he came to his death through his opposition to the powers of violence, which are summed up under the appellation of 'Satan'. It is not the violence of his death that brings salvation, but whole-hearted self-identification with the message of non-violence that he brought.

Girard sees Jesus' abjuration of the régime of violence in his denunciation of the Pharisees:

> Therefore I send you prophets and wise men and scribes, some of whom you will kill and crucify, and some you will scourge in synagogues and persecute from town to town, that upon you may come all the righteous blood shed on earth, from the blood of innocent Abel to the blood of Zechariah the son of Barachiah, whom you murdered between the sanctuary and the altar. Truly, I say to you, all this will come upon this generation. (Matthew 23:34–36)

The legerdemain by which Girard turns this passage of horrifying antisemitism into a message of anti-sacrifice and non-violence is amazing.[3] According to Girard, Jesus is here repudiating the whole edifice of human society which is built on violence. He is not particularly criticising the Pharisees or accusing them of killing prophets, only of belonging to a world in which the killing of prophets, echoing the primal sacrifice, is essential to the fabric and continuance of society. The mention of Abel, the first victim, and of Zechariah, the last victim mentioned in the Bible, shows that the reference is universal, and does not even apply to the Jews as a people (since Abel was not a Jew) but to mankind as a whole.

Girard, significantly, omits to include the opening of the quotation, which is, 'Woe unto you, scribes and Pharisees, hypocrites!', which might have made it too plain that these alleged remarks of Jesus are indeed directed against the Pharisees, not against some symbolic group. The fact that Abel is mentioned does not give the passage universalism; unless it is universalistic to blame the Jews, and their spiritual leaders the Pharisees, for all the evil committed since the beginning of the world. The effect of the passage, as reflected in the comments of churchmen throughout the history of Christianity, is to brand the 'generation' of Jews living at the time of Jesus with the guilt of violent opposition to Jesus. The branding of this 'generation' even continued in the statement put out by the Catholic Church at the Vatican II Council, which ostensibly cleared the Jews of the charge of deicide. This 'guilty generation', however, happens to have been one of the greatest and most authoritative in the history of Judaism, including such figures as Hillel, Gamaliel and Johanan ben Zakkai; and the authentic evidence is that they did not oppose Jesus, but gave him a sympathetic hearing. To slur over these 'curses' (as church rubrics have always called them) by a generalising interpretation that smooths out all their sectarian malice is an exercise in bowdlerisation. It is not the violence of Jewish society, or even of world society, that is in question, but the antisemitic violence of the author of the Gospel of Matthew who falsely attributed these words to Jesus, and thus set in train a history of Christian violence against the Jews.[4]

CHAPTER 13

THE ANTHROPOLOGY OF
THE NEW TESTAMENT

For Girard, the salvation brought by Jesus lies in his pacifist pronouncements, not in his death. Jesus, Girard believes, heralded a form of society not based on the sacrificial pact. It was thus his totally radical opposition to the sacrificial, violence-based structure of society that aroused such resentment in the establishment that they united to destroy him, but this act of destruction, though inevitable, did not itself produce salvation for anyone; nor does the New Testament (except possibly in the Epistle to the Hebrews) assert that it did so.

This reading of the New Testament involves some extraordinary twisting of the meaning of texts that appear to assert the salvific effect of Jesus' death, or which ascribe any violent behaviour to Jesus or to God the Father, or any intention of God the Father to sacrifice his Son on behalf of mankind in order to avert His own anger at mankind's sins. Girard is merciless to classical scholars when they try to avoid acknowledgment of sacrificial meanings in their beloved classical texts; yet, ironically, he provides, in relation to the New Testament, an outstanding example of the very same apologetic stance. It seems that his praiseworthy efforts to understand classical and Old Testament texts from an anthropological angle are brought to an abrupt halt when he approaches the New Testament. Yet, in important respects, the New Testament ought to be a happy hunting ground for anthropologists. Many of its narrative and discursive themes, as expressed in the Gospels and the Epistles, represent a throwback to sacrificial attitudes far more primitive than those found in the Old Testament.

Of course, Girard does notice this; but his reaction is to say that precisely because the New Testament 'uncovers' these deeper sacrificial themes, it is breaking through the conspiracy of silence that usually surrounds the sacrificial core of human community. The New Testament, Girard argues, continually points to the violence which underpins society, doing its work of cohesion only because society has tacitly agreed not to draw attention to it. This is the 'hypocrisy' which Jesus ascribes to the Pharisees, but which he regards as fundamental to all society, Jewish or non-Jewish. Here there is an affinity between Girard's thought and that of Freud, who regarded the New Testament as more primitive, yet more fruitful, than the Old Testament.[1] For the New Testament uncovers the violence against the Father, and the consequent expiation of the Son – a violence which the Old Testament concealed, ever since it wrapped in secrecy the murder of Moses by the Israelites in the desert. The difference is that Freud regarded the New Testament as superior to the Old by its very primitiveness, which allowed the 'return of the unconscious'; while Girard regards this primitiveness as a deliberate strategy. Freud regards the New Testament as similar to a tortured neurotic patient on the couch, coping with his problems by reliving the violent passions of his childhood; Girard regards the New Testament as playing the role of psychoanalyst who is encouraging the patient to express his sadistic fantasies and so transcend them.

In fact, however, the New Testament is far more like Freud's picture than Girard's, though one may doubt Freud's charitable prognosis that such regression gives promise of a breakthrough to a new level of vitality. There is a limit to the extent of which one can regard the illness as the cure. It is true that an illness (particularly a psychotic one) often displays overtly symptoms that remain hidden and repressed in a hampered but functioning personality. But the overt display of symptoms may signal the breakdown of a working psychological compromise, and the collapse of the personality into an infantile configuration.

Girard considers that the story of Jesus' death on the Cross differs from all other stories of sacrifice in that Jesus is an innocent and willing victim. In other stories, such as that of Oedipus (whom Girard wrongly regards as a primary sacrificial victim), the sacrifice is blamed for his own punishment, being laden with crimes. In this way, the sacrificers are excused for their violence. Jesus, however, as portrayed in the Gospels, provides no such excuse to his betrayers and killers, who are described as the instruments of evil cosmic 'powers', which in reality are simply the evil forces of society itself, which achieves and sustains its cohesion only through the primal violence. By bringing these powers into the open in their naked violence, Jesus unmasks them and thus punctures their claim to be peaceful and positive factors in the formation of human society. Thus Jesus' death does indeed bring salvation, but not in the sacrificial sense of absorbing the violence which would otherwise spend itself in indiscriminate feuding; instead his death points to a new form of society based on non-violence, and this is the definition of true salvation for humanity.

Girard overlooks, however, the many myths and rituals, other than that of Jesus, which emphasise the innocence and willingness of the victim. A biblical example is the sacrifice of Isaac by Abraham, in which the victim was in no way blameworthy. In Greek legend, there is the story of Leos of Athens, who sacrificed his three innocent and willing daughters, on the instruction of the Delphi oracle, to end a famine; and of Aristodemus of Messenia, who sacrificed his daughter to end a plague. While in other stories, there is certainly a tendency to blame the victim, this is not an essential element, but rather a way of excusing the sacrificer for an act of cruelty. Ideally, the victim should be not only innocent, but flawless in every way both spiritually and physically, for otherwise the sacrifice itself is flawed, being an ungenerous offering of an inferior gift to the deity. Thus there is nothing unique in the innocence and willingness of Jesus to undergo death. It is precisely in the most savage system of sacrifice, that of the Aztecs, that the innocence and willingness of the victims is most emphasised. The virtue of sacrifice is considered to be the willingness of the sacrificer to give up what is most precious to him, combined with the willingness of the victim to die for the sake of the community.

The picture that we receive from the Gospels and the Epistles is that it is the death of Jesus that saves humanity from the evil forces that surround it. This is an archetypal example of sacrifice. 'God so loved the world that he gave his only begotten Son, that whosoever believeth in him should not perish, but have everlasting life.' (John 3:16). The expression 'only begotten son' deliberately echoes the description of Isaac (Genesis 22:2), so that God the Father is pictured as playing the role of Abraham, the sacrificer of his son, Isaac. The situation, of course, is paradoxical, because God the Father plays the double role of sacrificer and demanding deity, to whom the sacrifice is offered; but such paradoxes are not uncommon in sacrificial myth. Jesus, at any rate, is the uncomplaining victim, like Isaac, whose death is gladly offered for the sake of the community, in this case mankind in general, i.e. 'the world', to whom God shows his love by his selfless gift of the life of his son. The benefit gained by the community from the sacrifice is eternal life; not a this-worldly benefit, but survival in a spiritual world after death. This is hardly a community benefit, since it is conferred on individuals; but this puts the Jesus cult into the category of the mystery-religions, which also endowed individuals with immortality. That John sees the saving function of Jesus as sacrificial is also shown by his expression, 'Behold the Lamb of God, which taketh away the sin of the world.' (John 1:29), a reference to Jesus as a sin-offering, bringing atonement for sins by his death. John, however, is merely echoing the formulation of Paul, 'He that spared not even his own Son, but has delivered him for us all . . .' (Romans 8:32), which itself echoes the sacrifice of Isaac by Abraham '. . . because thou hast done this thing, and hast not withheld thy son, thine only son . . .' (Genesis 22:16). No one denies that the Abraham–Isaac incident was a sacrifice. The difference is that it was a sacrifice that did not actually take place; whereas in the case of Jesus, the sacrifice did take place, at least in myth (though on the historical plane it was not a sacrifice but the execution of a rebel against Rome).

Certainly the sacrificial interpretation of Jesus' death was universally accepted by the Early Fathers who were the first interpreters of the New Testament, and it seems hard to accept Girard's contention that they all totally misunderstood the text. Indeed, Girard argues that they reversed its intention, foisting a sacrificial meaning on a text that was both non-sacrificial and anti-sacrificial. In fact, a non-sacrificial meaning did not even occur to them as a possibility, so that they were evidently transmitting a strong oral tradition of interpretation stemming from the time that the Gospels were composed. It was not until the Middle Ages that a lone voice, that of Peter Abelard, was raised to combat the sacrificial interpretation, on grounds of humanity and logic. Abelard has been wrongly described as representing a perennial strand of interpretation, when, as in some other of his opinions, this courageous and humane figure represented only himself, though he was the precursor of later trends, the Socinianism of the Renaissance period, and the liberal theologians of the present day.

One of the earliest interpretations of the Gospel story of Jesus' Passion is found in a canonical writing, the First Epistle of Peter. 'The price was paid in precious blood, as it were of a lamb without mark or blemish – the blood of Christ.' (I Peter 1:19). But this is no uncomprehending gloss, even though I Peter is not what it purports to be, but a Pseudepigraphic work. The author merely repeats what he found in the earliest writings of the New Testament: 'We have redemption through his blood, the remission of sins, according to the riches of his grace . . .' (Ephesians 1:7); '. . . through the redemption which is in Christ Jesus, whom God set forth as a propitiation by his blood . . .' (Romans 3:24); Christ 'loved us and delivered himself up for us, an offering and sacrifice to God . . .' (Ephesians 5:2).

These clear indications of sacrificial thinking are fully elaborated by the Early Fathers and the medieval Christian theologians. Through all the variations discernible in the theory of atonement from the 2nd century to the 15th, the basic concept of the mystical salvific efficacy of the death of Christ remains constant. The nature of this salvation is disputed, mainly because salvation is a many-faceted concept: it can be thought of as primarily a removal of the burden of sin, or as the attainment of spiritual freedom, or as an escape from the inevitability of death, or as an escape from bondage to Satan, or in many other ways, each of which led to a theory about the basic meaning and efficacy of the death of Christ. What they all had in common was that the doom of mankind (however defined) was removed by this death; and this attribution of a magical efficacy to a death is precisely the definition of sacrifice. Moreover, the once-for-all nature of the sacrifice, supplanting the piecemeal, renewable Jewish system of animal sacrifice, aligned the Christian sacrifice with other once-for-all sacrificial cults, namely the mystery-cults, in which the divinisation of the sacrifice renders further sacrifices unnecessary, requiring only a mental act of identification (called 'faith') by the initiate. It is not for nothing that the central Christian sacrament, the bread representing the body of Christ is called the 'host' (from the Latin *hostia*, 'sacrifice'), and that this rite reverts to the earliest known form of sacrifice, the eating of the god. This is not only sacrifice, but the apotheosis and centralisation of sacrifice as the chief mode of religious observance. In the Catholic Mass, every action of the priest, and every particular part of the service, is regarded as a dramatic allusion to the various circumstances of the Passion and death of Jesus. Even the kiss bestowed on the altar by the priest at one point, is regarded, according to the manuals, as partly recalling the kiss given to Jesus by Judas Iscariot when he betrayed him.

Church Councils also stressed the sacrificial nature both of the death of Jesus and of the Mass. 'If anyone shall say that a true and proper sacrifice is not offered to God in the Mass, or that what is offered is nothing else than giving us Christ to eat, let him be accursed ... If anyone shall say that the Mass is only a service of praise or thanksgiving, or a bare commemoration of the sacrifice made on the Cross, and not a propitiatory offering . . . let him be accursed.' (Council of Trent, *De Sacrificio Missae*).

These interpretations of the Gospel story of the Passion were not perverse, as Girard argues, but continuations of the doctrine found in the New Testament, which regards Jesus' death as a divine sacrifice bringing salvation to mankind. The New Testament is therefore a very fit subject for anthropological analysis, since its sacrificial concepts relate it to primitive cultures and to the religious practices of pre-history. The accepted paradigm both for Christian believers and for secularists is that the New Testament is less primitive than the Old; and this paradigm is based to a large extent on the belief that the New Testament moves beyond the sacrificial concepts embodied in the system of animal sacrifice codified in Leviticus. This condescending attitude towards the Old Testament is displayed in the nomenclature of 'Old' and 'New', which of course derives from the Christian 'two-covenant' dogma. It might be a salutary exercise for all biblical scholars and anthropologists to eschew the term 'Old

Testament' and use instead the term 'Hebrew Bible', as indeed some of them already do.

If it were allowed even as a possibility that the New Testament actually relapses into sacrificial concepts far older than Leviticus, New Testament studies would take off in a startling direction. In particular, antisemitism would be seen to have atavistic roots in the guilt-shifting connected with a certain stage of human sacrifice. The study of antisemitism would then emerge from its present condition of superficiality and mystification.

It is extraordinary, however, how the New Testament is constantly exempted by biblical scholars from anthropological analysis, which is directed exclusively towards the Hebrew Bible. A recent interesting anthropological study of the Hebrew Bible is *The Savage in Judaism: an Anthropology of Israelite Religion and Ancient Judaism* (1990), by Howard Eilberg-Schwartz. This book commendably refuses to be intimidated by recent purist objections to cross-cultural comparisons, and finds many features of anthropological interest in biblical institutions such as circumcision, ritual purity and animal sacrifice. Also, the author provides a useful survey of the history of Old Testament anthropology, showing, for example, that the allegedly primitive character of Israelite religion was used by 18th-century rationalists, such as Voltaire, as a weapon against Christianity. Even these bold thinkers, however, never investigated the New Testament in the same way; their attack on the New Testament consisted of pointing out that it relied on the flawed (because primitive) authority of the Old Testament.

Even Eilberg-Schwartz, however, follows in the footsteps of these 18th-century rationalists by refraining from bringing anthropological analysis to bear on the New Testament. His account of Christianity, to which he devotes some remarks at the end of his book, is all about its superior rationality to Judaism, particularly in the area of ritual purity. It never occurs to this Jewish author to consider that certain areas of New Testament thinking show inferior rationality or downright irrationality in comparison with Jewish thinking. So powerful is the theologically derived paradigm of progressive development (to which 19th-century evolutionary ideas gave added impetus) that the possibility of regression is unconsciously dismissed. The Christian doctrine of sacrificial atonement does not figure at all in Eilberg-Schwartz's account; he is able to see the savage in Judaism, but the savage in Christianity is invisible to him.

Most present day anthropologists (though, to his credit, not Girard) are dismissive of the work of Sir James Frazer in *The Golden Bough*. We all know the charges against Frazer: that he was an armchair anthropologist; that he was a naive rationalist, who thought primitive religion a mere botched kind of science; that he suffered from 'parallelomania', rashly linking similar phenomena in widely separated societies, though the contexts were structurally different. These charges are not without foundation, yet those who have made them have often had axes to grind of their own: ideologies of relativism, or even (as in the case of Evans-Pritchard) religious beliefs to defend. The fact is that Frazer was a great pioneer, who collected and ordered material of the utmost value that would otherwise have been lost. Moreover (as Eilberg-Schwartz has pointed out in some valuable comments), the warnings against cross-cultural comparisons have been much overdone, again often by people who have suspect motivations. The alleged uniqueness of every culture has often been urged as mode of covert return to the dogma of the uniqueness of Christianity, and the illegitimacy of all attempts to set it into context.

Frazer saw very clearly the savage in Christianity. He pointed out the obvious similarities between the central Christian myth of salvation and the promises of immortality offered by the mystery-cults, with their dying-and-resurrected gods, who suffered violence for the sake of mankind. Among New Testament scholars, there were some who were able to make the same connection, despite the indoctrination that usually prevents New Testament scholars from noticing any traces of primitive thought in Christianity. Richard Reitzenstein (1861–1931), in his much vilified book *Hellenistic Mystery-Religions*, pointed out the Hellenistic influence on Christianity, and particularly of mystery-religion and Gnosticism on Paul. He argued that the Eucharist was instituted not by Jesus, but by Paul, who claimed that he had received instructions about it from Jesus in a vision; Paul's vision of the Last Supper was later incorporated into the Gospel accounts. One of the many fascinating parallels noted by Reitzenstein related to Jesus' alleged instruction at the Last Supper, to drink wine symbolic of his blood, saying, 'Do this in memory of me.' Reitzenstein here cites a magical text, from about the time of Paul, '. . . in which Osiris gives to Isis and to Horus his blood to drink in a cup of wine, so that after his death they will not forget him, but must search for him with longing and lamentation, until, brought back to life, he is united with them'. This telling detail brings out the striking similarity between the Christian myth of Jesus and that of Osiris: both die a horrible death, betrayed by an intimate; both come back to life and provide an avenue for salvation. The Hellenistic associations of the Eucharist were further explored by Hans Lietzmann in *Mass and the Lord's Supper*, showing how a Jewish non-mystical ceremony, the Kiddush, was transformed into a mystical communion on the model of the mystery-cults.[2]

Wilhelm Bousset (1865–1920), in his *Kyrios Christos*, also drew attention to the links between Pauline Christianity and mystery-religion, especially in the terminology used, such as *kurios* ('lord'). Bousset shows that this designation for Jesus did not exist in the Jerusalem Church, but first arose in the Hellenistic Gentile Church, who derived it from mystery-religion. Bousset however is concerned only with the influence of 'Hellenistic mysticism', and does not appreciate the influence of the pagan sacrificial redemption myth, with its narrative core of violent death. This is true in general of the History-of-Religions school, as it has been called. Even Reitzenstein, despite his evidence from Osiris, does not see the violent death of Osiris as throwing light on the violent death of Jesus. There is here an unwillingness to recognise that, though Jesus' death was an historical event, it was mythicised in Pauline Christianity in a way that invites comparison with the deaths of other salvation gods of the era.

The History-of-Religions school of New Testament study was concerned to set Christianity in its environment, and see it as a 1st-century religious phenomenon, rather that a timeless, unique revelation. Thus the authors of this school were interested not only in Hellenistic influences, but also in Jewish influences on early Christianity. At first, the discovery of Jewish influences was felt by opponents of this school as just as threatening as the claims of Hellenistic influence. For both claims militated against the uniqueness of Christianity, relegating it to a historical phenomenon. But after a while, it was seen that the threat from Hellenism was far greater than the threat from Judaism. A few scholars, such as Rudolf Bultmann, were willing to accept that Christianity is essentially a Hellenistic religion, with only a colouring of Judaism. Most, however, rejected this assessment with horror. The concept of Christianity as 'the fulfilment of Judaism' had to be rescued, and at all costs, the picture of Pauline Christianity as a relapse into paganism had to be combated. Thus Albert Schweitzer, who had at first aroused much opposition by his reduction of Christianity to Jewish apocalypticism, was later regarded as providing a lifeline from a reduction to Hellenistic mystery-religion. Schweitzer himself rejected with indignation any attempt to show links between Christianity and mystery-religion, and for him even Paul was a hundred per cent Jewish figure. The hundreds of parallels in vocabulary between Paul and the Hellenistic cults were dismissed by Schweitzer as a mirage. Schweitzer was unable to see that his convincing argument about the influence of Jewish apocalypticism on Jesus applied only to Jesus himself and his followers in the Jerusalem Church, not to the Pauline Church, whose sources were chiefly Hellenistic.

Thus the insights of Reitzenstein, Lietzmann, Bousset and other New Testament scholars were buried. Hellenistic influence on the New Testament was discounted, unless it could be shown to have arrived via Judaism, which (it was argued) already contained a fair amount of Hellenism. Much effort was expended on showing that the concept of a divine Saviour was foreshadowed by the Wisdom figure of Proverbs, or the Son of Man of Daniel, or other angelic intermediaries. All this parading of angelic messenger figures or poetic personifications failed to bridge the gap between the Jewish concept of the Messiah as a human liberator who would institute the Kingdom of God on earth, and the Christian Messiah or Christ, a divine descending and rising figure who would bring immortality, and to whom the only parallels are to be found in pagan mythology and mystery-religion.

As for the redeeming sufferings of Jesus on the Cross, the figure of the Suffering Servant of Isaiah 53 has often been adduced to show that even this was foreshadowed in Judaism, and need owe nothing to the suffering gods of the mystery-religions. Commentators, Jewish and non-Jewish, have pointed out that this figure represents the Jewish people, who have suffered for the sins of mankind in the sense that their sufferings are an index of mankind's moral progress. There is no indication in Isaiah that the Suffering Servant is to supplant the Torah as a means of salvation, or that his sufferings are to become the central focus of religious belief. The theological function of the Suffering Servant passage in Judaism is to act as a counterweight to the explanation offered elsewhere in Scripture for the sufferings of the Jews: that it is a punishment for their sins. This explanation is indeed given great weight, and predominates in the liturgy, especially in that of the Fast of the Ninth of Av, the anniversary of the Destruction of the Temple, and is important as a spur to Jewish repentance and spiritual renewal. Yet it could never be a sufficient and complete reason for Jewish sufferings, as the experiences of the Holocaust have underlined. Another reason, emphasising the Jewish role as the pioneer and martyr of human progress, was needed, if only to prevent moral despair, a mood alien to Judaism. The Suffering Servant is not a sacrifice, for no one's sins are annulled by his suffering, nor is immortality promised for those identifying with his pain. Consequently, no evil doomed figure is required to carry the responsibility for his sufferings into the wilderness, as Judas went out into the night. On the contrary, the nations who have caused suffering to Israel are redeemed by their own voluntary repentance. The need for repentance, whether by the Jews or by their oppressors, has not been removed by a magical efficacy ascribed to the sufferings themselves.

This magical efficacy, deriving from the transgressional sanctity of violence, is what constitutes the definition of sacrifice. The breaking of the taboo against murder sets up a charge of dynamic power that dissipates the threat to the tribe; only a violent death can have this effect. But the salvation, being accomplished only by horrific transgression, needs a scapegoat to absorb the guilt of the sacrifice. This mechanism, ignored or covered up by anthropologists, historians of religion and Scriptural scholars, lies at the root of antisemitism.

CHAPTER 14

DID ANTISEMITISM BEGIN
IN THE MIDDLE AGES?

The work of Gavin Langmuir on the history of antisemitism has illuminated many aspects of the topic and can only be regarded with the highest respect. Yet one aspect of his findings is open to question. This is his view that antisemitism proper did not begin until the Middle Ages.

Langmuir sees antisemitism as particularly related to the 'blood libel', which first arose in the 12th century with the case of William of Norwich (1144).[1] His argument is that before this time there was anti-Judaism, which was based on rational premises, namely the religious disagreements which objectively exist between Judaism and Christianity. Only after the 12th-century watershed were the Jews demonised as subhuman perpetrators of imaginary crimes: crucifixion of Christian children, cannibalistic rites, poisoning of wells, spreading of disease. This demonisation, Langmuir argues, is so specific to the Jews that it cannot be regarded as merely a form of xenophobia, and has to be regarded as a special phenomenon deserving the name 'antisemitism'.

This is to oversimplify the matter by ignoring the element of myth in the Christian attitude to the Jews. Langmuir says, for example, that the Christian charge that the Jews brought about Jesus' death cannot be regarded as antisemitism since it was a factual charge which the Jews – at any rate in ancient times – did not deny (the point at issue being whether he deserved to be executed[2]). The point, however, is that the Jews were not simply accused of killing Jesus (as, for example, the Athenians killed Socrates). The charge was one of deicide, not one of wrongful execution. The Jews were accused of bringing about the sacrificial death of a divine visitor from outer space, a charge which they never accepted.

The Jews, by the charge of deicide, were mythologised into instruments of the cosmic power of evil. That their wickedness turned out to serve the cause of salvation only made the Jews more eerie, as predestined evil executioners of the divine sacrifice. Thus there is nothing 'rational' about the way the Jews were conceived from the very beginning of Pauline Christianity.

It took a long time for this mythological conception to transform itself into a widespread popular loathing of the Jews as subhuman. As Langmuir shows, many factors had to concur with the original mythological impulse before the irrational view of the Jews as intrinsically evil became a social force. But this does not mean that antisemitism began in the 12th century; it can be found in its purest irrational form in many Christian teachers long before that date, and its first expression is in the Gospels, where the Jews play the role of the betrayers of God. As a people allegedly possessed by Satan, the Jews were never regarded as merely having a rival religious outlook. Moreover, Langmuir appears unaware of the history of pre-Christian diabolisation of the Jews (as the people of the Demiurge) in Gnosticism.

Langmuir's approach has many merits. He does see that Christian antisemitism is rooted in Christian doctrine, and is not a mere matter of xenophobia, or, as it has become fashionable to say (in deep miscomprehension of Emmanuel Levinas), of fear of 'the other'. Langmuir's explanation of the timing of the great surge of antisemitic diabolisation in the 12th and 13th centuries is that this is a period when Christians began to feel agonising doubts about their own doctrine of the Eucharist. Because they doubted whether the bread really turned into the body of Christ and the wine into his blood, it was a comfort to hear that when the infidel Jews stuck pins into the communion wafer, it spouted a stream of blood. When Jews (allegedly) showed belief in the therapeutic efficacy of Christian blood, it became easier to believe in the magical efficacy of Christ's blood. The Jews, in Langmuir's view, acted as a screen on which were projected the innermost doubts and fears of Christians whose assurance of salvation had been threatened by the advance of philosophy and science, or by the existence of schisms in the Church.

This is a sociological approach (since it finds explanations in the disintegrating fabric of medieval society), but not an anthropological one. For it leaves out of account factors that reach back not only into the origins of Christianity in the ancient world, but even as far back as pre-history; factors that can be explained only by comparative study of religion and mythology in many societies widely separated in time and space. In particular, it neglects the factor of the role of the Jews in the Christian myth. The Jews in medieval society were not just an alien group on whom the society's current fantasies and anxieties could be conveniently projected. They were a group which, in a very real sense, was not alien at all, because they formed an intimate ingredient of the basic fantasy itself, the story by which the medieval Christian lived and was saved. The Jews featured as a sub-myth, or mytheme, without which the Christian myth could not function, and salvation could not be attained.

The distinction between sociology and anthropology is perhaps not entirely clear. Some have argued that the distinction is impossible to maintain, and that therefore sociology should be regarded as a non-subject, or as a sub-section of anthropology; others argue on the contrary that anthropology is a sub-section of sociology. I do not wish to enter into these professional debates, but will adhere to the commonly held distinction that sociology covers topics peculiar to Western society, in which changes in historical circumstances are taken into account; while anthropology covers the more unchanging institutions and myths of non-Western societies and primitive societies; and also, by comparative treatment, covers topics common to all societies. Social anthropology, on the other hand, is a mixed discipline in which concepts developed in the context of Western society are applied to primitive or non-Western societies. Christianity, then, as a community with roots in the ancient world, and even in pre-history, is a proper subject for anthropological enquiry into its rituals, myths and social stratification, including its subordination of the Jews into a sub-class.

Langmuir shows his sociological, rather than anthropological, bias by finding the causes of antisemitism in issues and anxieties peculiar to the historical circumstances of the Middle Ages. Thus he says that the Jews were persecuted because Christians, in this particular period, were becoming worried about the magical efficacy of the Eucharist. He does not ask, however, why the Jews, in particular, became the focus and remedy for these worries. He would perhaps answer that this was simply because the Jews were at hand, the only alien group living in Christendom on whom anxieties could be projected. But this is to regard the Jews as a kind of colourless screen, lacking specific characteristics in Christian eyes, and this was very far from being the case. It is to fall back, after all, on the view that xenophobia is the root of the trouble, or, to use the fashionable jargon, that the Jew was feared or despised as 'the other'.

But the Jews were not feared as some unknown quantity. They were intimately known, or believed to be known, by the Christian community, whose sacred writings contained voluminous reference to them. They were regarded as part of the Christian family, though the black sheep of the family. Judaism, indeed, was regarded as a subsection of Christianity. The Jews were the human, walking representatives of the Old Testament, which formed an essential part of the Christian Bible, and was regarded as Christianity's validation and credentials. If the Jews had been merely 'the other', their position would have been much less fraught with Oedipal anxiety. They were the parents of Christianity; disapproving parents who had to be induced to accept the children's rebellion, or else be overwhelmed by the children's malevolent fantasies. The panic and anger that arose among Christians when they first became fully aware (in the 13th century) of the role of the Talmud in Jewish religion can be understood in familial terms. The whole Augustinian compromise by which the Jews were tolerated in Christendom was threatened, because it was revealed that the Jews repudiated their parental role; the authentic child of the Old Testament, in Jewish eyes, was not the New Testament but the Talmud.

I am not suggesting, however, that awareness of the Talmud was responsible for the change that occurred in the ordinary Christian's attitude to the Jews in the 12th and 13th centuries, when the true demonisation of the Jews began, setting the stage for Auschwitz. Resentment of the Talmud was an issue mainly for the learned

Dominicans and Franciscans, who embarked on missionary efforts on a much increased scale in this period, and found the Talmud an obstacle. The demonisation of the Jews had much to do with the general intensification of Christian belief and enthusiasm, evinced in the Crusades and the rise of apocalypticism. Victories against Islam encouraged this mood, accompanied as they were by the conviction that the world-wide victory of Christianity was at hand. Langmuir's idea that Jew-demonisation arose from doubt rather than belief is not without merit, because the intensification of belief is often a sign of secret doubt. The encounter with the civilisation of Islam was bound to crack, to some extent, the assumption of Christian credal superiority. Yet the outward reality of this period was one of fervency and devotion. It was par excellence the Age of Faith, when the Church came nearest to its dream of subjecting secular authorities to its will. The ordinary people, previously pagan at heart, became truly Christian, developing new modes of devotion and deeply-felt fears of Hell. In this atmosphere, the toleration of the Jews which had existed on a personal level of friendliness, came to seem lax and irreligious. We have the phenomenon of the populist Louis IX of France, to whom hatred of the Jews was evidence of a good Christian heart, and whose anti-Jewish excesses were certainly no bar to his canonisation as Saint Louis.

Thus it seems somewhat perverse to attribute the rise of the blood libel in this period to Christian doubt rather than to Christian belief. The rise of the blood libel in this period does indeed appear to be related to the Eucharist, as Langmuir suggests. It is, after all, remarkable that the accusation against the Jews of cannibalism is precisely what Christians conceived themselves to be doing in the Eucharist, when they notionally drank the blood and ate the flesh of Jesus. It is much more likely, however, that the mechanism of displacing this activity on to the Jews was a transfer of guilt, rather than a way of appeasing doubt. This would merely be an extension of the general function of the Jews as guilt-absorbers in the Christian culture. The alleged murderers of Christ performed the very useful function of bearing the blame for a crime in which every Christian participated every time he fed on the victim in the Mass. But why was the accusation specifically concerned with the murder of children, rather than of adults? I have suggested[3] that this feature arose from a very contemporary development in Christian belief, namely the rise of Mariolatry. This suggestion combines the merit of Langmuir's theory (its contemporary sociological reference) with the deeper anthropological level of explanation advocated in this book.

The medieval stories and ballads about alleged Jewish murders of children (of which the best known is Chaucer's 'The Prioress's Tale') often involve also the Virgin Mary. Before the 11th century, the Virgin Mary played no prominent part in the Christian imagination. After that time, she rose to the position of a divine figure, the chief focus of prayer and hopes for forgiveness. Jesus himself became a terrifying figure, because he was pictured as the Judge of the Last Days. This applied, however, only to the adult Jesus. The infant Jesus, on the contrary, was strongly associated with the Virgin Mary and her role of protectress from evil, including the threat posed by the Jews. The Jesus who was eaten in the Mass began to be pictured as the infant Jesus. The displacement of responsibility for the sacrifice of Jesus on to the Jews thus now involved elements previously absent: the dismemberment and eating of a child and the drinking of his blood. Previously it was only the crucifixion of the adult Jesus for which the Jews were made responsible; now the cannibalistic fantasy which accompanied the eating of the Mass aroused such feelings of unconscious guilt, especially now that the victim was pictured as a child, that this sacrifice too had to be attributed to the Jews.[4]

The popular demonisation of the Jews was thus accomplished in the 11th and 12th centuries as a result of the success achieved at this time in spreading a frantic religiosity among the common people. The fear of Hell, the worship of the Virgin Mary and the hopes of an apocalyptic consummation of history all contributed towards this result. The demonisation had long existed in the writings of Christian teachers, and been assiduously preached by minor clergy to their parishioners. Now this teaching took effect, and was furthered also by Church art (with its portrayal of Jesus' New Testament enemies in Jewish garb and with caricatured Jewish features, while his Apostles and other supporters were portrayed as blond Nordics), and by the regular performance of Passion Plays, which now took on a new virulence. In these Passion Plays, the Jews, spearheaded by Judas

Iscariot, were portrayed torturing Jesus in prolonged and ingenious ways, until the spectators of these mass entertainments were roused to antisemitic frenzy, vented in post-performance pogroms. The Passion Plays were particularly vicious in Germany, the scene of the final outcome of medieval persecution, the Holocaust.

It was from this period that the Jews took on a subhuman and demonic aspect in the imagination of the Christian masses. Not only were they thought to be vampires, sucking the blood of Christian children; they were thought to have a noxious smell (the *foetor Judaicus*) and to have physical abnormalities, such as cloven hooves and male menstruation (the latter causing the loss of blood which necessitated vampirism). No fantasy was too lurid to be believed about the Jews. The result was a wave of popular persecution, triggered off by the Crusades during which there was huge loss of Jewish life, but continuing after that point on a more piecemeal basis. Those who profited most from the Jews, the kings and nobles, tried sporadically to protect them, and the Pope and upper clergy (being on the whole financially bound to the aristocracy) made occasional ineffectual pronouncements reminding the people of the Augustinian compromise, denouncing the blood libel as fantasy, and asserting the inadmissibility of forced conversions.

Even when forced conversions took place, this did not end the sufferings of the converted Jews. In Spain, many thousands of Jews became converted during the massacres of 1391, and the total number of conversions swelled to about 100,000 at the time of the Expulsion of unconverted Jews from Spain in 1492. These *conversos* (or, opprobriously, Marranos) became the chief victims of the greatest instrument of oppression before the Holocaust, the Spanish Inquisition, which functioned from 1481 until the 18th century. The Spanish converted Jews were not allowed to sink into the general population. It was never forgotten that they came from Jewish stock, and the success they achieved in Christian society (their legal disabilities having been removed by their conversion) roused bitter anger and envy. The situation was very similar to that in Germany and France in the late 19th and early 20th centuries, where the emancipation of the Jews, and their consequent rise in the professions, led to outrage and envy embodied in antisemitic movements. In Spain, from the 16th century onward, we find the first manifestation of the caste-stigma that continues long after the ostensible abolition of the caste-status. In later Europe this took the form of a racialist theory, based on pseudo-scientific theory. In Spain, it took a pre-scientific racialist form, based on the concept of 'blood'. Jewish 'blood' was regarded as a taint, not because it contained biological poison, but because it derived from a degenerate people, who had acquired an additional infusion of ineradicable Original Sin through their betrayal and murder of the Incarnate God.

The situation in 16th-century Spain, therefore, is very instructive about the later situation in post-emancipation Europe, where the taint of Jewishness persisted and even increased because of the resentment aroused by the spectacle of Jews posing as equals. Spain was the first run-through of what happens when the Jews are officially released from their position of stigma: a welcoming of freedom by the Jews, a flowering of their abilities, previously repressed, and then a backlash of resentment, a re-institution of the stigma, and a renewal of repression on an unprecedented scale. An enlightening book by B. Netanyahu has removed some common misapprehensions about the persecution of the Jews by the Spanish Inquisition. It was thought, by Jewish and non-Jewish historians alike, that the individuals persecuted were practising Judaism in secret, as the accusations against them alleged. Netanyahu shows, however, that in most cases the Jews were not practising secret Judaism at all; they were conscientiously practising Christianity. The accusations were brought by enemies motivated by jealousy or mere hatred. Part of the proof of Netanyahu's case is that the Jews who remained loyal to Judaism and suffered expulsion showed very little sympathy for their converted brethren who suffered from the Inquisition, considering this a just punishment for their disloyalty; but the chief proof lies in the records of the Inquisition itself, in which the trumped-up nature of the charges is hardly disguised. Those Jews, then, who thought to escape the Jewish lot through apostasy, only to die at the hands of the Inquisition, are the forerunners of the Enlightenment Jews who forsook their own tradition in order to partake as equals in the feast of Reason, only to find themselves more hated and vulnerable than ever.[5]

This pattern of stigma in the case of converted Spanish Jews can be seen even today in the Chuetas of Majorca. These are the descendants of converted Jews, and are devotedly pious Christians. But they have never lost their distinctive identity as the descendants of Jews. To intermarry with them is disgrace for Christians of pure Christian descent. They are not physically persecuted (for they have not excited envy in their professions, which are largely those of craftsmen), but they are regarded as low-caste and meet with undisguised contempt and social discrimination.[6]

In theory, Christianity is anti-racialist. Converts to Christianity, whatever their background, should theoretically be treated with honour and friendliness. The Jews, in particular, again in theory, should be particularly welcomed as converts, since their conversion is traditionally regarded as essential to apocalyptic hopes; to this end Missions to the Jews have been maintained in all Christian countries. A true example of how converts can be welcomed and fully integrated is to be found in Judaism, in which a historical succession of converts, sometimes consisting of whole nations, has not resulted in enclaves of discrimination, but in a unity in which descent from converts is lost in oblivion. Yet Judaism is often criticised as lacking the universalism of Christianity, in which ideally there is no discrimination between 'Greek and Jew'.

The reality was very different. Far from being accepted into the Body of Christ, the Jewish converts were never permitted to forget their Jewishness. The reason for this was that the Jews were already marked out within Christendom as a special caste. In Judaism, on the other hand, there is no analogous situation; the conversion of the 'Canaanite slaves' to fully Jewish status by emancipation from slavery might have proved analogous, but did not, since the prestige of acquired Jewish status in practice wiped out all memory of previous low-caste status. In Christianity, the Jews were not merely a low caste, but a hated minority endowed with mythical qualities of an abominable nature, arising from their role as *dramatis personae* in the central Christian myth. This stigma proved unexpungeable by conversion, just as the abolition of Untouchable status in Hindu India did not in practice remove the stigma belonging to the lowest caste.[7]

The analogy between the Jews and the Untouchables is, of course, far from complete. Yet it is very enlightening, because it explains the extraordinary persistence of antisemitism in the post-Christian secular world. It is necessary, however, to explore further the concept of modern antisemitism as the persistence of a medieval caste-stigma, and to consider in more detail whether the description of the Jews in medieval Christendom as a caste is in fact valid.

CHAPTER 15

WERE THE JEWS A CASTE?

The question of whether the Jews of medieval Christendom can be accurately called a 'caste' is a complex one. According to some definitions, the word 'caste' should never be used outside the religious system of Hinduism; according to other definitions, the word is susceptible of a more relaxed usage, in which other systems are deemed to show sufficient similarity to the Hindu mode of social stratification to permit the use of the word 'caste'.

What exactly is a caste? In particular, do the Untouchables of Hindu society, to whom the Jews of medieval Christendom (as it will be argued) most approximate, form a caste, or were they rather outcastes, who were ejected from the entire caste system?

The answer is that the Untouchables do indeed form part of the caste system. They comprise a great number of castes, of which the 'pariahs', of the Tamil region, are only one; for some reason, the name 'pariah' was adopted by English speakers as representing the whole class of Untouchables.[1] Confusion arises because the Untouchables are excluded not from the castes (*jatis*), but from the *varnas*, the broad categories in which the castes inhere.[2] There are four *varnas*, and Hindu writers frequently state, 'There is no fifth *varna*.' This is meant only to exclude the Untouchables from all honourable categories; it is denied that their castes comprise anything so dignified as a *varna*. The Untouchables, in fact, form an integral part of the caste system. Without their impurity, as Dumont points out, the Brahmins could not remain pure.

Undoubtedly, the Jews in the Middle Ages had certain societal characteristics that at least suggest comparison with the disadvantaged Hindu castes, i.e. the Sudras and the Untouchables, especially the latter. We may collect these points as follows:

1. They had a stigma attached to them, condemning them to a position of dishonour in society. Their official rank in Christendom was that of 'slaves'.

2. The stigma was reinforced by a myth derived from ancient times, and forming part of the central societal myth, explaining their dishonour. In the case of the Jews, the myth placed the Jews as the betrayers of Jesus, while in the Hindu myth, the Sudras (the lowest *varna*) were mythologically derived from the lower limbs of the deity whose dismemberment created humanity (the higher castes being derived from the upper limbs of the same deity).

3. The stigma was reinforced by social separation and distinctive marking. The Jews were segregated in special quarters, and were compelled to wear the yellow badge. The Untouchables too were segregated in special villages, and were recognisable by their garments.

4. Despite their stigma, the Jews formed a necessary element in Christian society. Their condition of degradation served the purpose of continually reminding Christians of the truth of their own religion; for the Jews exhibited God's punishment for their refusal to accept Jesus as Messiah, and also acted as living relics of the Old Testament Judaism out of which Christianity arose and from which it took its validation. Consequently, by the Augustinian enactment, the Jews were not outsiders, but an integral element in Christian society which needed to be preserved. At the time of the Second Coming of Christ, their stigma would be removed, together with their 'blindness'. Indeed, the conversion of the Jews was a necessary condition of the Second Coming. Similarly, the low-caste Hindus formed a necessary element of Hindu society, and the cycle of reincarnation gave them future hope of escaping their stigma. Further, the Jews practised religious rites that were given official

sanction in Christian society as *religio licita*, and therefore as a facet of Christianity itself (the Popes even claimed the right to supervise Jewish worship and to punish Jewish 'heresy', i.e. infringements of the set bounds of Judaism). Similarly, low-caste Hindus had their own forms of worship, including gods peculiar to themselves, which formed part of the general picture of Hindu religion, even though different from the highest form of worship, Brahmanism.

5. The Jewish stigma rendered the Jews available for tasks that were too dishonourable for Christians, yet were necessary for the functioning of the society as a whole. Thus Jews performed the necessary but taboo role of moneylending, thus providing a pool of money which could be confiscated by rulers whenever needed for purposes of war, building or administration. Jews were compelled to perform the disagreeable and guilt-making task of the public executioner. Similarly, the low-caste Hindus performed tasks that were taboo or polluting for the upper castes, such as leather making and lavatory cleaning, and also executing criminals.

6. The stigma attached to the Jews attained a persistent quality that has survived all attempts to remove it by political, legislative and even religious means. Thus, in Spain, after the mass conversions of Jews in the 14th and 15th centuries, the concept of 'purity of blood' (*limpieza de sangre*) arose to invalidate the acquisition of full Christian status and hoped for loss of Jewish status by the converts. Thus the religious concept of the equality of all Christians failed to counter the repugnance associated with low-caste status. Later, in the 19th and 20th centuries, the concept of 'race' arose to invalidate the acquisition by Jews of equal status in Enlightenment society. This persistence of stigma is a very strong indication of the presence of caste, and is paralleled in Hindu society by the persistence of low-caste stigma despite legislation to abolish Untouchable categories.[3] The persistence shows that the stigma has become so embedded in the societal conception of the group concerned that it has become indelibly connected with the group as if it were a natural characteristic.

On the other hand, it must be acknowledged that there are important respects in which Jewish status in Christendom was different from low-caste status in Hinduism.

1. Low-caste Hindus accepted their status, while Jews did not. Jewish status existed only in the eyes of Christians, who defined the Jews in terms of their own religious system. The Jews, however, had their own religious system, in terms of which their status was entirely different, and was not defined in relation to Christianity. While Judaism had a recognised slot in Christianity, Christianity had no slot in the religious system of Judaism. As far as their position in Christian society was concerned, the Jews regarded themselves as having a political relationship to the surrounding community, namely that of exiles, who were suffering an inexplicable level of hostility and oppression. Jews, however, took note of the fact that certain roles were expected of them, and they attempted to build their survival on fulfilling these roles, chiefly that of moneylending (except in Spain and Poland, where they were allowed to enter other professions and did so). Thus Jewish morale remained high, since, on the whole, they did not introject the dishonourable image of them that occupied the Christian mind. Consequently, whenever oppression was relaxed, the result was an outburst of Jewish achievement on the highest professional level; this in turn produced Christian envy and resentment leading to even bitterer oppression than before. This cycle does not apply to the same extent to the course of low-caste emancipation in Hindu society, where relaxation of caste oppression did not lead to startling large-scale changes in the professional activities of the lower castes.

2. Whereas the dishonourable status of low-caste Hindus involved impurity and therefore bans on intermarriage and commensality, it did not involve the accusation of criminality. As long as low-caste Hindus observed the rules of their caste, they were considered good Hindus, and in fact they were mostly pious and observant in their station. Consequently, they were despised but not diabolised. No stories developed accusing them of shocking depravities. The Jews

in Christian society, on the other hand, laboured under a myth accusing them of treachery and murder. This myth was always liable to be elaborated in pathological style, especially when the political situation fostered paranoia, religious frenzy and apocalyptic yearnings. This accounts for the massacres and expulsions of Jews, not paralleled in the treatment of low-caste Hindus, except in individual cases, where a low-caste person was felt to be stepping beyond his caste-bounds (here there is a parallel between Hinduism and Islam, which set bounds to second-class citizens or *dhimmis*; but whether the *dhimmi* system comes under the definition of caste will be considered).

3. It may be doubted whether the term 'caste' can be applied unless the stratification of society has religious sanction and indeed forms part of the religious system as a whole. Here the position of the Jews in Christendom was equivocal; in their own eyes, they were not part of the religious system of Christendom, but in Christian eyes, they were.

4. The Hindu caste system is based on a code of ritual purity, by which social mixing between the castes is regulated. Christendom, on the other hand, had no system of ritual purity.

5. In Christendom, it was possible for a Jew to escape from his disadvantaged position by conversion to Christianity, in which case, in theory, he became the equal of all other Christians. This is not possible in the Hindu caste system, where the status of Brahmin is conferred only by birth (in other castes, some individual exceptions can be made by which upgrading of caste can be achieved, but this does not have the theological significance of conversion to Christianity).

An important writer on the subject of caste is Louis Dumont, author of *Homo Hierarchicus*. He takes issue with other theorists, who have tried to subsume caste under notions of class or estate. He insists that while class is an economic term, and estate a political one, caste is essentially a religious term, arising from a religious concept of hierarchy. Consequently, he takes the view that caste is to be found only in Hinduism, and that in other contexts the term is inappropriate or at most metaphorical and inexact.

In Hindu theology, the castes are immutable and god-given divisions of the whole of mankind (not merely Hindus). The highest caste, the Brahmins, have the status of gods, and the lowest belong to a different breed. There is a certain amount of seepage between the castes, because intermarriage is permitted to some extent between adjacent castes, provided that the man marries a woman of lower caste. Thus in practice, the caste system is not racialist, but a kind of ideal stratification, in which the castes retain their identity despite some laxity of the rules of endogamy. The various castes tend to have characteristic occupations, Brahmins being priests, and others warriors, merchants, artisans, washermen, etc., but this economic division of labour is not the basic rationale of the caste system, for it is infinitely flexible. Rather the choice of occupation for a caste depends on the ritual purity rules attaching to the caste, and the extent to which various occupations entail ritual impurity.

If we accept Dumont's definition, we can see, for example, that the feudal system that determined the social stratification of medieval Christendom was not a system of caste. It was rather a system of estates – nobility, yeomen, serfs and slaves – which had no pretension to religious sanction, since it did not claim to include the whole of mankind, and did not claim the support of any religious myth. There were at times attempts to provide a philosophical justification for it on the ground that it rescued society from chaos, anarchy and mutual warring (an eloquent example is the speech of Ulysses in Shakespeare's *Troilus and Cressida*: 'The heavens themselves, the planets, and this centre/ Observe degree, priority, and place, . . .'), but no proof-texts from Scripture were adduced, and, on the religious plane, all Christians were of equal rank in the eyes of God.[4]

Within the feudal system, the Jews had a rank, namely that of slaves. But the allotment of this rank did not arise from the feudal system itself, but rather from theological considerations, which first relegated the Jews to inferior status, and then looked round the feudal organisation to find a suitable rank for such theologically-disadvantaged persons. Indeed, in the whole medieval world, the Jews were the only group whose status was decided on theological grounds, all others being regarded theologically as equal Christians. It would therefore seem that only the Jews exhibit a similarity to the Hindu caste system. For only the Jews owed their special status in Christian society to Christian considerations.

From the Christian standpoint, the Jews were a part of Christian society that was under a cloud. The disapproval under which the Jews were held was a permanent feature of Christian society, which might be removed in individual cases, but would remain for the bulk of the Jews for the foreseeable future, until the time of the Second Coming of Christ. The disapproval under which the Jews were held produced a stigma that marked them off: yet, unlike heretics, they could not be subjected to threats and violence to force them to come into line with Christian doctrine. The Jews were thus not exactly a caste, for that would imply approval of their mode of worship. They correspond more to the Untouchables of the Hindu culture, who were outside the regular categories of the system of *varnas*, yet not totally repudiated from the overall religious picture (since they were regarded as constituting a fifth, unnamed, *varna*).

The Untouchables are to be distinguished from the Sudras, the lowest of the regular *varnas*. The Untouchables consisted of certain castes considered to be so backward that they could not be admitted to *varna* status, and were therefore Untouchables. Unlike the Sudras, they were regarded with loathing and disgust, and were regarded as incorrigibly unclean.[5] This corresponds to some extent to the feelings of disgust and indignation held by Christians for the Jews, feelings that were at first moral and theological in character, but eventually degenerated into paranoid loathing, when belief in blood libels and the *foetor Judaicus* developed.

Yet the medieval Jews were not regarded, as the Untouchables were, as backward people. On the contrary, their high standard of culture and education was understood, and was indeed made use of by countless Christian administrators, philosophers and scientists, who were only too glad to avail themselves of Jewish help in times of need (only to reject the Jews when help seemed no longer required). Moreover, the Jews were often feared as somehow powerful, having mysterious international contacts, and even being able to harness supernatural powers, while the Untouchables were merely despised as far below the general cultural level. Thus there may appear to be many differences of detail between the position of the Jews and that of the Untouchables. Yet at the time of the Emancipation, even these differences tended to disappear. Through constant Christian oppression, the Jews had sunk, at least outwardly, in cultural level. They were no longer great merchants or great bankers, and they no longer led or participated in current movements of thought in philosophy and science. They had mostly become petty pedlars or dealers in old clothes, since all professional occupations were closed to them. The Enlightenment came much later for the Jews than for other people, and it was not until the late 18th century that the first movements were made towards their emancipation. Their image by this time had much deteriorated, so that even well-wishing liberals regarded them as degenerate and hardly capable of reaching an acceptable level of culture. In fact, the Jews, cut off from Western education, had maintained a very high level of intellectual effort by concentration on their own cultural resources in the Talmud and other rabbinic literature; so that when emancipation eventually came, they astonished even their well-wishers by the speed with which they rose in the professions. They thus confounded the predictions of Enlightenment antisemites such as Voltaire, who never anticipated such phenomena as the rise of Moses Mendelssohn and Salomon Maimon to the highest rank of European philosophy within a few years of their emerging from the Polish *shtetl*.

A typical example of Enlightenment contempt for the Jews is shown by the reaction of the exquisite Henry Adams to the Jewish migration from the Pale of Russia to the United States in the early 20th century. These immigrants seemed to Adams to be barbarous alien hordes, devoid of all culture, but with a lust for money and success that was both loathsome and enviable. Adams writes of himself, 'Not a Polish Jew fresh from Warsaw or Cracow – not a furtive Yacoob or Ysaac still reeking of the Ghetto, snarling a weird Yiddish to the officers of the customs – but had a keener instinct, an intenser energy, and a freer hand than he.' Adams did not know, or wish to know that this 'weird Yiddish' was a language with a longer history than the English language. He did not know that the 'furtive' Jew, who (he wrote) 'makes me creep', brought with him from the 'reeking' Ghetto a cultural tradition in both Yiddish and Hebrew in comparison with which the cultural acquisitions of the patrician Adams were parvenu. He did not in the least consider that these Jews were the victims of persecution, or that the Ghetto with which he taunted them was the symbol of their sufferings. Least of all did he expect that these Jews, or their children, once their thirst for the elementary decencies of life was slaked, would turn to the professions and the arts, would win Nobel prizes for science and literature, and would dominate the New York intellectual scene.

The cultural contempt felt for the Jews on the brink of their emancipation thus shows how far oppression had brought them to the status of pariahs, at least in Gentile eyes. The similarity between the Jews in Christendom and the pariahs in Hindu society thus increased the longer Christian domination lasted, and only decreased with the advent of secular society.

The advantages of viewing the Jews in the light of the Hindu caste system may be seen when one compares the situation of the Jews with that of the Gypsies. Dumont, in a casual remark, shows that he considers the Jews and the Gypsies to be similar minority groups within Western society, both being marginal and subject to contempt. It is surprising that a theorist of such high intelligence did not notice the huge difference between the two groups. The Gypsies have no theological importance within Christian society. They are in no way integrated within the Christian system, except in the trivial sense that they have adopted, in the main, Christian observances and assumptions, while retaining a way of life derived from their original status as a sub-caste of wandering entertainers in Hindu society. There was no Saint Augustine who felt it necessary to work out a theological position to account for and regulate the ranking of the Gypsies within Christian society. The Jews constituted a major problem for Christians, since they were the representatives of the religion from which Christianity took its origin. The persistence of Judaism as a religion commanding the allegiance, fervour and intellect of a formidable community was a phenomenon that challenged Christianity at its roots, keeping open the question whether the Christian defection from Judaism had been justified. The vitality of this question is shown by the fierce competition for converts that took place during the years when Judaism and Christianity competed on equal terms.[6] Even after the political triumph of Christianity and its official backing by the Roman Empire, the rival claims of Judaism continued to be strong, as was shown by the continuing recruitment of converts by Judaism, both from paganism and from the Christian Church itself (a phenomenon that prompted the antisemitic diatribes of St John Chrysostom). Even after Christian decrees punishing conversion to Judaism by the death of both convert and converter, a surprising number of conversions of Christians to Judaism took place.[7]

Having rejected the options of total expulsion or extermination of the Jews, the Church found room for the Jews in Christendom by carefully defining their status as an inferior group. At the same time, the Church forbade intermarriage and commensality with the Jews, though it did not forbid social and commercial intercourse with them altogether. Eventually, Christendom even found an economic niche for the Jews as administrators of the money economy, though this was never given religious sanction, and indeed was both encouraged and denounced in a contradictory way. The Jews were given an essential task to do, and were despised for performing it. There is here a most suggestive (though not complete) parallel to the way Hindu society delegates to its lower castes essential tasks that other castes regard as defiling. The great difference is that the ruling concept in Hindu society is that of purity and impurity, while in Christendom the purity concepts of Judaism had been largely (though not entirely) abandoned. Instead, the basis of contempt was moral; the Jews engaging in usury were regarded as wicked, not unclean (though concepts of uncleanness, always difficult to eradicate from society, eventually reappeared and functioned alongside concepts of wickedness). Morally, the Hindu attitude towards its disadvantaged and despised section of society is much superior to that of Christendom, for the Hindu pariahs are not demonised as hellishly wicked. Hinduism does not suffer from the endemic hypocrisy of Christendom, since to take advantage of ritually impure activities does not entail the moral contradiction of taking advantage of activities believed to be wicked. At root, this difference arises from the different circumstances of pariahdom in Christendom and Hinduism. While there is a case for arguing that there was an element of usurpation in the Hindu caste system (the lower castes being descendants of conquered indigenous peoples, like the Canaanites in Judaism), in Christianity the usurpation element was much stronger. Only by blackening the Jews to the utmost could Christianity uphold its usurpatory claims. Thus while integrating the Jews into its own religious system, it could do so only by perpetuating the myth of Jewish depravity, and this militated against the aim of a stable settlement with Judaism. It was inevitable that anti-Jewish paranoia would eventually push the compromise in the direction of persecution. This was especially so because the blackening of the Jews included a strong element of guilt-shifting, so that persecution of Jews always helped to lift the burden of guilt inherent in Christianity (about benefiting from the death of Jesus, eating his body and blood, benefiting from usury, etc.). The caste status of the Jews was thus unstable compared with that of Hindu lower castes, and was always liable to erupt into violence.

All in all, it is enlightening to regard the position of the Jews in Christendom as that of a caste. We may ask what particular rung of the Hindu caste system is most reminiscent of the Jewish position in Christendom. The answer seems to be that of the Untouchables, who were regarded as unclean even by the Sudras. It seems that while the Sudras derived from the indigenous population conquered by the Aryans, and therefore did not belong to the three Aryan categories of the 'twice-born', i.e. initiates in mystery rites, the Untouchables represented an even earlier population, despised and segregated even before the Aryan invasion. This reminds us of the position of the Jews in, say, Norman England, where the indigenous conquered Saxon population was largely assigned to menial tasks, yet the Jews were far lower even than the Saxons in prestige, not indeed because they represented an earlier indigenous population, but because they were the remnants of the old religion conquered by Christians, Normans and Saxons alike.

While the Sudras could achieve ritual purity, when required, by the appropriate washings, the Untouchables were permanently unclean. Higher castes had to avoid not only touching them, but even coming within a specified distance of them, graduated according to the holiness of the caste concerned, though these distance-rules were observed more rigorously in the pious South, where the preponderance of Sudras in the population increased the anxiety to demonstrate non-Untouchable status. The Untouchables were segregated into villages which they were not permitted to leave, just as the Jews in Norman England were segregated into quarters of certain specified cities. The Untouchables were employed in trades which were regarded as defiling, such as leather-working, so that their degraded status was in fact useful to Hindu society as a whole, which used their leather goods without scruple, except in the highest castes. Similarly, the Jews were employed in the taboo trade of moneylending, which was so useful indeed that medieval society could not function without it, though the Jews were unmercifully castigated and periodically punished for their wickedness in pursuing the profession into which they had been forced. It is an interesting instance of contrast in values that in Hinduism, moneylending on interest was regarded as an honourable profession, the perquisite of the third highest *varna*, the Vaisyas.

Though employed in useful trades within Hindu society, the Untouchables were treated with total contempt and loathing, being subject to constant beatings if they strayed, or were believed to have strayed, from their strict rules of confinement. But they were not entirely excluded from religious consolation. Like the Sudras, whose status was that of slaves, they could hope for promotion to higher caste-status in a future life (though certain texts suggest that such promotion was rare in the case of Untouchables). Here the Untouchables were better off than the Jews in Christendom (at least in Christian eyes). Christians believed that the Jews were destined to something even worse than exclusion from the Wheel of Life, eternal torment in Hell. Though it was believed that the Jews living at the time of the Second Coming would be saved from Hell by conversion, this did not work retroactively. All the Jews who had suffered under Christian rule would find even worse torments, eternally prolonged, after death.

The similarity between Jews and Untouchables has been obscured by the contrast in image between the two groups. Jews in Christendom are thought of as rich and even powerful, while Untouchables have an unequivocal image of wretchedness. Yet this contrast is misleading. The appearance of Jewish prosperity was a fleeting mirage, and was counterbalanced by suffering far greater than any undergone by the Untouchables, whose misery was at least stable and relatively free from mass violence.

Under the influence of Gandhi, the legal position of the Untouchables in India was altered, in the sense that they were to be regarded as a regular *varna*. This, as has been said by Dumont and others, is a reform of the *varna* system, not of the caste system, which remains fully in place. Religiously, the aim was to remove the impurity-stigma from the Untouchables, and enable them to enter temples, from which they had been excluded. Politically, the aim was to give them the vote and remove disabilities preventing them from taking part in social and political life. In practice, the social disabilities of the Untouchables remain. Intermarriage and commensality with them remains impossible even for Sudras. As Indian society moves slowly towards secularism, these disabilities will gradually be removed. At present, it is only the occasional gifted Untouchable (such as top cricketers) who can move freely in Indian society. Whenever a concerted effort is made by Untouchables to assert their legal rights, the response is often violent, especially as progress has led, as elsewhere, to an intensification of fundamentalism and fanaticism in reaction.[8]

This Indian situation throws much light on the antisemitism encountered by the Jews in the modern world. Once a group has acquired a stigma, making it into an Untouchable caste, the process of removing such a stigma is slow and punctuated by violence. The recognition of the caste-stigma attached to the Jews because of the Jewish–Christian religious conflict has been hampered by recent ideas of structuralism, which encourage a synchronic rather than a diachronic approach to societal phenomena. The position of the Jews in Western society cannot be understood, any more than that of the Untouchables in India, without consideration of the long history behind it, and especially of the religious ideas of which it is the outcome. Only when these religious factors are confronted will it be possible for modern secularists, in whom religious traces lie dormant and unrecognised and therefore all the more potent, to understand why antisemitism is still alive.[9]

CHAPTER 16

SIN-EATERS AND OTHERS

We have not found in the Untouchables of Hinduism a feature that is prominent in the role of the Jews in Christendom, the transfer of the guilt involved in a central salvific act of sacrifice. The Untouchables are not blamed for some primal crime which also functions as a means of salvation. Such a primal sacrifice does indeed exist in Hinduism, since the human race and the formation of the *varnas* is traced to the sacrifice by dismemberment of a deity. Sacrifice of animals plays a central role in the ritual of the Vedas, and it has the function of renewing the primal act of creation. The Hinduism which emerged from this early form of the religion eschewed or sublimated animal sacrifice, substituting vegetable sacrifice, which remained the main privilege and service to society of the Brahmins. But although guilt about blood-shedding changed the format of the sacrifices, it does not seem to have prompted a procedure of guilt-shifting. The sacrificing Brahmin of the Vedas is doing nothing shameful or horrifying, but performing a sacred task associated with the process of creation itself. It is not necessary, therefore (any more than with the sacrifice-glorification of the Aztecs) to find some scapegoat figure on which to transfer the guilt of blood-shedding.

Nor were the Untouchables of Hinduism blamed, like the Jews, for malfunctionings in society at large. Whereas the Jews were blamed for natural disasters, such as the Black Death, and for other people's crimes, such as the murder of children, or for political or economic setbacks, such as the victories of Islam or the French defeat in the Franco-Prussian War, there does not seem to be any tendency in

189

Hinduism to blame the Untouchables for things that go wrong. The Untouchables are despised too much for this. They are not considered to have any noticeable effect on anything that happens in the greater world. The Jews, on the other hand, are constantly suspected of plotting and achieving great, if evil, things. However downtrodden they may appear, there is the unquenchable belief that the Jews have great power which they are secretly employing in dark manoeuvres.

The reason for this is that the Jews play a prominent role in the central sacrificial Christian myth as betrayers and murderers of the Incarnate God. This means that however much they may be demoted into a caste of despised slaves, they can never be dismissed as insignificant. The ideal outcome, as far as Christians were concerned, would have been the acceptance by Jews of their sacrificial role and their consequent demotion in a spirit of repentance. The Christian legend that embodies this hope is that of the Wandering Jew. This figure, in some versions of the legend, even attains a certain dignity. Here is the Jew who fully accepts his destined role in history: to kill Christ[1] and then work out his penance without complaint. There is some contradiction between the hope expressed in this legend and the official Christian attitude towards Jewish converts to Christianity. If the Wandering Jew, as the legend has it, was a true penitent who accepted Jesus as God, why does he have to continue wandering and suffering? As a Jewish convert to Christianity, he ought, in theory, to find peace and equality in the bosom of the Church. In practice, the Church was able to assimilate only a very limited number of Jews. When Jewish converts joined in large numbers, as in Spain, they did not disappear into the Christian masses, but remained Jews, people of 'impure blood' in the eyes of Christians, continuing the Jewish function as blame-bearers, all the more hated for their Christian disguise. The Jews being unassimilable, the Christian fantasy was that, while remaining distinct, they would function as conscious, repentant witnesses to the truth of the Christian myth, accepting their role in it as the killers of Christ.

Something similar to this fancied role of the Jews as sin-bearers for Christendom can be seen in the phenomenon of the 'sin-eaters' in certain Christian communities. Some poor families managed to survive economically by becoming the bearers of sin for their village communities. This custom, or institution, was once widespread in England, Scotland, Bavaria and in immigrant communities of America. When a person in the village died, the sin-eater and his family would go to the house of death and sit on stools outside. They would be brought food, of which they would eat some immediately, and they would also be given money. It was believed that by eating the food, the sin-eater was assuming the sins of the dead person; he was therefore exchanging his hopes of eternal bliss for survival in this world. In later times, this became merely a custom, and was perhaps not taken literally, but the earlier form of the rite shows greater seriousness. The sin-eater was actually taken into the death-chamber, and a piece of bread having been placed on the corpse by a relative was handed to the sin-eater who ate it in the presence of the dead. He was then handed his fee and at once hustled and thrust out of the house amid execrations and a shower of sticks, cinders or other missiles.

This transfer of guilt obviously owes something to the scapegoat in Leviticus 16:21–22. But the scapegoat was not given a fee. A deeper analogy may be drawn between the 'sin-eater' and Judas Iscariot, who was given a fee for his service of treachery, which was also a deed of salvation (though the fee was displaced to the Jewish priests from the real beneficiaries, the recipients of salvation). There is evidence that in the heyday of the custom, the 'sin-eater' family was ostracised by the rest of the village. There could hardly be a better illustration of the role of the Jews in Christendom; ostracised and despised, they yet performed an indispensable role for the salvation of the community. Yet even the sin-eaters do not quite illustrate the poignancy of the Jewish role, for while the sin-eaters absorb the everyday sins of the village population, the Jews absorb the greatest conceivable sin (without which salvation could not be attained), the murder of God; and in medieval times, through the blood libel, the Jews even absorbed the more everyday guilt of the eating of God, the central and regular Christian sacrament.

A nearer parallel, in some ways, can be found in the Indian tribe, the Mapuches, who live in their reservation at Lago Budi in southern Chile. This tribe was investigated by the explorer and anthropologist Patrick Tierney, who described their customs in his *The Highest Altar*.

The Mapuches have retained their traditions partly because of their proud martial history. They were the only Indian tribe to achieve an independent treaty with the Spanish, who had failed to conquer them in battle.

The Mapuche tribe has performed ritual sacrifices in very recent times, and it was possible for Tierney to track down and interview an actual performer of human sacrifice, a woman sorceress, or *machi*, called Juana Namancura. She was evasive in her replies, but Tierney confirmed from witnesses that she had taken an important part in the sacrifice of a boy, José Luís Painecur, in 1960, on the occasion of a tidal wave that threatened the tribe. Tierney also ascertained that the Mapuche foundation myth involved the sacrifice by a Mapuche equivalent of Noah, together with his wife, of their young son, whereby a saving miracle occurred, the rising of the mountain on which they stood above the level of the flood. 'Humanity was saved by human sacrifice.'

The area is subject to earthquakes which are then followed by a tidal wave of great ferocity. In 1960 the earthquake was of unprecedented force, and was accompanied by the eruption of a dozen volcanoes. The ocean pulled back exposing miles of sea bed, and then, after a terrifying silence, roared inland carrying everything in its wake. The tribal chief, in conjunction with Juana Namancura, ordered a man called José Vargas to take his grandson José Luís Painecur to a spot called Cerro Mesa, a hill near the ocean with a flat top like an altar, the scene of ancient ceremonies. There the sacrifice was performed. The boy's arms and legs were cut off with knives by participants who handed the portions to the chief Trafinado, who waved them and threw them ceremonially into the sea. Juana collected the blood in a vessel which she sprinkled, with a branch, into the sea. The boy's heart and intestines were cut out and thrown into the sea. The torso was then stuck in the sea bed like a stake. This brutal form of sacrifice (differing from the usual throat-cutting method) was prescribed for such an emergency; the portions of the boy's body were being fed to the monster serpent Cai Cai Filu who had come out of the depths. Juana sang a song dedicating the sacrifice to the ocean. 'Take this boy now,/ We are helping you,/ We are paying you with this boy./ We are all orphans./ Why do you punish us, God?'

The rite concluded with a dance of naked armed men, under the direction of Juana, symbolising defiance of the monster. When arrested later by the Chilean police, Juana at first said, 'Great occasions need great remedies,' but later denied everything and was released after a few months.

The most interesting thing from the standpoint of this book is the ambivalent attitude of the Mapuches towards the sorceress Juana. On the one hand, she was hated and despised. Every time anything went wrong, from a crop failure to a family illness, the blame was attributed to her and her sorcery. No one spoke of her except in opprobrious, contemptuous terms. When finally Tierney found someone willing to give a detailed account of Juana's role in the sacrifice of José Luís Painecur, her action was condemned. Yet every time there was a tribal ceremony, she was seated in a place of honour. And at a time of extreme emergency, when the existence of the tribe was threatened, her orders and her superintendence of the sacrifice were obeyed without question at the time, however much condemned later.

There is here a strong parallel to the position of the Jews in Christian society, except that no acknowledgment of a debt of gratitude to the Jews for their (alleged) performance of the sacrifice is allowed even on ceremonial occasions. At the most, the Jews are spared from the extermination allotted to other heretics, and are promised a future reward in the Last Days. The prolongation of the life of the Wandering Jew (or *der ewige Jude* – the German term highlights the life-extension) reminds us of Cain, the murderer of Abel, who was given a sign to preserve him from the death-punishment. The Jews had to be preserved, not merely for the reasons of 'witness' adduced by Augustine, but because they were indispensable *dramatis personae* in the story of salvation, and were required to repeat their role eternally, not only in dramatic form in the Passion Plays, but also in the fantasised episodes of the blood libel.

It is not without interest that the Mapuche Indians, who resisted conversion to Christianity, did nevertheless incorporate one element of Christianity into their own religion. The chief volcano in their territory was believed to contain a tribe of evil spirits. After contact with Christianity, the Mapuches renamed these demons, 'the Jews'.

Patrick Tierney, who investigated the Mapuches so thoroughly, living with them and taking part in some of their ceremonies, broadened his research into South American rites of human sacrifice generally. He risked his life, not only in dangerous ascents of high mountains to discover startling evidence of Inca child-sacrifice, but also in investigating modern-day practice of human sacrifice procured mainly by drug dealers and mine owners to promote the success of their enterprises. He recorded, with a concealed tape-recorder, conversations with the notorious Maximo Coa, a *shaman* who specialised in human sacrifices, especially of women. This man turned out to be an original theologian, who saw clearly the connections between his own practices and the human-sacrificial doctrine of Christianity, though his affinities and traditional links were with the Incas and their sacrificial mountain worship. His own status was similar to that of Juana: he was a figure who excited both awe and hatred. Tierney calls him a 'Sacred Executioner'.[2]

So far we have found individual figures who absorb the guilt of performing human sacrifice, yet also, in recognition of their service to the community, acquire a dubious status of honour. Only in the case of the Jews, however, was this role attributed not to an individual, but to a whole community, who were consequently relegated to the status of a pariah class, as opposed to that of a banned and ostracised individual. The uniqueness of the hatred allotted to the Jews (i.e. antisemitism) is that it combines two elements found in abundance but in separation elsewhere: the stigma belonging to a pariah class, and the ritual hatred directed at the performer of the sacrifice.

There are many different rationales for the formation of a class of pariahs or untouchables. The Jews do share with other pariah classes the rationale of usurpation: the stigma of being a defeated and superseded group. But the usurpation myth in the case of the Jews differs from that of other pariah classes, in being of the Sacred Executioner type, a rationale of subjection arising from the salvation-sacrificial nature of the usurping religion.

What we can learn from other pariah groups, however, in the investigation of antisemitism, is the persistent power of *stigma*, once acquired by a class of people. If we see how stigma operates in other pariah groups, we shall cease to be surprised about the persistence of antisemitism in the post-Christian era, and we shall not find it necessary to explain antisemitism in the modern world chiefly in terms of modern factors. The religious factors of the Middle Ages were amply sufficient to set up a stigma which no amount of scientific enlightenment was able to remove – indeed, as argued earlier, the removal of the Jews' civil disabilities only made resentment against them greater. The cure of antisemitism will then be seen not in combating the stigma in itself on rational grounds, a largely ineffectual proceeding, but by laying bare the history of its origin, especially its religious roots.

An excellent example of the sheer persistence of societal stigma when attached to a group is the Japanese group of untouchables known as *baraku*. This illustrates the power of stigma even when detached from all other considerations, such as appearance, speech, race, age or disability. The *baraku* look and speak like any other Japanese, yet they are despised as the lowest of Japanese society. They are discriminated against in employment, segregated in special neighbourhoods, and barred from social intercourse and marriage. Yet the remarkable thing is that the *baraku* were created as a class by a purely arbitrary and bureaucratic decision during the Edo period of the 17th century. Some social planners of this period theorised that a class of untouchables was needed in order to bring content and happiness to the lowest rungs of the Japanese feudal system, the traders and shopkeepers – so that they could feel superior to somebody. Certain areas were set up in the larger cities into which arbitrarily chosen families were herded and designated as *baraku*. They were confined to leather work, like the Indian Untouchables, and were officially designated as *eta* ('dirty'), so a purity aspect was introduced. In time, the unfortunate *baraku* did indeed sink in moral and cultural level, as one might expect, and were the least educated elements in Japanese society. Yet with the arrival of Westernisation after the Second World War, government attempts were made to emancipate the *baraku* and improve their cultural standards, with considerable success, for they have now entered the professions in great numbers, despite continuing discrimination by employers (now using computer networks to compile lists to enable them to weed out undesirable applicants). The prejudice against them, however, remains as high as ever, and they remain unmarriageable and socially taboo. They still live in segregated neighbourhoods, and those who have tried to move have met with hostility.[3]

The *baraku*, as an arbitrarily created class, should not be confused with another pariah group in Japanese society, the Ainu, a conquered people with distinctive physical characteristics that mark them out from the main Japanese population. The stigma attached to the Ainu can be accounted for on grounds of mere xenophobia, the fear of the 'other', which is so inadequate to explain a religiously-based prejudice such as antisemitism. The pariah status of the *baraku* is at the opposite extreme, a stigma based on no cultural, physical or even religious consideration, illustrating the sheer power of stigma in itself. The only hope of removing the stigma of the *baraku*, therefore, is education in the history of the stigma itself. If Japanese people became better acquainted with how the *baraku* caste originated, there would be some chance of shaking this irrational prejudice.

A bizarre example of the persistence of stigma, even when fortuitously transferred, can be found in the history of antisemitism itself. The rag-pickers, or *fripiers*, of Paris were at one time exclusively Jewish, and formed a despised group. After the expulsion of the Jews from France in 1394, employment as rag-pickers fell into the hands of non-Jews, all practising Catholics. These Catholic rag-pickers, however, were given the nickname of 'les juifs', their guild was called 'the Synagogue', and they were treated with much the same contempt and social ostracism as their Jewish forerunners. The profession of rag-picking had acquired the Jewish stigma, and anyone employed in it became an honorary Jew. When the *fripiers* were taunted, in 1652, by a young man called Jean Bourgeois, as 'gentlemen of the synagogue', they gave him a beating. He then took successful legal action against them, which infuriated them so much that they ambushed and murdered him. This led to an antisemitic campaign, in which pamphlets were written to denounce the atrocities of 'the Jews'. One of these pamphlets thundered: 'There is no one who does not know that the Jews are the opprobrium of all nations and have been so for sixteen hundred years and more.' Another pamphlet satirically put a defence in the mouth of 'the Jews': 'Of what are we guilty? Moses in his day sacrificed animals, and we have sacrificed a man. Is it not said in the same book that our predecessors had the power to sacrifice Jesus Christ, their King and ours? Why do we not have the power to put a man to death?' Yet there is no question that the *fripiers* were not Jews, but Catholics of unimpeachable descent, organised in a guild dating back to the 14th century – set up, in fact, when the Jews were expelled and their trade handed over to Christians. Such is the power of stigma.[4]

There is no stigma more persistent than that of a pariah caste, because it becomes entrenched in society in which every class is seeking prestige and superiority. The upper classes jealously preserve their status, while the lower classes are even more anxious to seize some evidence that there are some still lower than themselves. This accounts, for example, for the dismaying phenomenon of black antisemitism in America, despite the fact that the Jewish record of support for emancipation of the blacks has been exemplary. Thus to combat antisemitism, it is not enough even to uncover its historical origins, though that is the main and basic task. There is also the problem of combating the problem of snobbery, which is based on lack of self-respect, and which uses all possible societal data to prop up a sense of occupying a position of dignity in society.

It would be a mistake, however, to concentrate on snobbery, or sense of class inferiority, as the *main* cause of antisemitism, as some theorists have done. One still has to ask why it is the Jews who have been the focus of such contempt that even the unfounded suspicion of being a Jew, or having remote associations with Jews, has been enough to rouse contempt. This brings us back always to the historical circumstances which saddled the Jews with such a burden of contempt and hatred. These lie in the religious conflict between Christianity and Judaism, the seed-bed of the baleful Christian usurpation myth which branded the Jews as Christ-killers.

CHAPTER 17

CONCLUSION:
THE HOLOCAUST WAS NO MYSTERY

The New Testament set up the Jews as an accursed people, destined for extraordinary punishment. Already within the New Testament writings, the destruction of the Temple is regarded as a fulfilment of this curse, and later the exile of the Jews from their land (which in fact did not take place until the Arab conquest in the 7th century) was antedated and regarded as further fulfilment of the curse. It was not the New Testament itself, however, that turned the Jews into a pariah people, though it set the scene and laid down all the conditions for this development. The Jews became a pariah people as a result of the triumph of Christianity in the Roman Empire, after the advent of Constantine, becoming for the first time a subject people in a Christian empire.

Even then it took a long time for the Jews to become a pariah group within Christian society. Despite the continual hostile preaching of Christian teachers at every level[1], over a period of centuries, the Jews retained a human and even dignified image in the eyes of the pagan-minded populace. Finally, the propaganda took effect. The 11th century can be designated as the turning-point, when the Jews began to be demonised on a wide societal scale. They became an ostracised group, banned from social intercourse, intermarriage, and every honourable profession. As has been argued, the closest analogy to their position is that of the Untouchables in Hinduism, who, however, were far better off, in that they were not saddled with the guilt of deicide, and were not demonised, or subjected to the kind of violent persecution suffered by the Jews in Christendom.

The Middle Ages continued longest for the Jews in Czarist Russia, where they continued to live in medieval conditions until the 19th century, when the haven of the democratic United States of America opened up for many of them, who fled from the Pale and the pogroms in search of freedom (to meet with the grimacing distaste of such as Henry Adams). The continuity between medieval pariahdom and modern antisemitism can be seen quite plainly in Russia, where the composition of the spurious *Protocols of the Elders of Zion* took place, the standby and bible of modern antisemitism. But the greatest outbreak of antisemitism took place not in Russia, but in Germany, where the continuity is not quite so obvious, and has therefore been denied by all those concerned to detach antisemitism from its Christian antecedents. In Germany, the Jews were not huddled into ghettos, but were represented in the highest professions as judges, professors, scientists, doctors, writers, critics, statesmen. They exulted in their freedom and gloried in their German patriotism. It was here that they were rounded up, sent off into Eastern camps, and done to death in circumstances reminiscent of medieval pictures of Hell, with every accompaniment that bitter hatred could devise of humiliation, starvation and torture.

To blame the Germans exclusively for this is a way of avoiding responsibility by other Christians. It is true that Germany bears the disgrace of the worst persecution of all, and this is a continuation of the peculiarly vicious tinge of German persecution of Jews in medieval times. It was in Germany that the first of the massacres associated with the Crusades took place. In Germany, the Passion Plays had a particularly sadistic edge, and the portrayal of Jews in art and caricature had a brutal, obscene relish. Yet this is only a German gloss on a universal Christian campaign of hate.

The flourishing of German Jewry, in the illusory 'German–Jewish symbiosis' described with irony and sorrow by Gershom Scholem, has served to distract attention from the historical continuity of antisemitism. Causes have been adduced that belong to the modern era, whereas in fact Nazi persecution and antisemitic propaganda was a relapse into medieval thinking and behaviour, prompted by resentment of the Jewish attempt to take advantage of Enlightenment promises and step out of their medieval role as pariahs.

It has been pointed out[2] that the Nazi measures curtailing the rights of the Jews as democratic citizens were in all respects echoes of medieval ordinances. Further, the actual propaganda used to vilify the Jews, including the blood libel, was taken directly from medieval literature, and from the antisemitic diatribes of Luther.

In view of this continuity, it seems necessary to say that there was no mystery about the Holocaust. If a people has been subjected to constant vilification and demonisation over a period of centuries, so that a popular loathing has been instilled so deeply as to operate like an instinct, it is no surprise that eventually a movement will arise that has as its aim the extermination of this alleged pest and enemy of humanity. If a nation has suffered humiliating defeat in a great war, and is also suffering economic hardship, it is not in the least surprising that a scapegoat will be found in an unarmed minority group that, in the minds of the people, still bears pariah status deriving from profound religious salvation-bringing conceptions, or that a political movement capitalising on national distress will fail to utilise such a dynamic unifying political weapon as the loathing and distrust of the Jews.

In relation to the Nazi 'Final Solution', it is necessary to raise a matter that, in a sense, runs counter to the general thrust of the present book. I have stressed the fact that the Jews were a necessary element in the Christian religious economy of the Middle Ages, and that this explains the preservation of the Jews from the fate suffered by the Albigenses and other heretics. St Bernard of Clairvaux is the leading example of this Christian concern to save the Jews from annihilation; important here was not only the 'witness' borne by the Jews, but also the belief that the Second Coming could not take place without their conversion. It was because of this belief in the need for Jewish survival that the Jews became a caste in Christendom – a pariah caste, to be sure, but one that was needed, like the Untouchables of Hinduism, to complete the religious spectrum.

Hitler's decision to annihilate the Jews altogether may thus be seen as a departure from the traditional Christian policy towards the Jews. Yet in fact it was not a complete departure, for the scenario of 'the Final Solution' was also present in Christianity. It is found in the millenarian movements that arose from time to time, and which focused on the concept of 'the Antichrist', based chiefly on the exegesis of II Thessalonians 2:3–12. This doctrine receives its earliest exegetical expression in the church Fathers (Irenaeus, Hippolytus, Lactantius). The Pauline passage was widely interpreted to mean that at the end of days a Jewish Antichrist would arise, who would be regarded by the Jews as the Messiah, and who would lead a powerful Jewish army against the forces of Christianity which would be led by Christ himself. It was also believed that the result of this conflict would be the total annihilation of the Jews, men, women and children, by the Christian forces.

This scenario contradicts the more usual scenario that the Jews would be converted to Christianity at the time of the Second Coming. Yet, in one way, the two scenarios agreed: that Jews would cease to be necessary at the time of the End. They would disappear, either as converts, or as victims of annihilation. The existence of the Jews as a pariah caste in Christendom was necessary in ordinary times; but in the Last Days, the Church Triumphant would have no further need of the Jews.

Thus Hitler did have a model in one strand of Christian tradition for his conception of the Final Solution. Indeed, the millenarian tradition was particularly strong in Germany, where Hitler's ringing phrase 'the Thousand-year Reich' had a millenarian resonance, derived ultimately from the New Testament (Rev. 20:4–6), but recalling also the movement of the Anabaptists led by Thomas Münzer, who was executed in 1525 at Frankenhausen, and later leaders, Johann Matthiesen and Johann Bockholdt. The idea of a populist movement inspired by millenarianism, and including the hope of ridding the world finally of the Jews, was by no means invented by Hitler, though he developed his own secular version of it.[3]

Millenarianism was never fully acceptable in official Christian circles (despite its respectable antecedents in the New Testament and the church Fathers) because it tended to be associated with popular demands for social justice, and sometimes identified the Antichrist with the Pope, instead of with the Jews. Official Christianity therefore opted for the more peaceful scenario in relation to the Jews: they would eventually be converted, but would meanwhile function as a necessary element in Christian society, i.e. as a pariah caste. Hatred built up against the Jews in their pariah function (unstable as this was compared with the settled status of the Untouchables in Hinduism) and this was the chief condition for the Holocaust. But the violent fantasies associated with millenarianism also played a part, and contribute to make the Holocaust even less of a mystery.

A number of factors have combined to prevent the obviousness of the antecedents of the Holocaust from being widely accepted. Most Jewish publicists and scholars have shrunk from attributing the Holocaust to Christian teaching and societal arrangements. Bernard Levin, for example, writes at intervals about the Holocaust in *The Times*, and his message is always the same: the Holocaust is an unfathomable mystery. At a higher level, Jewish thinkers such as Elie Wiesel and Emil Fackenheim have also made a mystery of the Holocaust, assigning as its cause some deep element of Evil in the Universe. Fackenheim and others have even called for a modification of the theology of Judaism, giving greater metaphysical status to the existence of Evil. This has been welcomed by Christian theologians, who see here a turning by Jews towards the theology of the Cross. Some Christian theologians, in their eagerness for Christian–Jewish rapprochement, have seen the sufferings of the Jews in the Holocaust as echoing the Crucifixion, and some statements of Elie Wiesel seem to support this interpretation. It was only a step from this to see the Holocaust as not a specifically Jewish experience, but as also part of the history and mission of Christianity. Some Christians, especially those of Jewish origin, but also including some who, despite general Christian indifference, attempted to support the Jews, died in the death camps. The death of these Christians, most of whom died as Jews not as Christians, was held to support the claim to Christian participation as victims in the Holocaust. In this spirit, a group of Carmelite nuns attempted to set up a convent on the site of Auschwitz, and were surprised to encounter Jewish opposition, which however nobody explained as deriving from the Jewish conviction that the Holocaust was an outcome of Christian teaching, rather than a proof of its truth.

The Holocaust is indeed part of the history of Christianity, but not in the sense intended by those Christians who seek to appropriate the Holocaust for Christian theology. The Holocaust is the greatest crisis that Christianity has ever faced, far greater, for example, than the Reformation.[4] The Christian response to the Holocaust will decide the future of Christianity, or whether it has a future. Many Christians are aware of this, and are reformulating the doctrines of Christianity, especially those of Christology, in the light of the appalling results of past doctrines. But there is still very little understanding of the role of the New Testament and the Early Fathers in the development of the demonisation of the Jews. Some Christian writers (for example, Rosemary Ruether, John Gager, and Jack Sanders) do acknowledge now that the Gospels are antisemitic. John Gager, together with Krister Stendahl, Lloyd Gaston and others, while fully accepting the antisemitism of the Gospels, tries to find a philosemitic enclave in the writings of Paul, with little success. The fashionable escape from the antisemitic vituperation of the Gospels is to attribute it to 'intra-Jewish rivalry' – one more attempt to blame antisemitism on the Jews! If the reformulation of Christian doctrine is left to a tiny minority of scholars, and has no effect on the Christian canon, it is hardly likely to produce much impact on the Church as a whole, especially as the vast majority of Christians (in South America and Eastern Europe, for example) are still untouched by the modern critical approach.[5]

The Roman Catholic Church has made valiant efforts since Vatican Council II to reform its teaching and liturgy, but unfortunately without accepting responsibility for the past. All the oppression of the Jews in the Middle Ages was due to a 'popular misunderstanding'.[6] One may ask why, in that case, so many prominent Christian churchmen, some of them canonised as saints, promoted the oppression. One is impelled to point out, further, that a religion must be judged by its moral effects. As Jesus himself said, 'You shall know them by their fruits.' If a religion, after teaching the people assiduously for centuries, has the Holocaust as its end-product, it is too easy to blame the matter on the unlettered masses.[7]

Christian antisemitism is not the only kind there is, but it is the kind that produced the Holocaust. None of the other kinds (Greek, Roman, Gnostic, Muslim) reduced the Jews to pariah status or invested them with the same stigma and loathing, setting them up for outbursts of popular or governmental violence. The level of Christian anti-Jewish propaganda, its endorsement in sacred texts, and the length of time over which it was disseminated, have no parallel. Given this history, it is ludicrous to profess amazement at what happened. Only a resolute decision to ignore history can account for such amazement; and unfortunately recent trends in 'theory' encourage the suppression of history.

Explanations of antisemitism are legion, but they can be regarded as hovering between two poles. On the one hand, antisemitism can be regarded as a unique and mysterious phenomenon, for which no rational explanation can be advanced. In this view, all attempts to find causes in either contemporary or historical factors can at the most provide only incomplete explanations; in particular the extraordinary persistence of antisemitism in all kinds of diverse historical and geographical circumstances remains inexplicable. This view of antisemitism as a mystery can be held by secularists, such as Bernard Levin, but is more commonly held in support of some religious position, sometimes Christian, but also sometimes Jewish.

At the other extreme is the view that antisemitism is wholly explicable in terms of proximate causes. On this view, each generation has its own antisemitism, and it is a mistake to try to connect all these antisemitisms into a continuous historical chain; in fact, there is no such thing as antisemitism as a historical phenomenon spanning the centuries. Thus events in the Middle Ages are totally irrelevant to antisemitic manifestations in the 20th century. Antisemitism is basically a form of xenophobia, a reaction to 'the other', or those considered not to belong. Since the Jews have in some way (usually explained in terms of Jewish shortcomings, e.g. 'exclusiveness') remained strangers in society for longer than anyone else, they have encountered more varieties of xenophobia than others, but these varieties must be treated piecemeal, not linked in an inadmissibly metaphysical way. The study of antisemitism consists of the separate study of generational antisemitisms, each analysed in relation to the sociological circumstances of its day.[8]

Alternatively, the view of antisemitism as basically xenophobia may express itself in terms of the study of 'stereotypes'. Here the assumption is that just as other alleged national characteristics express antagonism of the in-group towards adjacent but alien cultures

(Irishman: stupid; Scotsman: mean; Frenchman: lecherous, etc.), so alleged Jewish characteristics form a stereotype arising from mere unfamiliarity and non-identification. This theory is not wrong as far as it goes; certainly one component in antisemitism is xenophobia or reaction to the unfamiliar. But to put this forward as the complete answer to the problem is superficial, because it does not explain why the Jew, in Christian society, always remains the stranger, however much he may attempt to assimilate, even to the extent of becoming a Christian.

My own standpoint, expressed in this book, rejects both the above standpoints. Antisemitism is not either unique or mysterious, because it embodies elements that are all found elsewhere, though not in combination. A group, historically distinct, playing a despised yet necessary role in a larger society, which prescribes its status through religious texts – all this is by no means unique, for the same character-isation can be made of the Untouchables of Hinduism. A group that has claims to historical priority, and therefore has to be deprived of dignity in the interests of a usurping majority – this is even commoner, as is the attachment of a usurpation myth to such a depressed minority to explain and excuse its supersession. The particular myth attached to the Jews for usurpation purposes is again not at all unique. It is the myth of the Sacred Executioner, the dark figure saddled with the guilt of the divine sacrifice, and this role appears in the ritual and mythology of many cultures, wherever guilt is felt about a central rite of sacrifice. What is unique, however, is the application of this myth for the purposes of usurpation and the creation of a pariah caste.

While admitting the affinity of antisemitism to many other societal manifestations in other cultures, I reject the second extreme of explaining antisemitism by local sociological factors, different in dif-ferent societies, so that the unity of antisemitism as a historical phenomenon is destroyed. This is a superficial approach that atomises the historical record and fails to consider antisemitism as a phenom-enon spanning many centuries. Such an approach offers no hope of any fundamental solution to the problem of antisemitism, because it leaves the problem as a hydra whose heads may be chopped off one by one, but continually grows new heads. While I agree that there are several kinds of antisemitism, I urge that Christian antisemitism is by far the most significant in its historical results, including the Holocaust. While Islamic antisemitism is by no means unimportant, and has grown more significant in recent years because of the advent of Israel, it does not have a Holocaust on its conscience. Moreover, it does not offer itself for solution in the same way as Christian antisemitism, because fundamentalist belief has hardly yet felt the shock of modernism in Islam, and critical approaches are essential for the solution of what is at heart a religious problem.

Christianity does offer some hope of a solution, because it has entered the post-fundamentalist phase. It is possible, therefore, to approach the analysis of Christian religious texts in a scientific spirit, and to expose their sacrificial content. Despite 200 years of New Testament non-fundamentalist criticism, this task has hardly begun, because scholars, however fearless in dissecting texts and assigning them to various documents, still balk at facing their core of savagery. The anthropological analysis of the New Testament is the indispensable prologue to the understanding of antisemitism.

The historical circumstances in which the split took place between Judaism and Christianity are also important in explaining how Christianity came to demonise the Jews. The need of Gentile Christianity, converted by Paul to a non-political other-worldly religion of salvation, was to cut its ties with Judaism and so display itself to the Romans as unconnected with Jewish nationalism and strivings for independence. Consequently, the role of the enemy (still attached by Jewish Christianity to the Romans) was transferred to the Jews, but in an immeasurably enhanced form, since the enemy was no longer political, but cosmic, aiding Satan in his opposition to the divine scheme of salvation. Even more eerie was the legerdemain by which the very efforts of the Jews and Satan to prevent salvation were instrumental in bringing it about. The total effect of the fusion between sacrificial salvation-religion and political self-exculpation was to turn the Jews into an accursed people, doomed by their whole history for the role of archetypal traitors. This concoction was also useful as a usurpation myth, explaining why Judaism had to be superseded by Christianity as the true Israel. Thus the stage was set for the time when the Jews of Europe were to lie at the mercy of a triumphant Christianity, which would turn them into a caste of slaves, saddle them with dishonourable tasks, and eventually demonise them to the point at which massacre after massacre became inevitable, culminating in the Holocaust.[9]

ENDNOTES

Chapter 2

1. For discussion of the origin of the word 'pariah', and its use, or misuse, in European languages, see p. 217, endnote 1.
2. Weber's view of pariah status now appears over-rigid. See, for example, Charsley (1996), on the extent to which 'Untouchability' was a European concept. Moreover, Weber much exaggerates the acceptance by pariahs of their own status. Movements of escape (into other religions, for example) existed even before modern times (see Juergensmeyer, 1982). Nevertheless, Weber's general concepts retain their value, and his application of them to the discussion of Jewish status remains a rare attempt to see the Jewish problem in anthropological terms.
3. See Nietzsche, *Der Wille zur Macht*, Aphorisms 955–57. Nietzsche's view was the origin of Lanternari's *The Religions of the Oppressed* which gave rise to the deprivation theory of religion, attacked by Mary Douglas in *Natural Symbols* (1973).
4. Momigliano (1987) points out that the Jewish law itself, the Torah, was always of a character inconsistent with self-imposed pariah status, since it presupposed a fully-functioning Jewish State. 'Believing Jews never gave up their sovereign rights and never admitted to being without political institutions of their own. This excludes that subjective acceptance of an inferior, non-political status which seems to be essential to Weber's definition of the Jews as pariahs' (p. 235). On the other hand, Momigliano does not envisage the possibility that Jews might be correctly termed 'pariahs' from a Christian standpoint.
5. Also, Weber's sympathetic approach to the rabbinic literature, contrasting surprisingly with the tradition of German scholarship (e.g. Schürer,

208

Ferdinand Weber, Billerbeck), is hardly consistent with his scheme of inward-looking Jewish legalism from Ezra onwards.

6. This expression is used only once, and not by Ezra himself, but by the 'princes'. For an explanation of this, and of the alleged separatism of the Book of Ezra, see Maccoby (1996), where an explanation is suggested of Ezra's reticence about the religious nature of his objection to the 'foreign wives' on grounds of idolatry (syncretism). The document under-lying the book (as others have noted) is a report to the Persian court officials, who would not be pleased to find syncretism described as mere idolatry, since syncretism was the official policy of the Persian Empire.

7. The prohibition of marriage with non-Christians was asserted by Cyprian, Tertullian, the Council of Elvira, the Councils of Laodicea, Hippo, Orléans, Toledo, Rome, the Gratian Collection. Paul's pro-nouncement '. . . neither Jew nor Greek, neither bond nor free, neither male nor female' is often quoted as an endorsement of exogamy, but wrongly, since it does not include non-Christians. Paul indeed prohibited intermarriage: 'Be ye not unequally yoked together with unbelievers' (II Cor. 6:14), though he declined to break up existing marriages (I Cor. 7:12), in the hope that conversion would result; if such a marriage broke up, however, he declared the marriage to be void.

8. For example, the Council of Elvira (CE 306) forbids Christian people to eat with Jews (Canon L). This prohibition was constantly reinforced in later councils.

9. Momigliano (1987) makes this point in a slightly different way: 'In *Ancient Judaism* he [Weber] even suggests that resentment meant less to the Jews than to the early Christians: the rabbis fought against the religious internalisation of revenge while "the less sophisticated early Christians" indulged more openly in it. As, according to Weber himself, Paul freed the Christians from the pariah status of the Jews, the unavoid-able conclusion is that there is no necessary connection between pariah status and ethics of resentment' (p. 233).

10. See Maccoby (1988), pp. 144–147.

11. See Weber (1963), pp. 115–116.

12. Form criticism is the analysis of texts in terms of the literary and religious forms or genres which they exemplify, e.g. hymns, curses, laments, proverbs, laws, tales, myths, legends; such analysis helps to identify the social setting in which each text functions, e.g. worship, education, entertainment, politics, law courts. The pioneer of the method of study of the Psalms was H. Gunkel, but the method has also been widely used in New Testament study.

13. See Reif (1993), pp. 34–37.
14. The discovery of the Ugaritic literature at Ras Shamra, Syria, in 1929 led to a radical re-dating of many of the Psalms, since the Ugaritic texts, dated to about 1200 BCE, showed strong stylistic similarities to the Psalms. Some Psalms previously thought to belong to the Hasmonean era were re-dated to a thousand years earlier. The relationship of the Psalms to Ugaritic literature was particularly studied by M. J. Dahood (1966–70).
15. For example, 'It is worse to rob a Gentile than a Jew, because of profaning the Name of Heaven' (i.e. casting discredit on the God of Judaism), Tosefta, Bava Qamma, 10:15. For further examples, see Jewish Encyclopedia, s.v. 'Gentile'.

Chapter 3

1. Though the Dutch Republic began to show unusual tolerance to Jews from the 17th century onwards, citizenship was not granted to Jews until 1796, following the example of revolutionary France.
2. See Fischel (1972).
3. In his pamphlet 'Der Judenspiegel', 1862. In 1879, he brought the word 'anti-Semite' into political use by founding the League of Anti-Semites (Antisemiten-Liga).

Chapter 4

1. Tosafot on Babylonian Talmud, Kiddushin 41a. The Tosafot ('additions') consist of voluminous additions to the classic commentary of Rashi (acronym for Rabbi Shelomo ben Yitzchak, 1040–1105) on the Babylonian Talmud. The school of Rashi were mostly French and German, but some English scholars also contributed. The Tosafot often provide historical insights into conditions in the Middle Ages.
2. Jacobs, 1893, p. xxii.
3. See Strack, 1909, Trachtenberg, 1966.
4. The requirement of Jews to act as public executioners is paralleled in the Hindu system by the requirement of the Chandalas, an Untouchable caste, to perform the same service (Dutt, 1931, pp. 143, 275). It is noteworthy that in Jewish law, public executions must be carried out by the chief witnesses for the prosecution in any case leading to

conviction on a capital charge (Deut. 13:9), a law that is at the opposite extreme to the transfer of responsibility and guilt to the despised.

5. For an explanation of the term *varna*, and its relationship to the castes, or *jati*, see pp. 71 and 89 and Chapter 15.

Chapter 5

1. See Maccoby (1991), Chapter 1, 'Gnostic Antisemitism'.

Chapter 6

1. Douglas (1993).
2. See Mishnah, Yadayim 4:4.
3. See Babylonian Talmud, Yevamot 78b.
4. See Visuvalingam (1989).

Chapter 7

1. The allegation that the Torah was given by angels is repeated in Acts 7:38 and 53. For a full refutation of the view, put forward by some scholars, that the giving of the Torah by angels is to be found in Jewish tradition, see Maccoby (1991), pp. 40–43. The Jewish sources actually say that the Torah was given by God, who was *accompanied* on Mount Sinai by angels.
2. The Noachic covenant was the revelation of God to Noah (Gen. 9:8–17) in which God promised not to cause another Flood, and also gave mankind the Seven Laws of the Children of Noah. Thus Judaism recognises two divine covenants, one for mankind in general and the other, at Sinai, for the Jews as priest-nation.
3. See Diodorus, *Bibliotheca*, 34:1, 1ff.
4. See Maccoby (1992) for a full treatment of the development of the Judas Iscariot legend, both within the Gospels and in later literature.

Chapter 8

1. See Goulder (1994), taking up the previous standpoint of Brandon (1951).
2. For a full treatment of the Jerusalem Church and its relation to Paulinism, see Maccoby (1986).
3. See Maccoby (1982), pp. 11–40.
4. It is tempting to find a parallel in the story of the death of Dionysus at the hands of the Titans, who fought a war against the Olympian gods. Dionysus was miraculously resurrected, and this death and resurrection formed the basis of a salvation cult of which one of the main rites was the *omophagia*, a ritual meal, consisting of the body of the god, reminiscent of the Christian Eucharist instituted by Paul. The Titans and their allies the Giants represented the old gods ousted by the Olympian gods. It might be argued, therefore, that we have here a parallel to the relegation of the Jews, the old defeated religion, to the position of communal Executioners or Betrayers of the Incarnate God, Jesus. Like the Titans, the Jews demonstrate their unfitness to retain their authority by their treacherous and savage murder of the Saviour, and simultaneously perform an indispensable function, since without them, the salvific sacrifice would not have occurred. However, this parallel cannot be pressed, as the Titans are probably a late addition to the Dionysus myth (see Harrison, 1963, p. 17, arguing that the killers of Dionysus were originally not Titans but *titanes*, 'white-clay men').
5. For the full argument that Judas never betrayed Jesus, see Maccoby (1992). The chief points are: (1) Paul's silence about Judas, combined with his statement (I Cor. 15:5) that the Resurrection appearance of Jesus was to 'The Twelve' (as opposed to the Gospels' insistence that it was to 'eleven', Matt. 28:16, Mark 16:14, Luke 24:33, Judas having defected); (2) the evidence in the Gospels of the gradual development of the Judas story; (3) the evidence of an innocuous, loyal Judas (Saint Jude), of whom the treacherous Judas was a split-off version.
6. For the thesis that the historical Judas Iscariot was a loyal follower of Jesus who became the third leader of the Jerusalem Church and was the author of the Epistle of Jude, see Maccoby (1992).
7. For the full evidence of this see Maccoby (1980), pp. 206–210. Jesus' saying, 'The Sabbath was made for man, not man for the Sabbath' was not originated by Jesus, but was a saying current among the Pharisees to support Sabbath-healing. See Maccoby (1988), pp. 170–172, for

discussion of the rabbinic sources of this saying (Mekhilta on Exod. 31:13; Babylonian Talmud, Yoma 85b).

Chapter 9

1. For the full argument that Jesus, like other Jewish messiah-figures, aimed to fulfil the prophecies of Zechariah and others by miraculously overcoming the Romans and becoming King of the Jews in Jerusalem, see Maccoby (1980). That he foresaw and aimed at his own death is part of the later transformation of Jesus into a sacrificed deity on the model of the Hellenistic mystery-religions.
2. See Sanders (1992), pp. 170–189. Sanders, for example, quotes an inscription found in Jerusalem: 'Theodotus the son of Vettenus, priest and ruler of the synagogue, son of a ruler of the synagogue, son's son of a ruler of the synagogue, built the synagogue for reading of the law and for teaching of the commandments, also the strangers' lodging and the chambers and the conveniences of waters for an inn for them that need it from abroad, of which [synagogue] his fathers and the elders and Simonides did lay the foundation.' He comments, 'The inscription supports the evidence of the literature: it was the priests who taught the law.' The inscription says only that Theodotus built the synagogue, not that he taught the law in it. The title 'ruler of the synagogue' (*archisynagogos*, Hebrew *rosh ha-keneset*) was given not to the Sage or rabbi who taught, but to its main financial supporter and administrator. Theodotus was wealthy and public-spirited, and he no doubt paid the salary of the rabbi, who would be a relatively poor man, not commanding the funds necessary to build and maintain a synagogue. The fact that Theodotus was a priest tells us something about the wealth of the priesthood at this time, but not about its learning or teaching authority. For the title *archisynagogos*, which was sometimes held by a wealthy woman, see Brooten (1982).

    Much of Sanders' 'evidence' is derived from Josephus, whose testimony is in fact contradictory. Being a priest himself, he much exaggerates the teaching authority of the priests, while having to admit that the Pharisees 'have the multitude on their side' (*Antiquities of the Jews* xiii.297). Of course, there were some small groups, including the Dead Sea Scroll sect, who did regard the priests as teaching authorities, and rejected the authority of the Pharisee scribes altogether.

Chapter 10

1. Burkert (1983), pp. 140–147.
2. See Milgram (1976).
3. Yet against this there would appear to be the statement (b. Keritot 7a; see Maimonides, *Mishneh Torah*, Teshuvah 1:2, summarising the Talmudic discussion) that the Day of Atonement atones for the less serious intentional sins (of offences against God, rather than against man) even without repentance. But this means that for these sins a general, rather than a particular, repentance, is sufficient; i.e. the general attitude of repentance associated with fasting on the Day of Atonement.

Chapter 11

1. The Gnostic affinities of Colossians have been obscured by the mistaken view that the polemic of 2:16–19 is directed against some kind of Gnostic sect. This polemic is actually directed against the Jerusalem Church.
2. See Kümmel (1975), pp. 340–46 for a persuasive defence of the Epistle's Pauline authorship.
3. The Christian tradition that they left Jerusalem shortly before the war, warned by an oracle, and went to Pella has been shown to be a legend. See Brandon (1951) and Lüdemann (1980).
4. This is an interesting literary touch. The effect of it is to insert a moment of void between the ending of the old dispensation and the beginning of the new. In Luke, this moment of nothingness takes the place of the despairing utterance of Jesus: 'My God, why hast thou forsaken me?', which he omits. There is a similar apprehension of total void in the Jewish legend of the Destruction (Lamentations Rabbah, 2:57). 'A certain man was ploughing and his cow lowed. An Arab passed by and said to him, "Jew, Jew, untie your cow, untie your plough, untie your coulter, for the Temple has been destroyed." He untied his cow, he untied his plough, he untied his coulter. The cow lowed a second time. The Arab said to him, "Tie up your cow, tie up your plough, tie up your coulter, for the Messiah has been born."' Here the nomad Arab and the untying of the plough signify the end of agriculture and the return of civilisation to chaos, but immediately a new era begins with the birth of the Messiah.
5. The Gospels exonerate Pilate completely. It was only in the 3rd century

that the Gospel story was read, chiefly by Eusebius, as partly a criticism of Pilate, who, on this reading, weakly allowed himself, against his better judgment, to be influenced by the Jews. This reading was so far from being universal among Christians that the Ethiopian Church actually canonised Pilate as a saint.

6. It is particularly ironic, in view of the reality of Jewish resistance to Rome and Pauline withdrawal from this resistance, that John 19 portrays the Jews as more Roman than the Romans, reminding Pilate of his duty to the Emperor. The Jews have somehow taken over the imperial role, which the Romans have abdicated.

7. See Rowland (1985), p. 176–177; Kümmel (1974) p. 94.

Chapter 12

1. See Graves (1955), 71.1.
2. Girard (1987), p. 167.
3. Girard (1987), pp. 159–62.
4. Girard devotes an article (*Biblical Interpretation* 1, 3 1993, pp. 339–352) to the subject 'Is There Anti-Semitism in the Gospels?' Here he develops his view that the apparently antisemitic passages, such as the Curses against the Pharisees, the parable of the Vineyard and the accusation in John that the Jews are the sons of the Devil, are not directed against the Jews as such, but against the violent constitution of society in general. In a response in the same issue (pp. 353–357), Joanna Dewey remarks justly, '. . . Girard's interpretation of the Jews in the Gospel narratives as paradigmatic of all humanity seems to me particularly liable to reinforce anti-Semitic views. On the one hand, it renders the Jews invisible, merely a cipher for humanity in general; on the other hand, it (or the Gospels) makes the Jews the symbol for the violence committed by all of humanity. A reading of the Gospels such as Girard's seems to me to encourage anti-Semitism, regardless of Girard's intention.'

Chapter 13

1. See Freud (1939).
2. When the Spanish Christian invaders arrived in Mexico in the 16th century, they were horrified to find there a sacrificial cult involving the torture and killing of human victims, whose hearts were extracted as

offerings to the sun-god. The Aztecs, however, saw strong similarities between their own religion and that of the invaders; and these similarities helped considerably the missionary efforts of the Spanish clergy. In particular, the idea underlying the Eucharist, that drinking the blood and eating the flesh of the sacrificed god gave the devotee spiritual sustenance, was most congenial to the Aztecs. The Christian reverence for the Sacred Heart of Jesus struck a most responsive chord, while the story of the crucifixion of Jesus, and the preceding Stations of the Cross, reminded them vividly of their own tortures of sacrificial victims. See Tierney (1989), pp. 426–58, and Boone (1984).

Chapter 14

1. Langmuir points out correctly that the blood libel proper begins with the case of Fulda, 1215, when the Jews were first accused of drinking blood of Christians and using it for ritual purposes. Before this the charge had been that they crucified a Christian child.

2. See Babylonian Talmud, Sanhedrin 43a, where it is said that Jesus was deservedly executed by stoning by order of the Sanhedrin on charges of sorcery and 'seducing others to idolatry'. This unhistorical account is a 3rd-century concoction intended to counter Christian missionary propaganda, but it does show that the Jews did not rule out the possibility that Jesus was executed by Jewish authority on religious grounds. It was only when Jewish scholars, on the basis of New Testament study, began to doubt whether Jesus had ever claimed divine status for himself, that the scenario typical of modern Jewish scholarship took shape: that the Church had falsified the teaching of Jesus, who regarded himself as a human messiah and liberator, and that Jesus himself was loyal to Judaism. This 'Jewish view of Jesus' actually began as early as the Middle Ages with the work of Profiat Duran (c. 1350–c. 1414).

3. Maccoby (1982), pp. 156–60.

4. For other theories of the causation of the blood libel see Dundes (1991). Magdalene Schultz connects the accusation to the cruelty and neglect characteristic of non-Jewish parents in the early Middle Ages. In the 12th century such ill-treatment of children was beginning to give rise to guilt which was transferred to the Jews. Ernest A. Rappaport relates the blood libel to 'repetition compulsion'. The efficacy of the death of Jesus as the means of renewing the divine life is the central Christian belief; but in times of doubt and panic, there is a drive to repeat the sacrifice,

expressed as a fantasy of continual sacrificial performances by the Jews, repeating their original mythological role. Alan Dundes gives a version of my own theory in *The Sacred Executioner*, adding the concept of 'projective inversion', by which the victim of violence is blamed. These theories, however, do not explain why the blood libel arose precisely in the 12th century.

5. Some Spanish historians have produced apologias for the Spanish Inquisition claiming that the figures for the burning of Jews have been greatly exaggerated. These apologetic claims are themselves highly distorted, being based on juggling with the definition of the word 'Jew' (does a Jew who has been converted to Christianity count as a Jew in the statistics or as a Christian?). If we define 'Jew' to mean 'converted Jew' (the only sensible course), the figures are horrifying. The number of heretics burned during the existence of the Spanish Inquisition (1480–1771) was over 30,000 of whom the great majority were Jews. In addition, about 17,000, who escaped, were burned in effigy, and about 300,000 were sentenced to punishments including scourging and being sent to the galleys.

6. Patai (1962).

7. It could be argued that the failure to integrate the *conversos* of Spain was due to their sheer numbers. Similarly, the mass conversion of Muslims of Spain led to such a failure of integration that they (the Moriscos) were eventually expelled. However, the two cases are very different. The Jews converted by their own decision (being given the admittedly hard alternative of expulsion) while the Muslims were all converted by force. The Muslims made no effort to adopt Christianity except nominally, while the Jewish converts adopted a thoroughly Christian way of life. In the case of the Jews, it was the unconverted who were expelled, while in the case of the Muslims, it was the nominally converted (who of course reverted immediately to Islam when outside of Spain). The fact is that the Jewish converts embraced Christianity if not in belief, then at least as their way to acceptance in Spanish society and professional life, only to find this acceptance largely denied them.

Chapter 15

1. 'It is noteworthy that in the Gangetic plain, for instance, by far the most numerous caste of Untouchables, which constitutes the greater part of the agricultural labour force, is that of the *Camar* or "leather" people,

while in the Tamil country the typical untouchable caste is that of the *paRaiyar* or "those of the drum" (*paRai*) (from which we have "pariah"), drum skins being of course impure, and the Untouchables consequently having the monopoly of village bands.' (Dumont 1980, p. 54).

2. The *varnas* actually go back to a time before the caste system developed. The first three *varnas* comprise the classes, or estates, into which the Aryans were divided before they entered India. After their conquest, another *varna* was added, comprising the conquered peoples, known as the Sudras.

3. It was on this issue that Mahatma Gandhi lost his life. His work to remove the disabilities of the Untouchables led to his assassination by a Brahmin extremist.

4. Medieval theorising about 'the two swords' (see Luke 22:38), did adumbrate a kind of caste system, since it sought to include the position of the Emperor in a religious scheme based on Scripture, validating the power of Emperor as well as Pope. This is similar to the situation in Hinduism, where the religious authority of the Brahmins and the political authority of the Kshatriya *varna* are in tension, both having religious sanction.

5. Even lower than the Untouchables were the hill-tribes, which were not admitted to the caste system at all.

6. See Simon (1986), pp. 65–97, Feldman (1993), pp. 228–413, Golb (1987).

7. Golb (1987).

8. A more radical attempt to solve the Untouchable problem was that of Dr. B. R. Ambedkar, who advocated secession from Hinduism by the Untouchables into other religions, chiefly Buddhism. Another secessionary movement, the Ad Dharm, promulgated a new religion specifically for the Untouchables. See Juergensmeyer (1982).

9. While the similarity between Jews and Untouchables has gone unnoticed, some have perceived a similarity between Jews in Christendom and *dhimmis* in Islam. Both Jews and Christians were *dhimmi* groups in Islam, given status as inferior but permitted minorities and exempted from forced conversion. There is certainly a similarity between *dhimmi* status and the Augustinian toleration of the Jews. Moreover, the successful attempt of Jews to rise above *dhimmi* status by setting up an independent state in what was regarded as Muslim territory gave rise to resentment comparable with the diabolisation of professional Jews in Enlightenment Europe. The differences are that Islam did not attempt to regulate Jewish or Christian religion in the Augustinian manner, did

not carry contempt and loathing of Jews to the paranoid extent found in Christendom, did not restrict the professions of Jews to anywhere near the same extent, and in general did not turn the Jews into a caste of Untouchables. The comparison between the Christian and Hindu models is therefore more enlightening, though comparison between *religio licita* and *dhimmi* (or for that matter between *dhimmi* and caste) is by no means without merit.

Chapter 16

1. The Wandering Jew actually pushes Christ on his way to crucifixion, but this is clearly symbolic of the Jewish role in furthering the Crucifixion. See Hasan-Rokem & Dundes (1986).
2. Patrick Tierney, who was puzzled at first by the ambivalent treatment accorded to the ritual sacrificers, generously acknowledged that he found the explanation in my book *The Sacred Executioner*. He included much of our discussions of his South American material in his book.
3. See Pilkington (1995).
4. See Poliakov, vol. 1 (1962).

Chapter 17

1. For a full account of the vilification of the Jews by the Early Fathers and medieval writers, see Ruether (1974) and Maccoby (1990). The Jews were accused of habitual crime (especially idolatry and sexual vice) by Eusebius, Aphrahat, Chrysostom, Irenaeus, Justin, Ephrem. Chrysostom even accuses them of cannibalism. As James Parkes has shown (Parkes, 1934), the frequent accusations that the Jews persecuted the early Church were baseless. The theory that the Jews were under a curse, and had been punished by the destruction of their Temple, by exile and by slavery was pervasive, and was even held by the relatively enlightened Thomas Aquinas.
2. See Nicholls (1993), pp. 203–207, detailing fully the correspondences between canonical laws against the Jews and those of the Nazis, including prohibition of intermarriage and commensality, burning of books, marking out by special clothing, segregation, and prohibition of sale of real estate to Jews.
3. I first introduced the concept of Hitler's millenarianism in *The Sacred*

Executioner (1982), pp. 171–175. The idea was later developed by Robert Wistrich in his *Hitler's Apocalypse*, London 1985.

4. The Reformation led to changes in the Christian canon of the New Testament, which had been the subject of hot debate in the early centuries of the formation of the Church. When I have suggested on occasion, in public debate with Christian scholars, that revision of the canon is necessary in the light of the Holocaust, the response has been one of horror and incomprehension.

5. The unthinking hostility to Jews of the great majority of South American Catholics, whether traditional or 'liberationist', has been brought home to me by my friend Professor Federico Castro of Venezuela, himself a person of truly liberal vision who has suffered greatly from oppression.

6. This was the phrase used to me by Dr Eugene Fisher, Secretary of the Secretariat for Catholic–Jewish Relations, in a public dialogue with me and others in the City University of New York Graduate School. According to Fisher, my analysis of Christianity as a human-sacrificial cult in which the Jews act as Sacred Executioners was entirely correct as far as popular Christianity went, but has no relevance to official Christianity. See Braham (1986).

7. The conduct of the Roman Catholic Church during the Holocaust is as relevant to an assessment as its conduct afterwards. Pope Pius XII set the seal on the centuries-long oppression of the Jews by the Church when he steadfastly refused to make any protest to Germany about the Holocaust, even after full details of it were known to him. Even when the Jews of Rome were put into trucks and sent to die in Auschwitz, he did not intervene, though certain Catholics of Rome begged him to do so. He did however sponsor the hiding of some Jews who escaped the trucks. Even when the Allies were occupying Rome, and news came of preparations for the murder of the Jews of Hungary, he did not intervene, except to deplore racialism in general terms. He was entreated by Catholics as well as Jews to pronounce excommunication against any Catholic actively participating in the Holocaust, but did not respond, though such an announcement might well have influenced many Catholics who were looking for guidance. See Friedlander (1966), Lewy (1964). See also Gutteridge (1976), for the equally supine policies of the German Protestant churches.

8. A particularly jejune version of this view has appeared recently, advocated by those Jewish writers seeking to attach themselves to the theory of 'Orientalism' of Edward Said (see, for example, Cheyette, 1993). On this view, the antisemitism of the 19th and 20th centuries has been a

manifestation of colonialism; Jews have been despised because representative of uppity Orientals, challenging Occidental 'empowerment'. Even writers such as G. K. Chesterton, Hilaire Belloc and T. S. Eliot, whose antisemitism was openly religious in motivation, have been analysed along these lines. The term 'antisemitism' has even been altered to 'Semitism', to put it in line with Said's term 'Orientalism'. Said himself, of course, repudiates such allies, preferring to regard Jews as arch-colonialists, a view which at least points to a feature of the antisemitic myth ignored by the above Jewish theorists, that the Jews are always regarded as having mysterious and awesome power, not as being backward natives. Of course, this is not to deny that the fundamental Jewish religious stigma was overlaid at times by considerations of mere class snobbishness, as evinced in the novels of Trollope. Every generation, and even every class, has its own distinctive way of being antisemitic, but these nuances do not provide the explanation of the persistence of antisemitism itself.

9. See Daniel Jonah Goldhagen's *Hitler's Willing Executioners: Ordinary Germans and the Holocaust*. Reviewers of this book (which appeared while the present book was going through the press) have mostly misrepresented it as laying blame for the Holocaust entirely on the Germans. In fact, as the early chapters make clear, the author blames the Holocaust primarily on Christian medieval diabolisation of the Jews, and he stresses the continuity between medieval and modern antisemitism. Only secondarily does he blame the Germans, whose special history rendered them particularly vulnerable to a modern racialist version of the medieval loathing. Goldhagen's detailed evidence of the uncritical complicity of the average German in the Holocaust provides strong corroboration of the effect of centuries-long Christian antisemitic indoctrination.

BIBLIOGRAPHY

ABRAHAMS, ISRAEL, *Studies in Pharisaism and the Gospels*, London 1917, 1924.

ADAMS, HENRY, *The Education of Henry Adams*, Boston, 1918.

ADAMS, HENRY, *Mont-Saint Michel and Chartres*, Boston, 1905.

ANSELM, SAINT, *Opera*, ed. F. S. Schmitt, 6 vols., Edinburgh, 1938.

AQUINAS, THOMAS, 'Letter to the Duchess of Brabant', in A. P. d'Entrèves, ed. *Selected Political Writings*, (tr. J. G. Dawson), Macmillan, New York, p. 85.

AUGUSTINE OF HIPPO, *City of God* (tr. Henry Bettenson, ed. David Knowles), Harmondsworth, 1972.

BASHAM, A. L. (ed.), *A Cultural History of India*, Oxford, 1975.

BAUER, YEHUDA, *The Holocaust in Historical Perspective*, London, 1978.

BOONE, ELIZABETH H. (ed.), *Ritual Human Sacrifice in Mesoamerica*, Cambridge, Mass., 1984.

BOUSSET, WILHELM, *The Antichrist Legend*, London, 1896.

BOUSSET, WILHELM, *Kurios Christos* (Eng. tr.), Abingdon, 1970.

BRAHAM, RANDOLPH L., ed., *The Origins of the Holocaust: Christian Anti-Semitism*, New York, 1986.

BRANDES, GEORG, *Sagnet om Jesus*, Copenhagen, 1925; Eng. tr. *Jesus, a Myth*, London, 1927.

BRANDON, S. G. F., *The Fall of Jerusalem and the Christian Church*, London, 1951.

BROOTEN, BERNADETTE J., *Women Leaders in the Ancient Synagogue*, Chico, 1982.

BULTMANN, RUDOLF, *The History of the Synoptic Tradition*, Oxford, 1958.

BURKERT, WALTER, *Homo Necans: The Anthropology of Ancient Greek Sacrificial Ritual and Myth*, Berkeley, 1983.

CARMICHAEL, JOEL, *The Satanizing of the Jews*, New York, 1995.

CHARSLEY, SIMON, '"Untouchable": what is in a name?' *The Journal of the Royal Anthropological Institute*, 2, 1, 1996.

CHEYETTE, BRYAN, *Constructions of 'The Jew' in English Literature and Society*, Cambridge, 1993.

COHEN, JEREMY, *The Friars and the Jews: The Evolution of Medieval Anti-Judaism*, Ithaca/London, 1982.

COHN, NORMAN, *The Pursuit of the Millennium*, London, 1957.

COHN, NORMAN, *Warrant for Genocide: the Myth of the Jewish World-Conspiracy and the Protocols of the Elders of Zion*, London, 1967.

DAHOOD, MITCHELL J., *The Psalms*, Anchor Bible, 3 vols., New York, 1966–70.

DAVIES, ALAN T. (ed.), *Antisemitism and the Foundations of Christianity*, New York, 1979.

DEWEY, JOANNA, 'A Response to René Girard, "Is there anti-Semitism in the Gospels?"', *Biblical Interpretation*, 1, 3 (1993), pp. 353–356.

DIODORUS SICULUS, *Bibliotheca Historica*, (Loeb edition), 12 vols., Cambridge, Mass., 1933–67.

DOUGLAS, MARY, *Purity and Danger*, London, 1966.

DOUGLAS, MARY, 'Atonement in Leviticus', *Jewish Studies Quarterly*, 1,2: pp. 109–130, 1993/94.

DOUGLAS, MARY, *Natural Symbols*, New York, 1973.

DOUGLAS, MARY, 'The Forbidden Animals in Leviticus'. *JSOT* 59 (1993), pp. 3–23.

DOUGLAS, MARY, 'The Stranger in the Bible'. *Arch. europ. sociol.*, XXXV (1994), pp. 283–298.

DUMONT, LOUIS, *Homo Hierarchicus: The Caste System and its Implications*, Chicago/London, 1980.

DUNDES, ALAN (ed.), *The Blood Libel Legend: A Casebook in Anti-Semitic Folklore*, Madison, 1991.

DUNN, JAMES D. G., *Christology in the Making: An Inquiry into the Origins of the Doctrine of the Incarnation*. 2nd ed., London, 1989.

DUTT, N. K., *Origin and Growth of Caste in India*, Vol. 1, London, 1931.

EILBERG-SCHWARTZ, HOWARD, *The Savage in Judaism: an Anthropology of Israelite Religion and Ancient Judaism*, Bloomington, 1990.

ELIOT, T. S., *The Complete Poems and Plays*, London, 1969.

FELDMAN, LOUIS H., *Jew and Gentile in the Ancient World: Attitudes and Interactions from Alexander to Justinian*, Princeton, 1993.

FISCHEL, W. J., 'Cochin', in *Encyclopaedia Judaica*, Jerusalem, 1972.

FLANNERY, EDWARD, H., *The Anguish of the Jews*, New York, 1963.

FRAZER, SIR J. G., *The Golden Bough*, 3rd ed.: Part III, *The Dying God*, London, 1911. Part IV, *Adonis Attis Osiris*, London, 1907. Part VI, *The Scapegoat*, London, 1913.

FREEMAN, JAMES M., *Untouchable: An Indian Life History*, London, 1979.

FREUD, SIGMUND, *Moses and Monotheism*, London, 1939.

FRIEDLANDER, S., *Pius XII and the Third Reich: A Documentation*, London, 1966.

GAGER, JOHN G., *The Origins of Anti-Semitism*, New York/Oxford, 1983.

GASTON, LLOYD, *Paul and the Torah*, Vancouver, 1987.

GILBERT, ARTHUR, *The Vatican Council and the Jews*, Cleveland and New York, 1968.

GIRARD, RENÉ, *Things Hidden since the Foundation of the World*, London, 1987 (originally *Des choses cachées depuis la fondation du monde*, Paris, 1978).

GIRARD, RENÉ, *Violence and the Sacred*, Baltimore/London, 1977 (originally *La violence et le sacré*, Paris 1972).

GIRARD, RENÉ, 'Is there Anti-Semitism in the Gospels?', *Biblical Interpretation* 1, 3 (1993), pp. 339–352.

GOLB, NORMAN, *Jewish Proselytism – a Phenomenon in the Religious History of Early Medieval Europe*, Cincinnati, 1987.

GOULDER, MICHAEL, *A Tale of Two Missions*, London, 1994.

GRAVES, ROBERT, *The Greek Myths*, 2 vols., London, 1955.

GRAYZEL, SOLOMON, *The Church and the Jews in the Thirteenth Century*, New York, 1966.

GREEN, A. R. W., *The Role of Human Sacrifice in the Ancient Near East*, Missoula, 1975.

GUTTERIDGE, R., *Open Thy Mouth for the Dumb: The German Evangelical Church and the Jews 1879–1950*, Oxford, 1976.

HARE, DOUGLAS, A. R., *The Theme of Jewish Persecution of Christians in the Gospel according to Matthew*, Cambridge, 1967.

HARRISON, JANE, *Themis: A Study of the Social Origins of Greek Religion*, London, 1963.

HASAN-ROKEM, GALIT & DUNDES, ALAN (ed.), *The Wandering Jew: Essays in the Interpretation of a Christian Legend*, Bloomington, 1986.

HAY, MALCOLM, *The Foot of Pride*, Boston, 1950.

HAYNES, STEPHEN R., *Jews and the Christian Imagination: Reluctant Witnesses*, Basingstoke, 1995.

HEER, FRIEDRICH, *God's First Love*, London, 1967.

HENGEL, MARTIN, *Between Jesus and Paul*, London, 1983.

HERFORD, R. TRAVERS, *The Pharisees*, London, 1924.

HILTEBEITEL, ALF (ed.), *Criminal Gods and Demon Devotees*, Albany, 1989.

HOWDEN (HOEVEDEN), ROGER, *Chronicles of the Reigns of Henry II and Richard I*, ed. W. Stubbs, 4 vols., London, 1868–71.

HUBERT, HENRI AND MAUSS, MARCEL, *Sacrifice: Its Nature and Functions*, USA, 1964 (originally 'Essai sur la Nature et la Fonction du Sacrifice', *L'Année Sociologique*, Paris, 1898).

HUTTON, J. H., *Caste in India*, London, 1963.

JACOBS, JOSEPH (ed.), *The Jews of Angevin England*, London, 1893.

JEREMIAS, JOACHIM, *The Parables of Jesus*, (rev. ed.), London, 1972.

JUERGENSMEYER, MARK, *Religion as Social Vision: The Movement against Untouchability in 20th-century Punjab*, Berkeley, 1982.

KATZ, JACOB, *Exclusiveness and Tolerance*, London, 1961.

KLASS, MORTON, *Caste: The Emergence of the South Asian Social System*, Philadelphia, 1980.

KÜMMEL, W. G., *Introduction to the New Testament*, London, 1975.

LANGMUIR, GAVIN I., *Toward a Definition of Antisemitism*, Berkeley, 1990.

LANTERNARI, V., *The Religions of the Oppressed: A Study of Modern Messianic Cults*, London, 1965.

LÉVI-STRAUSS, CLAUDE, *The Savage Mind*, London, 1966.

LEWY, G., *The Catholic Church and Nazi Germany*, New York, 1964.

LIEBESCHÜTZ, H., 'Max Weber's Historical Interpretation of Judaism'. *Year Book* of the Leo Baeck Institute 9, 1964.

LIETZMANN, HANS, *Messe und Herrenmahl*, 3rd ed., Berlin, 1955.

LOISY, A., *Les mystères païens et le mystère chrétien*, 2nd ed., Paris, 1930.

LÜDEMANN, GERD, 'The Successors of Pre-70 Jerusalem Christianity: A Critical Evaluation of the Pella-Tradition', in *Jewish and Christian Self-definition*, ed. E. P. Sanders, vol. 1, London, 1980.

MACCOBY, HYAM, *Judaism on Trial: Jewish-Christian Disputations in the Middle Ages*, London, 1982 (2nd ed., London, 1993).

MACCOBY, HYAM, *The Sacred Executioner*, London, 1982.

MACCOBY, HYAM, *The Mythmaker*, London, 1986.

MACCOBY, HYAM, *Early Rabbinic Writings*, Cambridge, 1988.

MACCOBY, HYAM, 'Antisemitism', in *A Dictionary of Biblical Interpretation*, ed. R. J. Coggins & J. L. Houlden, London, 1990.

MACCOBY, HYAM, *Paul and Hellenism*, London, 1991.

MACCOBY, HYAM, *Judas Iscariot and the Myth of Jewish Evil*, London, 1992.

MACCOBY, HYAM, 'Holiness and Purity: the Holy People in Leviticus and Ezra-Nehemiah', in *Reading Leviticus*, ed. John Sawyer, Sheffield, 1996.

MAJUMDAR, D. N., *Races and Cultures of India*, Bombay, 1958.

MAYER, ADRIAN C., *Caste and Kinship in Central India*, London, 1960.

MILGROM, J., *Cult and Conscience: the Asham and the Priestly Doctrine of Repentance*, Leiden, 1976.

MILGROM, J., *Leviticus 1–16*. The Anchor Bible, New York, 1991.

MOMIGLIANO, ARNALDO, 'A Note on Max Weber's Definition of Judaism as a Pariah-Religion', in *On Pagans, Jews and Christians*, pp. 231–237, Middletown, Connecticut, 1987.

MONTEFIORE, C. G., *The Synoptic Gospels*, 2 vols., London, 1927.

MOORE, GEORGE FOOT, *Judaism in the First Centuries of the Christian Era*, 2 vols., Cambridge, Mass., 1927.

MORRIS, BRIAN, *Anthropological Studies of Religion*, Cambridge, 1987.

NETANYAHU, B., *The Origins of the Inquisition in Fifteenth Century Spain*, New York, 1996.

NEUSNER, JACOB, *From Politics to Piety*, New Jersey, 1973.

NICHOLLS, WILLIAM, *Christian Antisemitism: A History of Hate*, Northvale, N. Jersey/London, 1993.

NIETZSCHE, FRIEDRICH WILHELM, *Complete Works*, tr. Oscar Levy, 18 vols., New York, 1925.

PARKES, JAMES, *The Conflict of the Church and the Synagogue*, London, 1934.

PATAI, RAPHAEL, 'The Chuetas', *Midstream* 8, 1962, pp. 59–69.

PILKINGTON, EDWARD, 'Japan's "untouchables" locked into disadvantage by collective amnesia', The *Guardian*, July 2, 1995.

POLIAKOV, LEON, *The History of Antisemitism*, 4 vols., London, 1962–74.

REIF, STEFAN C., *Judaism and Hebrew Prayer: New Perspectives on Jewish Liturgical History*, Cambridge, 1993.

REITZENSTEIN, R., *Die Hellenistische Mysterienreligionen*, 3rd ed. Leipzig-Berlin, 1927. (tr. John E. Steely, *Hellenistic Mystery-Religions: Their Basic Ideas and Significance*, Pittsburgh, Pennsylvania, 1978).

ROBERTSON, J. M., *Pagan Christs*, 2nd ed., London, 1911.

ROBINSON J. (ed.), *The Nag Hammadi Library in English*, Leiden, 1977.

ROGERSON, J. W., *Anthropology and the Old Testament*, Oxford, 1978.

ROSENBERG, EDGAR, *From Shylock to Svengali: Jewish Stereotypes in English Fiction*, London, 1961.

ROTH, CECIL, *The History of the Jews in England*, 3rd ed., London, 1964.

ROTH, NORMAN, *Conversos, Inquisition, and the Expulsion of the Jews from Spain*, Wisconsin, 1995.

ROWLAND, CHRISTOPHER, *Christian Origins: An Account of the Setting and Character of the most Important Messianic Sect of Judaism*, London, 1985.

RUETHER, ROSEMARY, *Faith and Fratricide*, New York, 1974.

SANDERS, E. P., *Paul and Palestinian Judaism*, London, 1977.

SANDERS, E. P., *Judaism: Practice and Belief, 63BCE–66CE*, London, 1992.

SANDERS, JACK T., *The Jews in Luke-Acts*, London, 1987.

SCHIPER, I., 'Max Weber on the Sociological Basis of the Jewish Religion', *Jewish Journal of Sociology* 1, 1959, pp. 250–260.

SCHÜRER, EMIL, *Geschichte des jüdischen Volkes im Zeitalter Jesu Christi*, Berlin, 1886–90.

SCHWEITZER, ALBERT, *The Quest of the Historical Jesus*, London, 1948.

SIMON, M., *Verus Israel*, Littman Library of Jewish Civilization, Oxford, 1986.

SOMBART, WERNER, *Die Zukunft der Juden*, Leipzig, 1912.

STENDAHL, KRISTER, *Paul among Jews and Gentiles*, Philadelphia, 1976.

STRACK, HERMANN L., (tr. H. Beauchamp) *The Jew and Human Sacrifice*, London, 1909.

STRACK, HERMANN L. AND BILLERBECK, PAUL, *Kommentar zum Neuen Testament aus Talmud und Midrasch*, 4 vols., München, 1922.

TIERNEY, PATRICK, *The Highest Altar: The Story of Human Sacrifice*, New York, 1989.

TRACHTENBERG, JOSHUA, *The Devil and the Jews*, New York, 1966.

URBACH, EPHRAIM, *The Sages: Their Concepts and Beliefs*, Jerusalem, 1975.

VISUVALINGAM, SUNTHAR, 'The Transgressive Sacrality of the Diksita: Sacrifice, Criminality and *Bhakti* in the Hindu Tradition', in *Criminal Gods and Demon Devotees*, ed. Alf Hiltebeitel, Albany, 1989.

VERMES, GEZA, *Jesus the Jew*, London, 1973.

VERMES, GEZA, *Jesus and the World of Judaism*, London, 1983.

WEBER, FERDINAND, *Jüdische Theologie auf Grund des Talmud und verwandter Schriften*, Leipzig, 1897.

WEBER, MAX, *The Protestant Ethic and the Spirit of Capitalism*, (1904–5); Eng. tr., New York, 1930.

WEBER, MAX, *The Sociology of Religion*, tr. Ephraim Fischoff and intr. Talcott Parsons, Boston, 1963 (first published 1922).

WEBER, MAX, *Ancient Judaism*, tr. and ed. H. H. Gerth and Don Martindale, New York, 1967.

WELLHAUSEN, JULIUS, *Die Composition des Hexateuchs*, Berlin, 1889.

WELLHAUSEN, JULIUS, *Prolegomena to the History of Ancient Israel*, New York, 1957 (first published 1885).

WELLS, G. A., *The Jesus of the Early Christians*, London, 1971.

WHITELY, D. E. H., *The Theology of St Paul*, Oxford, 1974.

WILLIAMS, A. L., *Adversus Judaeos*, Cambridge, 1935.

WILSON, STEPHEN, *Ideology and Experience: Antisemitism in France at the time of the Dreyfus Affair*, Toronto, 1982.

WISTRICH, ROBERT S., *Hitler's Apocalypse*, London, 1985.

WISTRICH, ROBERT S., *Antisemitism: The Longest Hatred*, London, 1991.

YERKES, R. K., *Sacrifice in Greek and Roman Religions and Early Judaism*, London, 1953.

INDEX

Aaron, 66, 80
Aaronite priesthood, 75
Abderus, 149
Abel, 153, 193
Abelard, Peter, 159
Abraham, 66, 75, 84, 157, 158
Abrahams, Israel, 102
Adam, 147
Adams, Henry, 183, 199
Ad Dharm, 218
Adiabene, 75
Adonis, 91, 92, 97, 150
Ainu, 196
Akedah, 123
Albigensians, 16
Alexandria, 40, 133
Ambedkar, B. R., 218
America, 199
Amish, 109
Ammonites, 76
Amorites, 88
Anabaptists, 201
angels, 82, 83
Angevins, 52
Anselm, 52
anthropology and sociology,
    168
Antichrist, 201
anti–Judaism, 166
Antioch, 133
Antiochus Epiphanes, 40, 41
Antiochus Sidetes, 40, 88
antisemitism, 149, 166, 138

and accusation of deicide, ch 11
    passim
and snobbery, 197
caused by Jews themselves, 38, 114
Christian and Muslim compared, 43
definition of, 45
Gnostic, 41
Hellenistic, 40, 41
Islamic, 43
Japanese, 48
Marxist, 47
Nazi, 46
black, 197
outside Christianity, ch 3 passim
post-Christian, 48
spelling of, 45
usurpation, 15
xenophobia, distinct from 45
Apache Indians, 127
Aphrahat, 219
Apion, 41
apocalypticism, 170
Apostles, 97
Aquinas, Thomas, 17, 113, 219
Arab conquest, 89
archisynagogos, 213
Archon, 69
Aristodemus, 157
Aristotle, 36
Aryans, 186
Assyrians, 14
Athenian tragedy, 138
Athens, 116, 146, 147, 148

Athronges, 83
Atonement, 127
  ransom theory of, 119
  vicarious, 118
Attis, 91, 92, 97, 150
Augustine, 169, 184, 193
Auschwitz, 169, 202
Avicebron, 113
Aztecs, 121, 157, 189, 216

Baal, 91, 95
Babylonians, 14, 20, 115, 132
Balaam, 66
Balder, 91, 95, 96
Barabbas, 97, 98, 99, 114
baraku, 195
Bar Kokhba, 32, 83, 132
Baur, F. C., 93
Belaset of Oxford, 60
Belloc, Hilaire, 220
Bernard of Clairvaux, 17, 200
Betrayer, 96, 97, 98, 115, 146, 149
Billerbeck, Paul, 209
Black Christ, 96, 145
Black Death, 189
Blood Libel, 53, 60, 166, 191, 193, 200
blood, shedding of, 124
Bockholdt, Johann, 201
Boer, 80
Boone, Elizabeth H., 216
Bouphonia sacrifice, 146
Bourgeois, Jean, 196
Bousset, Wilhelm, 163
Braham, Randolph L., 220
Brahmins, 49, 74, 75, 79, 176, 181, 189, 218
Brandes, Georg, 131
Brandon, S. G. F., 133, 212, 214
Brooten, Bernadette J., 213
Bultmann, Rudolf, 164
Burkert, Walter, 121, 214, 143, 145, 146, 147
Byron, 72

Caiaphas, 130
Cai Cai Filu, 192
Cain, 42, 66, 149, 193
  as Sacred Executioner, 96
Canaanites, 63, 80, 88, 89
Canaanite slaves, 78, 79, 80, 81, 174

cannibalism, 170
canon, 219
capitalism, 33
Carmelites, 202
caste, *passim*
  in Gnosticism, 70
  in Judaism, ch 6 *passim*
Castro, Federico, 220
Cathars, 70
Chaeremon, 41
Chandalas, 210
Charsley, Simon, 208
Chasidic communities, 110
Chaucer, Geoffrey, 171
Chesterton, G. K., 220
Cheyette, Bryan, 220
China, 39, 48
Christ, 83, 90
Christian humanists, 113
Christianity
  and the sacrificial death of Jesus, 130
  antisemitism in, 15, 46, 82, 109
  as Edom, 14
  conversion in, 75
  Gnosticism, 43
  laws against intermarriage of relatives, 57
  liberal, 117
  polemic against Judaism, 23, 28, 29
  usurpation myth, 42, 46, 64, ch 8 *passim*
  usury by proxy, 54
  usury, view of, 56
Chrysostom, St. John, 185, 219
Chuetas, 174
Church art, 171
Church Councils, 160
Coa, Maximo, 194
Cochin, 38, 39
Colossians, 214
colour-prejudice, 79
Constantine, 198
conversos, 172
Crispin, Gilbert, 52
Crucifixion, participationist theory of, 125
Crusades, 170, 172
Cush, 80
Cyprian, 209
Cyrus, 27, 66

Dahood, Mitchell J., 210
damnation, 117
Daniel, 15
Dasyu, 74, 79
David, 66
Day of Atonement, 97, 123, 124, 132, 214
Dead Sea Scrolls, 114, 131
Demiurge, 66, 83, 111
  as laughing stock, 69
Dewey Joanna, 215
dhimmi, 87, 218, 180
Diana, 95
Diodorus, 40, 211
Dionysus, 91, 92, 95, 150, 212
Disraeli, 137
Documentary theory, 23
Doeg the Edomite, 75
Dominicans, 170
Douglas, Mary, 76, 208, 211
Dravidians, 74, 79
Dumont, Louis, 176, 180, 184, 188, 218
Dundes, Alan, 216 219
Dunn, James, 102, 112, 118
Duran, Profiat, 216
Dutch Republic, 210
Dutt, N. K., 210

Early Fathers, 158
Eastern Europe, 203
Edom, 14
Edomites, 76
Edward the Confessor, 54
Egyptians, 14, 76
Eilberg-Schwartz, Howard, 161
Eliezer, Rabbi, 106
Eliot, T. S., 126, 220
Elvira, Council of, 209
Enlightenment, 183, 199
Ephrem, 219
Epistle to the Colossians, 129
Epistle to the Hebrews, 119
Epistle to the Romans, 83
Esau, 66
Esther, Book of, 40
Ethiopian Church, 215
Ethiopians, 80
Eucharist, 142, 162, 167, 169
  congenial to Aztecs, 216

Eusebius, 214, 219
Evans-Pritchard, 162
evil, powers of, 128
Exchequer of the Jews, 58
Exodus from Egypt, 65
Expulsion from Spain, 172
Ezra, 23, 24, 25, 26, 113, 209

Fackenheim, Emil, 202
Feldman, Louis H., 218
'Final Solution', 200
Fischel, W. J., 210
Fisher, Eugene, 220
Foetor Judaicus, 172, 182
form criticism, 105, 209
Four Kingdoms, 15
Franciscans, 170
Franco-Prussian War, 189
Frazer, Sir James, 143, 146, 162
Freud, Sigmund, 148, 149, 156, 215
Friedlander, S., 220
fripiers, 196
Fulda, 216

Gager, John, 203
Gamaliel, 100, 101, 154
Gamaliel the Second, 101
Gandhi, 188, 218
Gaston, Lloyd, 203
Genesis, 88
'German-Jewish symbiosis', 199
Germany, 172, 199
  degree of responsibility for Holocaust, 199
Gibeonite, 77
Girard, René, 143, 144, 145, 146, 148, 149, 151, 152, 155, 162, 215
Gnostic Christianity, 83
Gnosticism, 41, 42, 46, 65, 66, 67, 82, 92, 118, 128, 130, 214
  as form of cosmic antisemitism, 70
  view of Jesus, 69
  view of Judaism, 69
  view of death of Jesus, 70
  view of Jews, 71
gnosis, 42
God-fearing Gentiles, 27
God the Father, 158
Golb, Norman, 218
Golden Age of Spain, 19

Golden Legend, 149
Golden Rule, 111
Goldhagen, Daniel Jonah, 221
Goulder, Michael, 212
Gratian Collection, 209
Graves, Robert, 215
Greece, 115
Greeks, 14
Gutteridge, R., 220
Gunkel, H., 209
Gypsies, 184

Hadrian, 41
Ham, 63, 80
Hanina ben Dosa, 103
Harrison, Jane, 143, 145, 146, 212
Hasan-Rokem, Galit, 219
hasid, 103, 108
healing on the Sabbath, 101
Hebdomad
    see Demiurge, 69
Hebrew Bible, 147
    preferable to 'Old Testament', 161
Hebrew slaves, 78
Hell, 170, 199
Hellenism, 42
Hengel, Martin, 102
Henry II, 52, 54, 59
Henry III, 59
Hercules, 95
Herford, Travers, 102
Herod Antipas, 99, 130
Herod the Wicked, 99
Herodians, 98, 99, 152
High Priest, 99, 100, 111, 112, 113
    as collaborator with Romans, 115
Hitler, 200
    and millenarianism, 219
Hillel, 101, 154
Hillel, House of, 103
Hindu castes, 71, 80
Hinduism, 15, 49, 50, 75, 79, 176,
    189
    attitude to Israel, 50
Hindu-Jewish relations, 50
Hippo, Council of, 209
Hippolytus, 149, 201
History-of-Religions school, 163
holiness code, 28
Holland, 39

Holocaust, 172
    and Crucifixion, 202
    and Hungary, 220
Holy of Holies, 132
'holy seed', 25
Honi the Circlemaker, 103
Horus, 163
host, 160
Hubert, Henri, 143, 145, 146
human sacrifice, 143, 147, 148
hylics, 70

Iago, 137
Ibn Gabirol, 113
Idumaea, 75
immortality, 125
Incas, 194
Innocent III, 52
    Ezra compared with, 26
'intra-Jewish rivalry' 203
Irenaeus, 201, 219
Isaac, 75, 84, 157, 158
Isaiah, 83
Ishmael, 66
Isis, 163
Islam, 43, 87, 170, 189, 218
Israel (country), 206

Jacob, 14, 66, 75, 84
Jacobs, Joseph, 57, 210
jati, 71, 176
James, brother of Jesus, 93
    as Prince Regent, 94
Japan, 48, 195
Jethro, 75
Jeremiah, 147
Jeremias, Joachim, 104
Jerusalem, 84, 93
Jerusalem Church, 91, 93, 94, 95, 97,
    105, 115, 131, 132, 133, 164
Jesus, 84, 90, 91, 96, 203
    alleged conflict with Pharisees, 103
    as a descending and ascending deity,
    90
    as a religious reformer, 109
    as High Priest, 121
    as historical person, 99
    as innocent sacrificial figure, 98
    as Judge, 171
    as King of the Jews, 94, 149, 213

as martyr, 116
as Pharisee teacher, 102, 104, 106
as reformer, 110, 116
as sacrifice, 120
as saviour-god, 95
brother of Judas, 97
crucifixion of, 91
as messiah-figure, 98
executed by the Romans, 91, 98
incomprehension of disciples, 94
in Talmud, 216
Jewish view of, 83
messianic aim, 108
parables of, 104
preaching of repentance, 108
trial of, 100
Jewish Christianity, 206
Jewish women, 60
Jews, 11, 16, 84, 119
as people of God, 112
and the crucifixion of Jesus, 91
as heretics, 52
as slaves, 55
as usurers, 53
blood of, 173
demonisation of, 53, 60, 87, 171
expulsion from England, 59
function of, in medieval England, 19,
51, 58, 60
rebelliousness of, 91
high cultural level, 55, 60
in Hebrews, 120
massacres of, 58
as pariah class, 16, 61, ch 15 passim
paranoid fantasies about, 12
Paul's view of, 83
prosperity in Middle Ages, 19, 51
stigma of, 174
under a curse, 99
witnesses to the truth of Christianity,
16, 17
Job, 24, 27
Johanan ben Zakkai, 154
John, Gospel of 91
John the Baptist, 130
John Hyrcanus, 23
John, King, 59
Jonah, 24
Josephus, 102, 113
Judah the Prince, 32, 101

Judaism, *passim*
as this-worldly religion, 72
as *religio licita*, 178
and business ethics, 35
conversion in, 75
doctrine of chosenness, 74
historical sweep of, 92
attitude to interest on loans, 35, 55
contains no colour prejudice, 75
non-dualistic, 81
pariah groups in, 81
Paul's view of, 83
pluralistic, 28
role of King in, 72
slaves in, 77
rabbinic, 108
Judas Iscariot, 91, 92, 94, 95, 97, 121,
148, 160, 165
as Betrayer, 95
as symbol of Jewish people, 137
designated by Jesus, 140
in the Passion Plays, 172
Judas Maccabaeus, 23
Judas of Galilee, 83
Judas Thomas, 97
Jude, 212
Juergensmeyer, Mark, 208
Justin, 219

Khazaria, 75
Kiddush, 163
King, Martin Luther, 116
Koestler Arthur, 45
Kohanim, 75
Kolbe, Father, 137
Kshatriya, 74, 218
Kümmel, W. G., 214, 215
kurios, 163

Lactantius, 201
Laius, 149
Lanternari, V., 208
Langmuir, Gavin, 46, 166, 167, 168,
170, 216
Lanzmann, Claude, 99
Laodicea, Council of, 209
Last Supper, 162
Leos, 157
Leviticus, 88
Levinas, Emmanuel, 167

Levin, Bernard, 202, 204
Lévi-Strauss, Claude, 143, 148
Lewy, G., 220
lex gentium, 28, 37
Lietzmann, Hans, 163
limpieza de sangre, 78
Loki, 95, 97
Louis IX, 170
Lüdemann, Gerd, 214
Luther, 200

Maccoby, Hyam, 209, 211, 212, 213,
    216, 219
Magi, 90, 95
Maimonides, 113
Maimon, Salomon, 183
Malebisse, Richard, 58
mamzer, 76
Manetho, 41
Mapuches, 191
Mariolatry, 171
Marr, Wilhelm, 45
Marranos, 172
Matthiesen, Johann, 201
Marxism, 47, 48
    and messianic longings, 72
Mary, 97, 171
Mass, 160
Mauss, Marcel, 143, 145, 146
Melchizedek, 42
Mendelssohn, Moses, 183
messiah, 66, 201, 214
Mexico, 215
Mithraism, 95
millenarianism, 200
millennium, 15
Miriam, 80
Miriam of Norwich, 60
Mot, 95
Moabites, 76
Momigliano, Arnaldo, 208, 209
Montefiore, Claude, 102
Montefiore, Hugh, 45
Moore, George Foot, 102
Moriscos, 217
Moses, 80, 83
Münzer, Thomas, 201
mystery-religion, 95, 97, 118, 150, 151
    participatory nature of, 127
    violence in, 126

Naaman, 27, 75
Nachmanides, 113
Namancura, Juana, 192
Nazism, 46, 47, 72, 109, 200, 219
Netanyahu, B., 173
Nehemiah, 26
Nethinim, 81
Neusner, Jacob, 102
New Testament and anthropology, 155,
    206
Nicholls, William, 219
Nietzsche, Friedrich Wilhelm, 46, 71,
    208
    Weber influenced by, 22
Noachic covenant, 211
Noah, 63, 66, 147, 192, 211
Normans, 186

Odin, 97
Oedipus, 148, 149, 156
Oenomaus, 149
omophagia, 212
Original Sin, 107, 108, 139
Orléans, Council of, 209
Orpheus, 150
Osiris, 91, 92, 95, 96, 97, 150, 163
'other', the, 169, 204

Patai, Raphael, 217
Painecur, José Luis, 192
Palestine, 32
Palestinian Arabs, 64
Pariahs, 60, 87, 176, 218
Parkes, James, 45, 219
Passion Plays, 47, 139, 171, 193
Paul, 56, 94, 99, 106, 107, 111, 203
    and intermarriage, 209
    and sacrificial myth, 129
    and the usurpation myth, ch 7 *passim*
    conflict with Peter, 93
    conversion of the Jews, 17
    Jesus as saviour-god, 95
    on death of Jesus, 117
    on slavery, 117
Pauline Church, 91, 93, 95, 115, 132
Pétain, Marshal, 100
Peter, 93, 94, 100, 101
Pella, 214
Persia, 115, 209
Pharaoh, 72

Pharisees, 98, 99, 100, 101, 130, 132, 141, 152, 153, 156
  as religious authority, 109, 111
  as representing cosmic evil, 114
  continuity with Rabbis, 103
  theories for hostility to Jesus, 102, 103
pharmakos, 148
Philistines, 14
Pilate, 91, 96, 115, 130, 135, 136, 140, 214
  canonised, 215
Pilkington, Edward, 219
Pius XII, 220
pneumatics, 70
Poliakov, Leon, 219
Powell, Enoch, 107
priests, 98, 99
privilegium paschale, 97
Prodigal Son, 108
Protestantism, 36
'Protocols of the Elders of Zion', 43, 199
Psalms, 210
psychics, 70

Quran, 43

Rabbis, 113
Rappaport, Ernest, A., 216
Rashi, 113, 210
Reformation, 203, 219
Reif, Stefan C., 210
Reitzenstein, Richard, 162
re-judaization, 104
Remus, 97, 149
repentance, 123, 165
Resurrection, 125
Richard, I., 58, 59
ritual purity, 161
  in Hinduism, 180
Roman Catholic Church, 203
Roman centurion, 136
Romantic movement, 72
Rome, 14, 78, 85, 89, 93, 115, 133
  exonerated for death of Jesus, 135
Rome, Council of, 209
Romulus, 97, 149
Rowland, Christopher, 118, 215
Ruether, Rosemary, 203, 219
Rufus, 51

Ruth, 24, 75
Russia, 199

Satan, 135, 167, 206
Sacred Executioner, 96, 139, 145, 148, 149, 194, 205
sacrifice
  definition of, 159, 165
  human, 117
  willingness of victim, 121
sacrifices in Temple, 122, 123
Sadducees, 98, 99, 103, 130, 152
Said, Edward, 220
salvation, various theories of, 159
Samaritans, 152
Samuel, 73
Sanders, E. P., 102, 105, 113, 213
Sanders, Jack, 203
Sanhedrin trial, 100
Star Chamber
  origin of name, 59
Scapegoat, 97, 124, 191
Scholem, Gershom, 199
Schultz, Magdalene, 216
Schürer, Emil, 208
Schweitzer, Albert, 164
Scrolls, 102
Second Coming, 200
Set, 95
Seth, 42, 66
Stendahl, Krister, 203
Sennacherib, 77
stereotypes, 204
Seven Laws of the Children of Noah, 211
Shammai, House of, 103
Shelley, 72
Shem, 63
Shoah, 99
Shylock, 23
Simon, M., 218
Sinai, 84, 211
sin-eaters, 190
sin-offerings, 123
Six Day War, 132
slaves of Solomon, 81
Socinianism, 159
Socrates, 116, 166
Solomon, 78
Son of Man, 164

Sophocles, 149
South America, 203
Spanish Inquisition, 172, 217
Sphinx, 149
stigma, power of, 194
Strack, Hermann L., 210
Sudras, 64, 74, 177, 186, 218
Suffering Servant, 164
syncretism, 209

Talmud, 56, 100, 169
Tamil region, 176
Temple, 78, 80, 81, 89, 131, 143
Tertullian, 150, 209
Thebes, 149
Themistocles, 148
Theodotus, 213
Theudas, 83
'Thousand-Year Reich', 201
Titans, 95, 212
Tierney, Patrick, 191, 216, 219
Titus, 132
Toledo, Council of, 209
Torah, 165, 208
    observed by Jerusalem Church, 94
    whether given by angels, 211
Tosafot, 55, 210
Trachtenberg, Joshua, 210
Trafinado, 192
transgressional sacralism, 81
Troilus and Cressida, 181
Trollope, Anthony, 221
Tübingen school, 93, 94
'two swords', the, 218

Ugaritic literature, 210
Untouchables, 79, 174, 176, 177, 189,
    198, 217

acceptance of status, 16
Urbach, Ephraim, 102
Uriah the Hittite, 75
usurpation myth, 44, 63, 194, 206
usury, Talmudic view of, 55

Vatican Council II, 154, 203
Vaisya, 74, 187
Valentinians, 70
Vargas, José, 192
varna, 71, 74, 79, 176, 182, 189, 218
Vedas, 189
veil of the Temple, 132
Vermes, Geza, 102, 103
Virgin Birth, 90, 95
Virgin Mary, 97, 171
Visuvalingam, Sunthar, 211
Voltaire, 161, 183

Wandering Jew, 149, 190, 193, 219
Weber, ch 2 passim
Wellhausen, Julius, 23
Wells, G. A., 131
Wells, H. G., 39
White Christ, 96, 145
Whitely, D. E. H., 125
Wiesel, Elie, 202
William of Norwich, 166
Wisdom, 118, 164

xenophobia, 166, 204

yellow badge, 52

Zealots, 152
Zechariah, 83, 153, 213
Zionism, 12
Zipporah, 80